THE
COLORBLIND
CAREER

**What Every
African American,
Hispanic American,
and Asian American
Needs to Succeed
in Today's
Tough Job Market**

OLLIE STEVENSON

with DANA

Peterson's
Princeton, New Jersey

Visit Peterson's Education Center on the Internet (World Wide Web) at
http://www.petersons.com

Library of Congress Cataloging-in-Publication Data

Stevenson, Ollie, 1945–
    The colorblind career : what every African-American, Hispanic-
American, and Asian-American needs to succeed in today's tough job
market / Ollie Stevenson, with Dana Huebler.
        p.   cm.
    Includes index.
    ISBN 1-56079-700-2
    1. Career development.   2. Minorities—Employment—United States.
I. Huebler, Dana.   II. Title.
HF5381.S775   1997
650.14′089—dc21   97-10992
                                                                    CIP

Editorial direction by Carol Hupping   Composition by Gary Rozmierski
Production supervision by Bernadette Boylan   Creative direction by Linda Huber
Copyediting by Kathleen Salazar   Interior design by Cynthia Boone
Proofreading by Joanne Schauffele

Printed in the United States of America

10 9 8 7 6 5 4 3 2 1

Contents

■ ■ ■

iii

ACKNOWLEDGMENTS

■ ■ ■

I believe that books that have the capacity to reach and enhance the lives of many people, as I hope this one does, can only come about through divine guidance. For me, that source is God, and I give thanks to Him for choosing me to be involved in developing and writing this material.

I was very fortunate to work with an extremely talented and dedicated team of people who infused their spirit and expertise with mine to make this book into a reality. First, my thanks to Carol Hupping, executive editor at Peterson's, who was inspired to provide a work of value rather than just another book and thus gave careful scrutiny to every step of the process to reach that end. Carol, thank you for refusing to compromise. Next, to my agent and mentor, Michael Snell, who chose to help develop my career as a writer and, in so doing, guides me in taking on increasingly more challenging projects. Michael, thank you for having the confidence in me to recommend me for this project and for coming up with the title, which perfectly captures the essence of the book. And finally, to Dana Huebler, my collaborator, who smoothed out my writing (rewriting when necessary), made critical suggestions that enhanced the material, and ensured that the message would be clearly understood. Thank you, Dana, for your professional help, but more than that, for your unrelenting support, encouragement, and dedication to the end. I could not have completed this project without you.

Even with my experience at counseling people from all cultures, I knew that writing this book and addressing the diverse needs of persons of both genders from many cultures would be an effort beyond ambitious. So I got help from a multicultural team of advisers who have their fingers on the pulses of the spectrum of cultures in America. Their unique universal perspectives and information add rich value and insight that make the material more meaningful for readers of all races because it helps promote self-awareness and greater understanding of others. John Hill, thank you for working into the wee hours of the morning and in between a hectic consulting practice to review the material. Sharon Garcia, I know how challenging it is to squeeze out time from a hectic organizational restructuring—thank you for doing so. George Fraser, thank you for your encouragement and for taking time between your busy travel schedule and writing your own book to review mine. Hector Cantu, thank you for finding time for me even while confronted with the high-pace demand of publishing a magazine. Thanks to each one of you for adding your voice to this project and for doing it within the short time frame I provided. Your participation in supporting a goal for the good of many exemplifies the team spirit and willingness to give back that are two of the hallmarks of the truly successful professional.

The same special thanks goes to all the other role models whose profiles are included in the book. Your individual stories highlighting specifically what it took for you to succeed demonstrate how to turn the principles embodied in this book into practical applications to achieve success. Thank you for your time and very valuable contributions. You made the book real.

And my unending gratitude to the many, many people who supported me personally. To my friends and colleagues at Drake Beam Morin, Inc.: Bylle Snyder, Jay Soloway, Judy Kneisley—thank you for providing me with the diverse projects that enhanced my knowledge and enabled me to add to the value of this material; Judy Estrin, Gary Davis, and Michele DaRosa—I couldn't ask for better agents. I appreciate your recommendations, suggestions, and support. Kim Terry—thanks for your valuable and critical systems support, which at times bordered on crisis management. I could not have survived without your help. And to Sandy, Norma, Lynn, Nikki, Anita, John, George, Phyllis, and all you many, many other friends and associates who continually in small ways gave your support—thank you very much.

And finally, to my family, who made the greatest sacrifice of all in personal time—thank you David, Joyce, Kylie, and Fernando. I love you all for your understanding and patience.

Ollie Stevenson
January, 1997

PART I

GETTING
STARTED

W hat does it take to have a successful career in mainstream America? Why do some people seem to have all the luck and others can't make anything work? Is there a path to success that only a few fortunate people can travel? Is it mostly based on who you know, or are there other things that are key?

Part 1 of the book will help you find the answers to these questions and more. It is for those of you who are just starting out on a career journey—whether you've just finished school, have finally decided to commit to a career after a period of working simply to pay the bills, or are reentering the workforce after an extended absence.

The information in the following chapters will help demystify the process of building a solid foundation by laying out the tried-and-true methods that others have used to establish a successful career. You will learn what is expected in mainstream America, the importance of having a dream, how to identify your career goal, keys for recognizing some of the obstacles to success, and how to establish the pattern of success necessary for moving up the ladder and advancing.

■

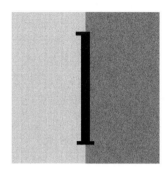

ACHIEVING THE COLORBLIND CAREER

E xactly what is a colorblind career? It is a career that reaches beyond color to enable you to achieve success in today's mainstream business culture. And, like it or not, to reach this success, you have to follow standards of behavior and attitudes and a set of business values that are based, for the most part, on the business values, work ethics, and the business mind-set of the white male. The simplest way to think of this business mind-set is to understand that the majority of people in a given situation set the standards for that situation; the ideas and values they adhere to become the mainstream standard. Currently, the majority of people in American big business are white, so the standards are most heavily influenced by them.

As more and more people of color enter the business arena and move to higher levels of influence, this mind-set will change to incorporate a greater diversity of values. As a person of color, you can be part of that change only if you're on the inside. Once you adhere to the standards—the values, attitudes, and behaviors—of today's corporate business culture, you will be in a position to add your unique perspective to it and, together with other people of color, slowly and steadily change it.

MAKE THE BUSINESS MIND-SET A WORKING REALITY

When I step into the arena of corporate America, I get into my best business mind-set because it's the most effective way to accomplish my goals in that environment. A simple example of this is what I do for lunch. Whenever I can, I make a point of having lunch with any one of my peers—male, female, older, younger, white, black, Hispanic, Asian, or whatever. This is one of the basics of the business mind-set: that you network with everyone. And guess what? It is actually very enjoyable, because my peers and I have a lot in common. Lunch is a great time to network. While casually enjoying each other's company, we discuss our common goal, which is how to improve our process so that our company can maintain its competitive edge in the marketplace (and so we can receive our reward for helping to bring this about).

Adopting the business mind-set for work is similar to wearing the right clothes for different occasions. Just as you wear different outfits to attend a formal dinner, walk on the beach, or go into the office, you adopt different mind-sets for various situations in your life. Depending on the circumstances at a particular moment, you decide whether it's appropriate to adopt your business mind-set, your cultural mind-set, or your social mind-set. The more you know about these different mind-sets and understand their importance, the easier it will be for you to choose which to adopt to fit a given situation.

THE BUSINESS MIND-SET

To adhere to today's standards and fit into the current corporate work culture, you need to adopt what I call the "business mind-set." I have outlined some of the major elements of the business mind-set below and, where appropriate, have included examples I've observed where people of color have unintentionally applied inappropriate standards. This is hardly an all-inclusive list. Rather, it contains the more universal elements that I have found apply in most situations. When you get into a specific industry and then a particular company, you'll want to pay attention to the unique culture you find there.

Be assertive and take responsibility for developing and advancing your career.

Some people are passive about developing a career; they enter the business world with the expectation that they are going to be led and guided up the ladder of success. It is possible to get step-by-step guidance in doing that, but you have to seek out that guidance yourself. This book, and all the books mentioned in it, will help you learn how to do that. But you cannot stop there. You'll have to read more books, talk to people, and watch and model behavior that works. And you'll have to make a commitment to advance your career.

(A note about reading: I believe that at least one book has been written on every subject you can think of, which means that at least one book out there that will help you do anything that you want to do. But you have to go to the bookstore or library and get the book and then read it. I list some books at the end of each chapter in *Resources* that I particularly like and that I think will be useful to you and your career.)

But even with the reading and the advice you get from others, you still have to take responsibility for putting it all together and making it work for you. For example, let's say you feel capable of performing a certain job within your company, and you're hoping that the management will notice that you're ready, available, and willing. Wrong.

You have to make them notice—and there are a number of approaches you could take to bring this about. You could try a direct

Continued

approach by asking to work in the area you're interested in or handle some of the responsibilities associated with the job. Or you could talk with people to find out how you can get on a project doing that kind of work. You could also write an article for your company newsletter (so the decision makers will notice it), demonstrating that you have the understanding and the capability to perform the job. Or you could talk with someone in one of your professional groups who is acquainted with the decision makers and could recommend you.

The important point is that if there is something you want, you have to research the ways to get it, choose the best strategy for your personality and the company culture, and then go for it. You must also be willing to take the consequences of your action (or nonaction), as well as accept any rewards. That's the essence of taking responsibility for your career.

Be willing to tell others about your skills and abilities. In other words, toot your own horn.

Learn the strategies appropriate in your environment for letting decision makers know what you do. Too much humility is not appropriate in the business world! And hoping to get recognized for your accomplishments without letting others know about them will probably get you nowhere.

If you want to advance, you need to subtly and strategically feed information upward to the decision makers about your interests and abilities so that when they are considering which employee has what it takes to assume certain responsibilities (usually this means who is ready for advancement), your name will come up.

I've worked with clients who've made me pull information out of them about their qualifications. They were reluctant to talk about their accomplishments because they did not want to sound like they were bragging. Refusing to communicate accomplishments can interfere with your ability to be competitive in an environment in which accomplishments are valued and often the ticket for advancement. "Tooting your horn" may feel awkward—especially at first—because it is a different behavior than you're accustomed to. But you can let people know about your abilities without being obnoxious or going against a value system that says you should not seek the limelight.

Consider these ways of communicating your accomplishments to the people who matter:

- Mention your achievements and the problems you've solved in status reports to your manager.

- Write an article for your company newsletter highlighting an activity you've been involved with.

- Talk with coworkers about how much you enjoyed participating on a particular committee or getting an opportunity to handle a certain responsibility.

- Send your manager a photocopy of written letters of commendation you've received from clients or others in the company. (And don't hesitate to ask someone to put his or her positive comments in writing.)

These are only a few suggestions; I'm sure if you think about it, you can come up with a few of your own. When you join a company, watch how others point out what their major and minor achievements are so that you can get a sense of what works in that particular culture. Then apply it to your situation. Just remember—making your accomplishments known is a very necessary part of the process of advancement.

Keep your cultural distinctiveness in the workplace, but adapt it to the mainstream corporate culture.

I am not suggesting you give up the values, pride, and dignity that make up your cultural identity—because I certainly do not intend to give up mine. I am a black woman and I love all that identifies me as a black woman. Whether you are Asian, Native-American, African-American, Hispanic, white, or a member of any other group, I certainly hope that you feel the same way about your culture—that you wear your cultural identity proudly. However, if your long-term goals include developing a successful career within the American corporate system, you must learn to switch from your cultural mind-set to a business mind-set while in the business arena.

What does it mean to switch mind-sets? It means—while in your business environment—switching to values, attitudes, and behaviors that fit the workplace, as long as they do not conflict with what you believe to be morally correct. For instance, consider the way you dress: Your clothes should always be consistent with the attire worn by the greatest

Continued

number of people within your industry, company, and job. Never call attention to yourself with your clothes (unless you're in a job where it's appropriate, such as a sales clerk in a trendy clothing boutique).

All people of color that I've known from all races have colorful wardrobes. And appropriately so, because bright colors look better with our skin tones. Even so, our wardrobes need to be tempered for the workplace. And with a little creativity, we can strike a reasonable balance.

Think of it this way: Waitresses have to wear uniforms on their jobs because it's appropriate attire for working in the restaurant business. As career-minded professionals, we need to wear a "business uniform" because it is appropriate attire for our jobs.

If rejected for a position, maintain pride in your accomplishments, analyze the situation, regroup, and persevere.

No matter how good you are, how talented, or how exceptional, you will not get every single job you go after. Accept this fact and it will reduce your chances of feeling frustrated when you don't get a coveted position. Even when you are the most technically qualified for a position, don't expect that it will automatically go to you.

A number of factors go into any hiring decision. First there's what I call "the mix." If a company already has a person on board with a similar background and qualifications to yours, managers may want to add someone else with a different background to round out the team. Chemistry can also be an important factor. Chemistry cannot be learned or manufactured—you're just going to hit it off better with some people than with others. With all things being equal, I'd probably hire the person I clicked with best. And even in a predominantly white environment, that does not always mean a white person. Think about it. Do you automatically click with every member of your race? Other factors an employer might consider include perceived motivational level, potential for adding value based on previous experience, outside business contacts, and potential for growth and advancement.

If you don't get a position, feel honored that you were part of the group selected for consideration. If you were involved in a selection process within your company, you may be able to network (or observe) within the company to find out why the other person was chosen. If you discover that it was because of office politics, forget it. That's life, and one day you'll be the chosen one. If, on the other hand, you learn that the person who got the job had qualifications that you're lacking, then get busy and get qualified for the next opening.

Take the initiative to introduce yourself in new situations.

Remember when you were in school and a new person joined your class? You and your classmates probably stared at the person with curiosity and maybe wondered what he was about, until finally something happened to break the ice. Eventually the newcomer found his way into a group of kids and that was that.

Things haven't changed much. When you join a company, you're the new kid. And considering that the demographics are still heavily skewed toward white people, you'll probably stand out even more than the new kid in school. Most likely, your fellow employees won't stare at you outright, but they will be just as curious. In spite of their curiosity, some of them may hesitate to approach you because they don't know what to say. In some environments, there will be white people who have had limited exposure to people of color, so you'll have to be the brave person. Take the initiative to introduce yourself and say how you're looking forward to learning the job. Tell people that you'd welcome any help they can give you in learning the ropes.

Don't be exclusive. People of color have natural relationship-building skills that allow us to easily network with everyone. Use them.

In his bestselling book *Success Runs in Our Race*, George Fraser shares a vision of networking that's worth aspiring to: "It is the brand of networking that calls upon you to give until it hurts, and then give until it feels good. It is the kind of networking that over time delivers to your doorstep your every dream and every hope."

I've found this approach to networking to be absolutely true for me, and it can be for you as well—if you apply the principles. But don't limit yourself to a few select people and your own limited social circle; otherwise, you'll narrow your opportunities. I've actually had clients of color who refused to network to get a new job. They perceived it as

Continued

asking for a favor and, thus, did not want to feel obligated or beholden to anyone. What an unfortunate attitude! Statistics show that over 70 percent of people seeking a job get it through networking. The statistics are even higher for prime jobs because these are often only accessed through a network.

If you don't network because you don't know how, read and apply the principles in Fraser's book. Make it a goal right now to meet and get to know a certain number of new people each month, each year. More than likely, somebody you know will eventually introduce you to somebody they know, who might just offer you the best opportunity you've ever had. All you have to do is continue to meet people until you make that right connection.

Use social gatherings as opportunities to be visible and meet more people.

Networking is a two-way street. It works because you're as important to your network partners as they are to you. Being committed to a profession means more than going to work from 9 to 5. Socializing is part of the mix. You have to let people get to know you, and you need to take the time to get to know them. This will not only enhance your chances for advancement, it will also make you more comfortable with the people that you'll be working with as you move forward in your career. Consider social gatherings an extension of your work week.

Seek mentors.

Ask for advice from people working in jobs like the one you want. Ask about skills that are rewarded and how to acquire them so that you can advance. A mentor serves as a guide and teacher to help you move forward in your career. You do not choose your mentors—they choose you. But they cannot choose you unless they know you need to be chosen. And how will they know unless you ask them for advice?

People love to give advice, to share their knowledge—it's a wonderfully uplifting thing to do. I look at it this way: Allow someone to experience the joy of helping guide your career. And don't limit yourself—be willing to accept whomever the universe provides to you as a mentor. Seek out a mentor of power. It is good if the person is someone of your race and ethnicity who has made it through the system. If not, look for two mentors—one of any race who can help guide your career and one of your race who can identify and help you overcome the obstacles facing people from your background.

Seek feedback on performance so that you can continually improve and grow.

No matter how significant your last accomplishment was, today it's old news. As long as you live, you need to be striving to do and be the best you can possibly be. Make feedback a part of your education. Mentors can be very helpful here because part of their role is to provide valuable feedback. But don't limit your search for feedback to the mentor relationship. Ask people in your peer group for feedback on ideas and activities—and be willing to take time to give it to them as well. Then, take the information you gather from your friends and colleagues and incorporate it into your objectives for growth.

If you are totally comfortable in your profession and everyone says that you're just great—just perfect at what you do—then I don't think you're being truly challenged. And if you're not really challenged, you're not growing. If you don't grow, you can't make the contribution you're capable of making. So find out what you can do better and then do it, or initiate your plan to expand the scope of what you do or to move up a rung on the ladder.

Adopting the Right Mind-Set Eliminates Barriers

We have excellent examples all around us of people who are part of a specific mind-set. Take newscasters, for instance. No matter which station you listen to, regardless of their race or gender, all newscasters sound pretty much alike and project a similar image. Black, Asian, white, Hispanic, male, and female—they have the same accent (or lack of accent), display similar mannerisms, and dress in the same conservative styles. They adhere to the newscasters' mind-set, which has its own distinctive language, clothes, behavior, and attitude.

I have counseled people of color in many industries about how to establish their careers and move them forward. The ones who operate from a business mind-set have benefited greatly with advancement and promotions. But more people need to learn to make this adjustment and get into the system. Such adaptability is essential because, ultimately, it is the way to eliminate barriers. As people at work start to share a common mind-set and speak a common language, they will more easily relate to each other, work better together, and solve some of the problems and break down the barriers that are associated with race and culture.

Keep in mind that the business mind-set is continually evolving and, as it evolves, more and more barriers will fall away. In other words, as the workplace becomes increasingly diverse, the business mind-set will change to reflect that diversity. And the changes will apply to everyone—so that someday, hopefully, the corporate culture will truly become colorblind.

THE WRONG MIND-SET CAN BE A BUSINESS BARRIER

Some people approach a job with an attitude that is not conducive to growth or their career well-being. This attitude is reflected in statements like:

- "I just want to be left alone to do my job and as long as I do that, no one should have anything to say."

- "I'm an educated, qualified person. I shouldn't have to tell anybody this—it's obvious."

- "What I wear doesn't matter. I'm just here to do the work."

- "All they're getting out of me is my 8 hours—then I'm outta here."

- "I don't care . . . what they think . . . who they are . . . what they say . . . about this job."

Any statement that begins with "I don't care" surely suggests a negative attitude. My father used to say, "I don't care don't have no home" (meaning that such an attitude is not appropriate anywhere). And that's exactly where a person can end up with these kinds of attitudes—without a home or, in this case, without a job (or without a job that is challenging and rewarding).

THE TANNING OF AMERICA

- By the year 2000, people of color in the U.S. workforce will have increased from 19 percent in 1980 to 27 percent.

- By the year 2010, people of color will make up 30 percent of the workforce.

- By the year 2010, people of color in California's workforce will have increased from 40 percent to 60 percent.

- California is likely to be the first state where white males will be in the minority in the workforce.

Source: Statistical Abstract of the United States, 1994, Bureau of the Census.

As people of color, we have already overcome many obstacles and with our spirit and faith, we will overcome more so that we can chart a bright future for ourselves. In my years as a career counselor, I have seen many people lose out on opportunities because they haven't learned enough about the business world and have, as a result, incorrectly applied the values of their cultural mind-set in their business dealings.

Three young women I've counseled are good examples: Gina,* a young black law school graduate; June, an Asian secretary with an advanced degree; and Amy, a Hispanic factory worker. Each of these women, mostly without knowing it, let her cultural values and background get in the way of achieving success.

I met Gina during a book tour. She approached me in an intense, serious manner with questions about how to succeed with her newly acquired law degree. I asked Gina about herself and her career goals and soon discovered that she had unrealistic expectations about what a company could offer her. She was frustrated in her career because she mistakenly believed that her education had already fully prepared her to handle a position in her chosen field.

As people of color, we are justly proud of graduating from college. But the real challenge—finding and keeping a job in corporate America—is only just beginning. Gina expected that once she found a position and established herself, the company would assume the responsibility of training her and helping her to advance. The other people of color listening to our conversation nodded in agreement, indicating that they, too, expected the same thing. In fact, all were applying the wrong set of values to the job—in other words, they had the wrong mind-set. They expected the same nurturing support they received in their cultural environments to be present on their jobs.

Gina had not been taught how to succeed. School gave her the technical skills needed for her work, and her family and culture gave her the necessary emotional support. But her cultural and school

---

* When only a first name is used in an anecdote in this book, the anecdote represents an amalgam of various experiences.

mind-sets were getting in the way of her career success because they had not prepared her to assert herself and get the help she needed. Instead, they had prepared her to be quiet and respectful and to wait for guidance.

To succeed in business, she needed to apply one of the values of the business mind-set, which is to be assertive and take responsibility for your own career. Bottom line: Gina needed to seek out training, get mentors, join professional groups—in essence, she needed to develop her own training program. Because her cultural mind-set had not prepared her to be assertive in this way or to understand the benefits of these types of activities, she was floundering.

June, an Asian secretary who was married and had a child, approached me at a conference. She had obtained an advanced degree in marketing but was unsure what step to take to start using her degree—or even whether she should launch her career right now. I offered her a number of suggestions for how she could apply her degree, but to each of my suggestions she offered no response. Finally, June told me she'd probably be better off if she could just make herself content with the job she had and with taking care of her family. Taking care of a family is truly an honorable thing to do—the problem is that this alone was not giving June the satisfaction she needed. Her career dreams were not being fulfilled.

June's cultural mind-set was supportive of her obtaining an advanced degree, but it didn't give her the drive to go out and get a job using that degree. To me, her emphasis on peace and harmony, which was revealed in our conversation and by her stating that "maybe I should just stay home and be satisfied," contrasted with the standards of the business mind-set, which rewards people for going out and actively competing for what they want.

Thanks to her educational pursuit, June's career prospects were promising, if she could get beyond her cultural mind-set. Amy's career, on the other hand, was derailed before it even got started. When she finished high school, Amy knew that she wanted to pursue a degree in engineering. However, she delayed her education and, following the example of most of her friends, started working temporarily in a factory. The temporary job turned into a two-year stint.

Amy explained her situation to me at a workshop I was conducting at her company for employees who were being laid off. When I told her about her options for going to school, she was dismayed that she had wasted so much time. She had been working to prepare herself financially to go to school, not realizing that there were ways of attending school without scholarships and grants while still working. She may have found out all I shared with her much earlier if she had known about and exercised another element of the business mind-set, which is networking with people (of any race or culture) to find mentors.

Wearing the Wrong Uniform Can Be Painful

I identified easily with the dilemmas that these three women faced. Like them, my culture gave me emotional support, but it did not provide me with the mind-set, knowledge, or tools to succeed in mainstream American business.

I remember some of the lessons and adjustments I had to make when I first started in my career. I refused an opportunity to work as director of a community services agency because I felt it was a man's job. Even though I had been handling the responsibilities of the position all along, since I did not have the official title, I considered what I was doing as only "helping out," a position with which I was more comfortable. Another time, I missed an opportunity—to join the staff of a Fortune 100 company as a public relations consultant to one of its senior executives—because I had no clearly defined career goal and, as a result, no sense of how the position could help my career.

Later in my career, I failed with a project because I had not realized I needed to gather a consensus. After designing a process to revamp a national system within the company, I got input from all the relevant people, but I didn't revisit them to confirm their support before I presented my recommendations to a team of executives. That was a mistake. They were caught off guard when the executives approached them for feedback on my idea. Finally, I missed out on a promotion because of my naiveté regarding company politics. I was the logical candidate (in my mind) for a position at the next level above mine, so it did not occur to me that I would have to campaign for it. I was quite shocked, then, when the position went to someone who did campaign for it. Take this lesson to heart and remember: If you ask, you may receive. If you don't ask, don't be surprised if you don't get anything.

I had no mentors or support system during that time, nor did I know that I needed any. I mistakenly thought that all that was necessary for success was knowing how to do a job and then working hard and proving my skills. My ignorance was compounded by my belief that there was men's work and there was women's work (and that men's work was the kind that required decision making and authority over others), which, of course, stopped me from pursuing certain career opportunities.

Some elements of my cultural mind-set actually limited my business growth. The professional associations I joined at that time (must I mention how long ago?) were made up mainly of other African-Americans like myself and focused mostly on issues of discrimination. As a result, I didn't gain much in terms of professional growth and knowledge. Plus, the groups generally had an attitude of "them" against "us," making it seem as if I'd be a traitor to ask one of "them" for help (see "They Can't Stop You from Succeeding"). So, like June, Amy, and Gina, I, without knowing it, applied the standards of my cultural mind-set rather than those of a business mind-set to my career. Because of this, I followed the wrong pattern as I struggled to succeed.

"THEY CAN'T STOP YOU FROM SUCCEEDING"
■

"The other day my wife and I were looking at homes in a nice area of Los Angeles, when she commented that the area would be a fine place to own a home but that 'they' don't want us living there. I've heard people use that

term before, and even though I know what it means, I don't give any thought to it; I certainly don't let it rule my life."

Keith sees this attitude—that "they" (white people) can hold blacks back—a result of the negative brainwashing that is an outgrowth of centuries of discrimination. He believes that blacks who allow themselves to be held hostage by the invisible "they" are giving white people the power of approval over them.

"Sure, there is hate and discrimination—on both sides—because there are radical whites as well as radical blacks, but these types are on the fringe of society and do not represent the norm," Keith says. "Most white people are concerned about their own needs—not about us. And we should likewise be concerned about our needs."

According to Keith, blacks and whites would be better off following the Japanese approach to handling problems, which is to just solve the problem and forget about whose fault it is. "Once the problem is solved," he says, "the Japanese then set mechanisms in place to prevent it from happening again. The way we solve problems in America is not as productive because it focuses more on finding fault and placing blame than on problem resolution."

For Keith, the force behind a person's success is his or her belief system, which is based on one's spiritual and mental wisdom. "My grandfathers achieved their goals in the face of all obstacles because of their belief systems: It was the only thing they had. They inspired my father and me to start our own businesses." Keith followed his grandfathers' example and started his own business when his consulting position lost its challenge.

Although Keith says he has never been discriminated against because of his race, he does point to an unpleasant experience that occurred when he worked in the aerospace industry under a manager who was abusive to all his subordinates. When he became the target of one of this manager's attacks, Keith challenged the man's behavior—behind closed doors—and was never singled out again. "I didn't make a big deal out of what had happened, but it was important for me to have the respect that I deserved, so I got it."

"I believe that I am able to influence a situation based solely on the dollars I can generate for a company. And since the American system rests on economics, not race, I believe anyone can accomplish his or her dreams *just by being an important team player. You don't have to be a partner (by being a member of the white business culture), as long as you're good at what you do."*

■

KEITH WEBSTER
African-American entrepreneur
President, Champion Technical Services, Los Angeles, California
Business: Facilities support, temporary services, manufacturing

Establish a Positive Pattern for Success

As my career progressed, I learned that an important part of taking responsibility for it was establishing early on the right pattern for developing and advancing. You, too, will see this pattern emerging, and you'll find yourself repeating it over and over as you advance level by level up the ladder of success. The pattern very simply is:

- Setting a goal based on your own desires or dreams

- Assessing your talent and ability to accomplish the goal

- Developing a plan to get the experience, education, and training you need

- Developing a strategy to get to the goal

- Being committed to attaining the goal, despite possible detours and setbacks

PEOPLE OF COLOR HAVE A GREATER CHALLENGE

My experience has taught me that adopting the business mind-set can be especially difficult for people of color because some of our key cultural values are different from those in the white culture. For instance, many Hispanic people have an ingrained respect for authority based on age and title, and this might inhibit them from making suggestions or from taking orders from someone who is roughly the same age or holds a similar rank. My Hispanic colleagues say that another problem for Hispanic women is the very male dominant and "macho" culture in which they were raised. Without strong female role models who are succeeding in the business world, many Hispanic women question their own competence and abilities in a "man's" workplace.

An Asian person's fear of losing face might stop him or her from taking business risks, or because of the cultural discomfort that results from being singled out or seeking glory, an Asian employee might feel reluctant to stand out in the business arena or actively seek promotion. A black person's inclination to work independently and do things his or her way makes it difficult to adjust to working in a team environment, seeking consensus in decision making, or adhering to an established standard for advancement.

Another challenge we all face, even those of us who have already adopted the business mind-set, is dealing with discrimination, racism, and prejudice. These problems exist—and, in view of human nature, probably always will. Some of this ignorance will be overcome as people of color advance in the workforce and the cultures blend and assimilate each other's values. In the meantime, it is important to know that you are likely to encounter discrimination at various points in your career. Sometimes you will have to confront it, and other times you will choose to ignore it. I will be addressing these issues at appropriate points in the book, and I've included two books in the Resources section that can help in dealing with issues of discrimination.

Putting It All Together and Starting the Journey

Understanding the problem is halfway to the solution. I believe that, as a person of color, you can equip yourself to meet the challenge of adopting a business mind-set in several key ways:

- **Educate yourself on how to handle discrimination.** There may be times when you need to deal with an issue that violates your civil rights. In those instances, you should contact: The U.S. Equal Employment Opportunity Commission, 2401 E. Street NW, Washington, D.C. 20507 or call 800-USA-EEOC to contact an EEOC field office (for the hearing impaired, EEOC's TDD number is 202-634-7057). Also, read books focusing on work and people of color (see Resources at the end of the chapter for some examples).

- **Educate yourself about the business mind-set by reading.** Books like *The New Professional: Everything You Need to Know for a Great First Year on the Job* by Ed Holton (see Resources) provide excellent advice for all people just starting their career journey.

- **Educate yourself by socializing.** Join groups—professional associations as well as some that are just for fun—that include people from more than one culture. Take the initiative to say hello first when you join a new group. Get to know others and be open to letting them know you. Look for the things you have in common and build relationships based on those things. These same people may be helpful to you later in your career when you need advice or support.

- **Educate yourself by getting involved.** Volunteer for activities in some of the groups you join. Learning to work together with people of another culture within the low-risk environment of a volunteer activity will prepare you well for working with others in the workplace. Volunteer for a responsible position on at least one committee a year.

Remember Your Roots

Making the daily mind-set switch as we travel from home to work and then back home again is something we need to be able to do in order to maintain our mental health and emotional balance. If you get too caught up in the business culture, you run the risk of allowing your cultural mind-set to slowly fade or disappear altogether.

In fact, one of the downsides of the business mind-set is that it is not nurturing. Because of this, we need to be involved in activities outside of work that help us stay in touch with the essence of our culture. As a black person, my spiritual nurturing (church and prayer) and getting together with family and a few friends to gab and make fun of ourselves totally revives me. Some of my friends from other cultures tell me they value the get-togethers for big family meals, with all the babies and the laughter and hugs and kisses. And of course, men of all cultures seem to get reinforcement from watching or participating in a sporting event together.

Whatever it is that is a normal part of your culture, that rejuvenates you and keeps you in touch with core aspects of your being, do it on a regular basis. We need to maintain our base of emotional support because we will need to rely on it often during our career journey. As people of color, our ultimate career challenge is to learn to handle the realities of the work world while maintaining our own cultural values.

"YOU NEED A GOOD FOUNDATION TO ACHIEVE YOUR GOALS"

■

Al developed a strong work ethic very early in life, when at 9 years old he started working alongside his father and uncles in the family's construction business. He credits this early work experience, as well as his participation in high school football, as integral to his character development. While the family business gave him work experience, playing football taught him to be a team player and to handle both victory and defeat. "A team sport is an excellent training ground for people (both men and women)," explains Al. "I learned how to deal with disappointment and, most of all, how to set a goal and keep working toward it until it is accomplished."

By the time he graduated from high school, Al had accumulated nearly ten years worth of experience in the construction industry. At 19, he left the family business and found a job with a construction firm, where he expected to progress quickly because of his past experience. When he did not, he was undeterred; he set a goal to become an independent businessman. "I knew then that I needed to have my own business. I refused to let someone else limit my progress; I needed to control my destiny."

"Two key factors that will help us get ahead is (1) having a sense of self and direction, which you develop from your family life, and (2) having a goal that really keeps you motivated. Whether the career goal is tangible or intangible, you've just got to realize that you'll have to work hard to get your goal, and that no one else is going to hand you success."

■

AL HARVEY
African-American entrepreneur
Partner, Desert Imports, Phoenix, Arizona
Business: Food, clothing, commercial office furniture

WHAT THIS BOOK CAN DO FOR YOU

Over the past twenty-plus years, I have counseled and coached many people. Most of my business life has been spent addressing career management issues in corporate arenas, either as a manager or consultant. I've also had an opportunity to help people with business start-up and expansion. Along the way, I've had the chance to counsel and coach white people—as well as people of color—from entry-level professionals to corporate executives.

My experience has allowed me to see the differences between the people who succeed and those who don't. It has also made me acutely aware of some of the attitudes and approaches in each one of the major cultures that inhibit growth. I realize that some of us have already accepted the realities of the business mind-set and are succeeding without losing our identity. You will read about some of these successful role models throughout this book. But a lot more people of color still need to learn what to do, and I've written this book to help address that need.

The primary objectives of this book are to:

- Help you understand the elements of the business mind-set in America
- Help you succeed in the work world by showing you how and when to switch from your cultural mind-set to a business one
- Provide insights and strategies to help you advance and maintain a satisfying and rewarding career—or move on to a new career—until retirement
- Draw on the courage, strength, wisdom, and the spiritual and emotional support that are part of your culture to help you make the changes necessary to achieve the career success

This book is structured in three parts to correspond to the three stages in most people's career lives. You can find yourself, no matter what stage you're currently in, somewhere in the book. You can look ahead to other stages to get the big picture or to see what's down the road for you, and you can revisit a stage if you change careers and find yourself, in some ways, beginning again.

I know absolutely without a doubt that you can achieve success in America, and I am happy to be a part of helping you to meet that challenge and realize your career dreams.

RESOURCES

I Went to College for This? True Stuff About Life in the Business World and How to Make Your Way Through It by Garrett Soden (Peterson's, 1994). Will familiarize you with many of the terms and processes of business and the work world and how they are used.

The Minority Career Book by Miquela Rivera, Ph.D. (Adams Publishing, 1991). Addresses the problems faced by people of color in the workplace and includes information on understanding cultural diversity (this is the other side of the coin: managing minority employees), the pressure of being the "only one," and answering the call to leadership.

The Minority Career Guide by Michael F. Kastre, Nydia Rodriguez Kastre, and Alfred G. Edwards (Peterson's, 1993). Provides basic advice and inspiration to launch and maintain a successful career. It also offers good perspectives on some basic career issues like goal setting, résumé writing, and job interviews.

The New Professional: Everything You Need to Know for a Great First Year on the Job by Ed Holton (Peterson's Guides, 1990). Focuses on getting oriented and becoming familar with your new company's culture. Includes common pitfalls for new professionals, how to earn respect and credibility, and fast-starter tips to help set your course through the first year of your career.

Success Runs in Our Race: The Complete Guide to Effective Networking in the African-American Community by George C. Fraser (Avon Books, 1996). Includes ways college students and professionals can network for a job, tips for whites networking with blacks; tactics for creating your own networking events, exercises for increasing your networking skills, best places to network, and working do's and don't's; plus Fraser's Top Ten Principles for Effective Networking.

SUCCESS STARTS
WITH A DREAM

M any who've dreamed of success have turned their dreams into realities, not because these individuals were more unique or special than others but simply because they were persistent. That is part of the beauty of living in America: All people have the opportunity to make their career dream a reality if they are hungry enough for it and willing to adopt a business mind-set to accomplish it (see "Living the American Dream"). Of course, the path to success is not without obstacles. Gender bias, racism, prejudice, discrimination—these are just a few of the roadblocks faced by people of color. Still, none of these obstacles is powerful enough to stop someone from achieving a dream if he or she is determined to get it.

In his book *Live Your Dreams*, Les Brown describes this determination as an absolutely compelling, deeply rooted, and powerful motivation. Paul and Sarah Edwards, in their book *Finding Your Perfect Work*, describe the motivation this way: "For some people, there is no crisis that catalyzes them to pursue their dreams. Quite the contrary, they simply decide they're no longer willing to compromise, delay, or forego what's in their hearts and souls. So they summon up their courage to make a specific choice that will change their lives."

Your dream may be fired by a compelling force that burns in your heart—driving you, inspiring you, and providing a constant source of motivation. Or it may be kindled by a subtler, but equally powerful, force—a quiet, abiding commitment that comes from a deeply rooted sense of inner purpose. Whether it's a fiery passion or a steady inner light, the important thing is that you have a dream that serves as a beacon, drawing you toward your own unique success.

In every walk of life, you can find numerous examples of people who have been drawn to a dream and then unwaveringly followed a path to success: the finely tuned, completely disciplined athlete who competes on a field of champions and wins by a breath, a split second, a last perfectly executed step; the musician whose musical rendition captures our souls with a sound so exquisite that we dare not breathe for fear of marring its perfection; or the scientist who, after years of painstaking analysis and self-sacrifice, suddenly finds the solution to a problem that changes the world in some way.

These feats of greatness are not the exclusive right of superstar sports figures, larger-than-life entertainers, or exceptionally brilliant scientists. Success is possible for all people who will not settle for less.

LIVING THE AMERICAN DREAM

■

Omar has achieved the American dream. He did it by placing a strong focus on education and professional growth and by striving to get along with others in his field. His advanced education, which includes a bachelor's degree from California State University, Long Beach, followed by a master's degree in engineering from Stanford University, has enabled him to turn an interest in math and science and a mechanical inclination that he inherited from his father into a career as a mechanical engineer.

His father, who never finished high school, strongly encouraged all three of his children to get a good education. Besides this lifelong support from his family, Omar was also motivated by a strong love of learning. Even so, getting his degrees proved to be a major challenge. He worked his way through school, spending two years in the army to help finance his education and then, while in school, earning extra money tutoring other students. "I liked school and really wanted to go, but it was hard. Sometimes I would ask myself why I was doing it and was it worth it. But you just have to set your goals and not let anything distract you, no matter how hard it is. In the end, it's worth the effort."

Now, with his schooling behind him and firmly established in his chosen career, Omar still does not see his education as complete. "In a sense, I'm just at another stage of training. I expect to learn 90 percent of what I need to know on the job. It takes about five years before you can say that you are an engineer. I'll be glad when I get to that point, but for now I'm satisfied to still be growing in my field."

He attributes part of his career success to his ability to get along well with his coworkers (his diverse work group is 90 percent white). "We all get along well. We work together, lunch together, and communicate well. I don't have a problem with any racial group. Race is not an issue for me: I don't think any outside forces can prevent me from accomplishing my goals because of my race."

■

OMAR MIRAMONTES
Mexican-American mechanical engineer
TRW, Redondo Beach, California
Business: Aerospace

A BRIGHT FUTURE FOR PEOPLE OF COLOR

We can be proud of the talented people of color who throughout this country's history—and especially in the past four decades—have made significant strides and won tremendous achievements. Role models exist at every level and within virtually every arena of American enterprise. Many achieved their goals in much more difficult times, facing far more obstacles and far fewer opportunities than people of color currently face. They realized their dreams through will power, perseverance, intelligence, and talent and, in doing so, changed the complexion of American business.

The collective result of these past achievements and the changes in the corporate culture is that in today's workplace, people of color have more and better career opportunities than ever before. As we move into the twenty-first century, we're in a position to achieve some of the biggest career successes of all time and to make outstanding contributions to American history.

This isn't to say that the road to success will be easy. Even though increased opportunity exists, the workplace of the next century will be more challenging than ever, for all people, no matter what their color. Instead of being supported by programs or implied promises of cradle-to-grave employment, everyone will have to compete and achieve individually by setting high goals and taking responsibility for turning their dreams into realities.

You will face additional challenges. Moving through your career, you will likely face some form of racism or discrimination. Prejudice and intolerance are alive and well in America—no one can deny that. We cannot mandate an internal change in people that will eliminate racism, but we can establish laws to protect ourselves from racist behavior that interferes with our pursuit of the American dream. Laws have been established to protect us and help us to challenge discrimination, and more will be established as necessary. Part of the beauty of the American democratic process is that we have the right to deal with these obstacles legally and, hopefully, to continue chipping away at them. Besides these obvious challenges, however, there are other, even greater, challenges that we, as people of color, face.

Stepping Out of the Cultural Box

One weighty challenge is breaking free of a cultural mind-set that limits professional growth. When you pursue a career that is not the norm for your gender or culture (as Judith Schulte did, a female Hispanic-American engineer profiled in chapter 6), you face additional obstacles—perhaps lack of support from family and peers, friction on the job, or, possibly, slower upward mobility. It takes courage and a great deal of fortitude to go after a dream that requires you to break from cultural tradition and pursue something that your family may not support. If you find yourself feeling drawn to such a calling, you can take steps to make the path easier and gain the support you need to follow your dream.

How do you do this? Make the effort to get your family's commitment and support by slowly involving them in the process. Discuss your plans with the parent or sibling whom you expect to be the most receptive to your endeavor. When you've gained the backing of that individual, ask for his or her help in anticipating the arguments of the more difficult family members and in developing a plan for how you will respond to their arguments.

Don't Be Limited by Stereotypes

You have to be courageous enough to move past programming that says that success is limited for you because of your race. It simply is not true. If Oprah Winfrey, a black woman, can make $45 million a year, I would say there is no limitation. If Connie Chung, an Asian-American anchorperson for national news, or Tiger Woods, a young biracial (Asian and black) golfer, can rise to the top of fields dominated by white men, I would definitely say there is no limitation. And if Colin Powell, a black man, can be encouraged by millions of Americans to run for the presidency of the United States, I would definitely say there is no limitation.

Some of you will also have to make the decision not to fall into a stereotypical job or let someone push you into one. Refuse to be a basketball player just because you're 6'5" if it doesn't fulfill your soul and make you happy. Refuse to pursue a degree in the sciences just because you're supposed to be good in math; do it only if you feel you will be operating at your highest level by doing so. Refuse to be a gardener or a cook just because you know others in your culture who are doing this work; do it only if it satisfies the creative urge within your spirit. Follow only that profession that is a calling—that work about which you can truly be passionate.

Working to accomplish a goal is the essence of being truly alive—without it, you are just existing. If you choose the right career for your life, one that comes from your heart, you will know it because the universe will respond by providing you the support you need to accomplish the goal. Be open to receiving that support from wherever or whomever it comes. And know that if you pursue your dreams, you enhance yourself as well as others and, ultimately, make the world a better place for everyone.

Of course, all of this means nothing if you haven't yet established or ever identified a definite career goal—or if you don't believe that you can come up with one. So in the following pages, you will find some tools and guidance to help you determine your career goal and gather the confidence to achieve it.

IDENTIFYING YOUR CALLING

A first step toward developing a career is establishing a goal you can commit to working toward. The right career for your life is the one that is based on a dream that comes from your heart. And the avenue for discovering that dream career may be closer than you realize. It may stem from desires you expressed or felt in your early childhood.

When I look at the steps that led to my current profession as a career consultant, speaker, and writer, I truly believe I was guided subconsciously along this path by my childhood aspirations. As a little girl, I wanted to be a missionary. And a teacher. And a philanthropist (at the time, I didn't actually know the title—I just knew I wanted to have enough money to help others achieve their dreams). Even though I didn't go into any of these professions, my career incorporates elements from all of them.

Think about the activities you involve yourself in—either through work, for fun, or as a volunteer. What aspects of these activities do you particularly enjoy? Can you trace them back to any desires you expressed during childhood? Statements made as a child are powerful because such aspirations are not yet tainted by any reality that says they cannot happen. They often reflect strong inner drives and can be indicators of where success will be found in your future. Think back to when you were a child—can you remember having a clear idea about what you wanted to be when you grew up? That childhood vision may be your key to true career satisfaction.

Blanca and Sean clearly remember their childhood dreams, and these dreams led them both to their present careers. As a child, Blanca often told her mother that she wanted to get a job hiring people so that she could give everyone she knew a job. Now, as a human resources professional, her job involves making employment recommendations and hiring people. Sean dreamed of enjoying personal freedom while making a lot of money to help his family. He realized these ambitions by going into sales—working on commission gives him freedom, and by working hard and excelling at his job, he is able to generate the high income he needs.

Perhaps you don't immediately remember having as clear a childhood vision as Blanca or Sean did. If not, the following questions may help you reexamine your childhood aspirations and identify areas to explore for developing a career that will motivate you to succeed.

- As a child, what did you tell your parents and friends when they asked what you wanted to be when you grew up?

- When you played with other children, what kind of games did you want to play and what role did you assume—the leader, the organizer, the follower, the helper, or the problem-solver?

- Did adults make comments to you about the kind of work you should do based on their observations of your actions (e.g., "Honey, you're always trying to take care of someone—you'll probably be a doctor or social worker when you grow up.")?

- In comparing what you wanted to be as a child to the types of functions that you perform well now, do you notice a pattern of skills or interests? (For example, as a child perhaps you wanted to be a fireman, and now you are involved in a community-based group that provides a messenger service and delivers meals to house-bound seniors. Both your dream as a youngster and your present work involve people-oriented activities, constantly helping others, and managing people or solving problems.)

MAKE SURE YOU WANT THE DREAM FOR THE RIGHT REASON

As you think about the career you dreamed of as a child, be sure to look at the origins of that dream. This way you can determine whether the underlying motivation is a valid one on which to build a career. Will it truly represent the type of profession that will give you satisfaction?

For instance, you may be thinking of becoming a firefighter only because you admired Uncle Pete when you were growing up—you wanted to be just like him. If you pursue a career as a firefighter for this reason, it probably won't provide you with the same satisfaction as it did your role model. On the other hand, if you wanted to become a firefighter because you loved the idea of saving people's lives and homes and working in emergency situations, then your career choice is most likely motivated by the desires of your heart. You can be certain you're being true to your inner self if you can see a relationship to firefighting in some elements of the activities you enjoy now, perhaps helping people in a volunteer activity or handling family and neighborhood emergencies.

Whether you build your career on a childhood dream or simply on something you enjoy doing, the motivation needs to spring from your heart to be truly fulfilling. If you formulate a goal based on the wrong motivation, it won't provide a solid foundation for you to endure the challenges you'll face ahead. Your attempt will eventually become a halfhearted effort, and because the universe does not judge—it just responds—your result will, in turn, also be halfhearted. Take the time to search within yourself for the answer.

Let the Dream Be Yours—Not Someone Else's

I've known people who have lost sight of their dreams or pushed them aside to follow career paths based on the hopes, needs, or expectations of others. A young man I knew who grew up with dreams of being an artist entered a profession his parents thought would guarantee him a good living. A young woman who had her heart set on becoming a lawyer struggled instead to become an actress to satisfy her mother's own thwarted ambition for a profession in the arts. Similarly, a young husband set aside his wish to teach and entered a more lucrative profession to accommodate his wife's need for economic security.

Clearly, these people are living someone else's dream. When others insist that you follow a path other than the one you have chosen for yourself, they are usually motivated by their own needs and not by yours. When people offer you career advice or urge you in a specific direction other than one you've chosen, you need to consider their suggestions in light of their biases and values.

For instance, a friend or family member who places a strong emphasis on practicality and security might encourage you to pursue a career in a field like engineering or finance, because they believe it would be an avenue to financial security. On the other hand, a person who values creativity over practicality might encourage you to follow a creative path in the arts. Whatever the case, pursuing a career to live someone else's dream or simply to ensure economic security will not provide the stimulation you need to keep you motivated.

The right career does not have to be a lofty ideal that will impact thousands; it simply needs to be based on what you want to do (see "Just Do What Makes You Happy"). Whether it comes from a need for creativity or practicality, it must bring psychological fulfillment based on your own dreams and unique personal talents. With a clear vision and true aptitude as your foundation, success can be achieved in any profession, as long as you are committed and willing to take the steps necessary to bring that talent to fruition.

JUST DO WHAT MAKES YOU HAPPY

■

"I can't say that I've ever really had a dream job in mind—I've just always looked for a job where I would be happy," says Phyllis, who believes that taking risks and doing what you love are the keys to success. "You have to be willing to put your best foot forward, take chances, and not be afraid to try something different. After that, if you're not happy, be willing to move on."

Phyllis acknowledges that most Asian-American women have careers in an analytical fields such as finance, accounting, or financial analysis or in helping professions such as teaching and human resources. But in spite of these cultural influences, she opted to pursue a career that led to sales. After deciding at age 16 that she wanted to work behind a sales counter, Phyllis applied for a job at a large department store. The person in charge of hiring told her that the company would not hire her to work behind the counter but could offer her a job in gift wrapping. She thanked the person nicely and went across the street to a competitor store, where she got the job she wanted. She chuckles when she says, "I still don't shop at that other store to this day."

After that, Phyllis developed her career by continually seeking out new opportunities that made her happy and that also advanced her career. "I always moved forward and haven't wasted time with a job that did not offer me what I wanted. Her attitude toward people and discrimination has helped her progress. "I refuse to see the racial attitudes of a few people as a factor that can stop my progress. Also, I don't view people in terms of what group they belong to—I deal with them as individuals. My two best friends in school were a Jewish girl and a black Catholic girl. I was the Asian Protestant, and people referred to us as the three musketeers. We were drawn together because of our ambition. We loved talking about our differences and really learned a lot from each other."

For Phyllis, sharing common values and goals can provide a stronger bond than race. She also believes that cultural diversity within business has the potential to improve relationships among people of different backgrounds. "In the new team environment, we have to be able to count on one another, or we're all going down. We need to be aware of other cultural backgrounds. It's our responsibility as individuals to find out about each other."

■

PHYLLIS MIYOSHI
Asian-American corporate executive
Account Executive, Drake Beam Morin, Inc.
Los Angeles, California
Business: Global transition consulting firm

Don't Postpone Choosing Your Dream

Karen's story is an example of what can happen when you live someone else's dreams. A nursing professional, Karen always wanted a career in the fashion industry but instead followed her mother's advice to enter the nursing profession so that she would have job security. As a nurse, Karen's credentials and knowledge enabled her to move rapidly into a supervisory position. However, as a supervisor, she felt frustrated and often received complaints for being abrupt with the staff. People on the job thought she was angry with them much of the time.

Karen may have been difficult to work with as a nurse, but in her off-hours she was a different person. Spending her evenings and weekends working as a freelance fashion coordinator, Karen seemed stimulated and happy. She assembled and maintained wardrobes for a select clientele that she had developed mostly through referrals. When she wasn't working directly with a client, she would spend hours browsing the clothing stores and discount marts, looking for bargains or special items for her clients. In spite of the demands it put on her time, working as a fashion coordinator energized Karen because she loved the work.

While Karen found some element of satisfaction in both nursing and fashion since both were service-oriented and required attention to detail, her heart was in fashion. Even so, she continued working full-time in nursing and freelancing in fashion until outside circumstances forced her to make a choice. After a twenty-five-year nursing career, the catalyst to change professions came when her hospital changed hands and the new management offered Karen the option to leave her job with a large severance. Realizing that it was now or never, Karen decided to follow her lifelong dream. Now, she earns a modest income as a fashion coordinator and supplements that with the income she gets from the real estate investments she made with her severance money.

Karen's story emphasizes the importance of choosing a career early based on your own interests and aptitudes rather than on someone else's expectations and advice. Obviously, doing work that you love and are good at will provide you with the greatest satisfaction and an ongoing sense of challenge and motivation. Your responses to the following questions will help you determine if the goal you have set is based on your own motivation or someone else's expectations.

- Do you love being involved in activities that are aligned with your goal—so much so that you spend much of your leisure time doing them? For instance, if you're planning to be an attorney, do you love going to the courthouse or the law library, following a trial for its points, or analyzing the merits of a case?

- Do you spend some of your leisure time involved in reading information that supports your goal? For example, a person who wants to start his own business might be found reading books on business start-up, finances, or developing a winning marketing plan.

- Do you volunteer your time in any activity associated with your goal? An aspiring photographer who wants to build her portfolio in order to compete on a professional level will be likely to volunteer to photograph a variety of occasions.

- Would you still pursue your desired goal if you could do something else and make more money?

CAN YOUR VISION STAND BEING CHALLENGED?

While some people let the dreams of others influence their career choices or pursue dreams that are not grounded, others allow their dreams to fall by the wayside for one reason or another: lack of confidence in their ability to achieve the goal, lack of knowledge about what it takes to succeed, or negative programming that limits their ability to succeed. If you give in to psychological obstacles like these, you'll probably never come close to achieving your goals. If, on the other hand, you work to overcome these roadblocks while keeping your vision strong, your chances for success are almost guaranteed.

It's unrealistic to expect that any positive goal won't be challenged by obstacles—that's a given. Just because you have a vision doesn't mean that it is going to be easy to bring it to fruition or that glory, fame, and fortune will come instantaneously. Most often, the road to success involves education and training, followed by hard work and a commitment to slow but steady progress.

Realizing this, how do you work to overcome any psychological obstacles that are blocking your progress? If your problem is lack of confidence, you can build it up by accomplishing small steps related to your goal. If your goal seems overwhelming to you, simply think of it in terms of one step at a time, moving ahead slowly but steadily in the right direction. As you grow more confident in your vision, you allow yourself to be open to more opportunities and support from wherever or whomever they come.

Another potential psychological obstacle that is easily overcome is lack of knowledge. Not knowing what it really takes to succeed in a profession that appeals to you is no reason to abandon it. Knowledge can be easily gained. Instead of being fearful about the unknown, take

ESTABLISHING LIFE-CAREER GOALS

The right career plan works in conjunction with your life goals and may be instrumental in accomplishing your life-career dream. Satisfaction with your plan may depend upon fulfilling some of your most important life goals. The following list represents areas where you may have such goals. While it is not all-inclusive, it should stimulate thought about important life goals that you need to consider when choosing a career path. Clarify the goals you have in each area, and then prioritize the areas in terms of their importance. This will help you to identify what will truly motivate you.

Spiritual　Goals that contribute to moral or spiritual ideals: being involved in a religious community, making a contribution to help humankind, making the environment better, becoming a better person in some way.

Physical　Goals that involve developing overall good health: eating right, exercising, engaging in sports and other group activities.

Financial　A short-term and long-term dollar and/or asset goal: How much money do you need to support the lifestyle you want and still have reserves for the future?

Family　Goals that involve marriage, children, parents, or other family members you have responsibility for and with whom you want to spend time.

Lifestyle　Goals that lead to a good quality of life: e.g., environmental circumstances, such as commuting time between work and home; where you want to live; ability to control work and schedule; balance between work and personal life.

Interests　Goals that involve personal hobbies, extracurricular activities, community service, a creative endeavor.

the steps to research your career and find out exactly what you will need to achieve success in your profession of choice. As you read on, you will discover more ways to find out what you need and how to develop your plan.

Look Out for Negative Programming

Probably the most insidious career challenge to a person of color is getting rid of lifelong negative programming that can dictate your career choices. As I touched on earlier, negative programming can be so ingrained that it causes unconscious responses. Some of the beliefs and messages that have been hammered into your head and programmed into your subconscious can stop you before you've even begun—messages like: "You'll only be able to go so far in the white world"; "That's a man's job"; "Everyone expects you people to be smart in math."

Negative programming is often hard to recognize. It may take the form of a subtle negative feeling, or, as in Leon's case, an automatic refusal to follow a path that would take him away from that which his family expected. Leon played the clarinet all through grammar school and high school. He had an obvious musical gift and enjoyed playing so much that he made special adjustments in his schedule to accommodate practicing and performing in the school band. His musical aptitude eventually earned him a full four-year scholarship to a major university.

He declined the scholarship, however, and instead stayed in his small hometown working at a laborer's job to help support his mother and younger sisters and brothers. Knowing that his mother and siblings depended on him, Leon chose work that would bring in steady income. He reasoned that a degree in music would not be practical because it did not offer any financial promise.

Obviously, Leon let lifelong programming strongly influence his career choices. A product of an environment that expected the eldest son to take on the responsibility of an absentee father, Leon grew up seeing himself as head of household. His mother called him "her little man" and created in him a burden of responsibility that would not allow him to follow any dream that would conflict with his family responsibilities. This negative programming made it impossible for him to pursue a "frivolous" career in music.

Identify Internal Barriers

No one can argue that overcoming barriers created by cultural tradition or racism in the workplace are significant challenges; however, they are external factors that are pretty easy to recognize. The biggest challenges that you will face may be internal ones—beliefs and ways of thinking that are blocking you from achieving your potential. Actually, you may not even be aware of these internal obstacles because they are so deeply ingrained in your psyche.

Try to identify these potential internal barriers by asking yourself some hard questions about what might be holding you back. Are you afraid to pursue your goal because it means making changes or venturing into something unknown? Are you being held back by inner voices telling you "You don't have what it takes to do that," "You'll never be anything," "You're not smart (talented, aggressive) enough"? Are you afraid that if you achieve success in your chosen career, you may face rejection in your community?

Being aware of these internal fears is half the battle. Once you can identify the fears that may be holding you back, you can take steps to overcome them. Realize that everyone is afraid at some point in their life. Everyone is confronted by some kind of programming they have to deal with—whether it was developed in the home, by the media, in school, or whatever. Such fears are a fact of life. But if you want to make your dreams a reality, you have to be willing to proceed in spite of the fear. And sometimes resisting that fear will actually propel you forward toward accomplishing your goal.

Overcoming this kind of negative programming may be difficult, but you'll need to do it before you can achieve your goals. Start by examining any negative reactions you have to your career dreams, then try to identify the motivation for the negative feeling, and, finally, determine if it truly makes sense for it to influence your career decision. *Latino Success* by Augusto Failde and William Doyle can help you learn to deal with this negative programming or with taking on a role that is not traditional for your culture. While the book highlights Latino people and focuses on issues specific to their perspective, it can be helpful for anyone trying to work through negative programming.

If you find that you have been influenced by negative programming and have felt torn about pursuing the career that you think is right for you, discuss your conflict with someone you respect to help you see the reasons behind your choices. It will be worth the effort to get on the right track early because, in the long run, working hard for something you believe in is actually easier than hardly working for something you don't want to do. In the first instance, you will be motivated because your heart is in your work; in the latter, you will eventually feel as if you've died spiritually—because your creative instinct will perish without the nourishment of a dream. If you say there is something that you want to do but have done nothing at all about it or you have no genuine enthusiasm for it, then you probably have the wrong goal. Look for another one that you can pursue with passion.

Evaluate Your Dream

Before committing to a goal based on your vision, evaluate your dream against the following statements to help determine if it can stand being challenged. If you can say yes to each statement, then you're ready to take the next step.

- You have resolved issues about conflicting responsibilities or finances and are ready to proceed.

- You have elected to follow your career dreams, even though some other type of work seems more lucrative.

- Comments from others that your career dream is unrealistic have only served to provide you with more areas to research before setting your goal.

DREAMS ARE AGELESS AND TIMELESS

Perhaps you have a clear vision of your career goals but have told yourself that you're too old or too far along in your career to pursue them. You convince yourself to stay where you are by talking yourself out of trying to attain new goals. Do these excuses sound familiar?

- "I'm not 20 anymore—it's too late for me."

- "I should be happy to just get a job and try to make the best of it."

- "Pursuing a dream is not for people with responsibilities like me; it's for those who can afford to take a risk."

- "Why should anyone hire me when they can get a younger, more enthusiastic person?"

Are you tempted to use any of these reasons for not allowing yourself to have a dream? A person over 40 who has a vision brings more than passion to the goal; she often brings maturity and wisdom as well. These qualities can make a person more goal-oriented and able to reach her goals, and they can provide added value for potential employers. If you are reentering the workforce or changing careers, there is no reason to be deterred by age.

Dare to Set a Goal Based on Your Dream

Once you've identified your dream, the next step is to bring that dream into focus and establish a realistic career goal based on it. To do this, you'll need to explore and research your chosen profession as a whole to determine which specific area of it will best support your goal and what steps you need to take to get there. The next few chapters will help you do just that.

RESOURCES

Finding Motivation

Latino Success: Insights from 100 of America's Most Powerful Latino Business Professionals by Augusto Failde and William Doyle (Simon & Schuster, 1996). Gives a unique perspective on what it takes for a Hispanic person to succeed. The concepts in the book are universal and will be motivational to anyone. Includes information that is especially good for addressing some cultural limitations and how to overcome them.

Live Your Dreams by Les Brown (Morrow, 1992). Provides a personal formula for success and happiness—positively charged with thoughts, guidance, and examples, plus an action planner to help you focus on your specific goals.

Personal Approach: A Game Plan for Unlimited Success by Johnnie Johnson (Dove Books, 1996). Written by a former Los Angeles Rams superstar, this book offers a game plan for unlimited success. While stressing preparation and self-control, it focuses on unlocking your potential.

Choosing a Career

Finding Your Perfect Work by Paul and Sarah Edwards (Tarcher/Putman, 1996). While this book is designed for people who want to work for themselves, it is also an excellent source for job seekers who want help in identifying careers that are right for them. I find this to be a good book for those just starting out on their career track because it has an entrepreneurial focus that's needed by everyone who wants to succeed in the twenty-first century, whether in a company or in their own business.

How to Choose the Right Career by Louise Welsh Schrank (Passport Books, 1991). Uses an interest indicator as a model. Guides you in narrowing your interests, then shows jobs that align with those interests, as well as the prospects for those jobs.

What Color Is Your Parachute? by Richard Nelson Bolles (Ten Speed Press, updated annually). Deals with the comprehensive process of finding a first job, as well as making a career change, and finding alternative ways to work when you can't find a traditional job. Provides a process for identifying and deciding where you want to use the skills you most enjoy.

Wishcraft—How to Get What You Really Want by Barbara Sher with Annie Gottlieb (Ballantine, 1986). A down-to-earth, step-by-step approach to setting a goal and implementing it. Shows how to translate dreams into practical realities. Deals with discovering strengths and skills and turning negative fears and feelings into positive tools. Shows how to diagram the path to your goal, map out target dates for meeting it, chart daily progress, create a support network of contacts and sources, and use a buddy system to keep you on track.

CHAPTER

FITTING THE DREAM
INTO REALITY

I dentifying your dream can be a wonderful process. It allows you to enter a realm where all things seem possible. But putting that dream into focus and translating it into a career goal can be agonizing. For instance, let's say you want to be a writer (the dream). The next step is to ask yourself what kind of writing you want to do (the goal). Magazine articles? Novels? Poetry? Educational books? Children's books? Finally, and possibly the hardest part: You need to figure out what it will take to get there (the objectives).

In translating my dream into a career goal, I went through a lot of self-examination and reflection, followed by more examination, research, and analysis before I finally decided what I wanted to do. After that, I evaluated my career goal against my life goals to determine if they would fit together to help me achieve my life-career dreams. This chapter will help you begin that same process. (Use The Action Plan as an ongoing summary of your analysis.)

THE ACTION PLAN

Use the following Action Plan form to help summarize the information you gather while researching your career goal. Photocopy it and continue revising the information as your process of discovery unfolds. When you have completed your final revision, it will help serve as a guide in deciding what kind of companies and jobs to pursue.

Revision No. _____
Date _____

    My ultimate career dream is to be a(n) _____. Attainment of this dream would satisfy my (love/passion) for _____ _____. It fits my natural ability/abilities in the following area(s): _____. I expect to reach my goal within _____ months/years.

    I have talked with _____ and _____ about the realities of what I want to do because they have already achieved success in the field. I have also talked with _____ and _____ because they know me, and I trust their feedback about my capabilities.

    Based on my research, I believe that I need additional education in the form of _____ and _____. I have investigated how I can get that education and have enrolled at _____ _____ to secure it.

    I know from my research that I need experience that will allow me to develop skills in _____ and _____. I have spoken with (my boss/a human resources representative/someone at a nonprofit organization/other) _____ about doing some work in the area of _____ in order to get the experience I need. Within _____ months of securing some experience, I intend to go after a job doing _____, which will give me more experience and move me closer to my goal.

    I see the following jobs of _____, _____, or _____ as interim jobs to help me reach the goal. My current job of _____ helps by _____.

    I've joined a professional group, called _____, which is providing me with an opportunity to develop a professional network as well as to work on activities that I will be able to include on my résumé.

Hard as it is, when you've determined a career goal based on your dream, you will have taken the next important step to getting where you want to be. Your career goal is the cornerstone of your success—but to build your career, you'll need other crucial building blocks, including the right education, relevant experience, and an action plan. Without these, you might end up taking a flying leap to nowhere or spinning your wheels in frustration at your lack of progress.

Setting your goal and reaching it will be your responsibility—and yours alone. By accepting this responsibility, you will set yourself apart from people who take the first jobs offered to them and then passively let their company or manager dictate the progression of their careers. Managing and directing your career will make you feel more in control of your destiny and, ultimately, happier and more secure in your work. To do this, you need to plan on carving out your career path, independent of a particular job or company, and not expect anyone—employer or colleagues—to help you make your dreams a reality.

The responsibility for accomplishing your goals may seem overwhelming at first. But believe me, if you proceed slowly and learn as much as you can about the career you think you want before really committing to it, you'll develop the insight to make informed choices and move forward in a direction that is right for you. In fact, a clear and practical understanding of what you need to reach your goal and what you can expect once you get there may actually strengthen your commitment and enhance your motivation.

LOOK FIRST, LEAP LATER

To get a sense of what it means to proceed slowly and build your commitment, consider the different approaches taken by two friends of mine—Kristine and Judy. Both dreamed of owning their own company. Kristine worked in the public relations department of a large manufacturing company. When she told coworkers of her ambition to own her own public relations firm, they found her passion and

THE REALITY CHECK

You stand a better chance of being happy and successful in a career you truly love. The questions below apply to anyone on a career quest, and your responses will let you know whether you have chosen a career that will put you on the track to success. Answer true or false to the following statements or questions.

1. I've decided what I want to do or at least the skills I am most excited about using and am looking forward to starting my career.
   (If you haven't decided what you want to do, then you're trying to steer a ship without a rudder. Reread chapter 2, talk with a counselor, and decide at least which skills you enjoy using.)

2. My friends and family are 100 percent supportive of my career choice.
   (Don't expect everyone to support your dream, especially if it conflicts with their needs.)

3. I have already done work in my chosen profession and/or actually volunteer my services because I enjoy using the skills so much.
   (If you really love your chosen profession, you can't help but do it—sometimes just for the sheer joy of it.)

4. I already have a degree relevant to my career path, so I don't have to worry about making education and training part of my development plan.
   (You may not have to get another degree, but the training and updating of skills never stops. It should always be a part of your plan.)

determination so forceful that no one dared challenge her plan by expressing a lack of faith in it. Still, some believed she didn't have the ability or experience necessary to realize her dream. In a sense, they were right, but Kristine took the steps necessary to build her skills and get the education and experience she needed to successfully strike out on her own.

She began by assisting with public relations for community functions on a freelance basis. The efforts reinforced her goal but also made her aware of her need for more specific training and education.

THE REALITY CHECK—Continued

5. I've identified the technical training I need and am currently enrolled in a program.
   (Start your technical training as soon as possible. Rearrange your lifestyle to accommodate that need. That's what committed people do.)

6. I've met people who are involved in my desired profession; I like them and the culture I will work in.
   (If you don't like the people in your profession, you may have chosen the wrong profession or the wrong application of your skills.)

7. I pride myself on being able to work with and maintain good interpersonal relationships with all people. I like people and it shows.
   (The ability to maintain good interpersonal relationships is an essential skill for progress.)

8. I am computer literate and have my own system at home.
   (If you don't have a system, make some sacrifices to get one.)

9. I have developed both a short- and long-range goal and a plan for accomplishing both.
   (If you're serious, you'll have at least drafted a plan of your short- and long-term goals.)

10. I have reviewed my development plan with someone who has been there.
    (Reality-testing your plans with someone who has been there can save you time and add value to your ideas.)

Instead of stopping her freelance work and enrolling in school full-time, Kristine decided to keep working while attending school. Her commitment steadily grew stronger and helped her to persevere through the long hours and to manage the many demands on her time. Eventually, she accumulated enough experience and know-how to start her own company.

Unlike Kristine, Judy jumped headfirst into pursuing her dream of owning her own realty company. She quit her job as a junior accountant, went to school to get her real estate license, and then started marketing single-family dwellings. Just three months into her new career, however, Judy realized she hated the real estate business.

She detested wearing a beeper and having to work evenings and weekends, and she could not get used to the insecurity of knowing that any deal could fall through at the last minute.

Judy was trying to drive a BMW dream with a Pinto commitment. The realities of her chosen career forced her to admit that the demands were not worth the rewards. Ultimately, she achieved some aspects of her dream by finding a position that drew on her real estate training. Judy gladly gave up the goal of owning her own company and returned to a more structured and secure position as an office manager with a large real estate development company.

TEST THE WATER

Kristine's and Judy's stories show how important it is to research a major career move before making a full commitment to it. Before you give up your current job or enroll in an educational program, take the time to see if your dream can be translated into a workable goal for you.

Begin exploring your dream career by making a list of questions you need answers to, then add to the list as your process of discovery unfolds. What are the various professional categories connected with your goal (e.g., if you're exploring the field of engineering, are you interested in mechanical, electrical, structural, civil, or systems engineering)? How much money can you expect to make at the beginning and, ultimately, at the height of this career? How easy or difficult is it to find work in this field?

Consider the education and experience you'll need to get you where you want to go careerwise and decide whether you want to invest the time and money needed to commit to it. Also, look at the work culture of your chosen career and ask yourself whether you would be truly comfortable working in that environment.

Essentially, the broad categories of your research should include but not be limited to:

- The education and experience necessary and what you can do to acquire it

- The culture of the industry (e.g., the type of people, the environment, the working hours)

- Your earning potential

- The best geographic locations for this field and whether you might have to relocate in order to advance in your chosen career

After you've listed all the questions that come to mind, start doing the legwork to find your answers. Go to your public library or college career planning center and ask the librarian for help in gathering information about your prospective profession. Ask to see trade journals so you can get a sense of the industry or past issues of the Sunday paper so you can look through the classifieds to find out about the job market in your area.

But don't stop there. Make a point of talking with as many people as you can about your goals. This is where, as a person of color, you may need to step outside of your cultural mind-set and expand your social activities so that you interact with people of other races and cultures. Talking about your goals with a diverse group of people that have a common interest will give you information that can help you as well as them in accomplishing career goals.

To hook up with people who share your goal or who are already doing what you want to do, contact professional associations that represent your career interest (check the *Encyclopedia of Associations* at your public library for information). Speak with professors who teach in the subject area where your interest lies. Network with friends to meet people who are already working in the profession or industry you want to go into. If you're working now, you may be able to talk with someone in your company's human resources department about new career opportunities in the company and ask for referrals to others who can help you in researching your goal.

Try to determine if what you want to do truly fits your personality. Evaluate the information you glean from talking with and observing people in your desired profession. Do they have a personality similar to yours? Do you like the activities and environment surrounding the profession? For instance, if you are an extremely social person, would you be happy in a job that required long periods of isolation?

You may find, as you do your research, that you really don't want to invest the time or money or make the sacrifices necessary to achieve the goal you've selected. Maybe the effort just seems more than you're willing to make or the work culture does not suit you. But don't let this stop you from continuing toward your goal. It may simply mean that, like Judy, you've discovered that you'll be happier pursuing an alternative goal—one that allows you to follow your interests and use your talent and skills but in a different capacity than you at first envisioned. If this is the case, use the research you've already compiled as a starting point to explore alternative ways of using your skills, possibly in a different but related capacity or on a part-time, freelance, or volunteer basis.

WHAT TYPE OF INDUSTRY: DOES IT MATTER?

Why is it so important to get a sense of the working culture that you'll be in once you achieve your professional goal? Because if you feel comfortable in the working environment and share with your colleagues a similar outlook, personal style, and sensibility, you have the greatest chance of being happy in your work.

Also, the compatibility of working style, personality, and values works both ways. How the employer feels you will "fit" into the organization will strongly influence the hiring decision. Generally, if you have common interests with the interviewer or interests that align well with the culture of the organization, you will you make a more positive impression. And if you choose an industry because it is aligned with your personal values, then you will probably also understand the culture and feel compatible with the people in it.

In fact, as a person of color who has to switch from a cultural mind-set to a business mind-set, one of the greatest benefits of being part of an industry that complements your values and personal style (cultural mind-set) is the tremendous psychological advantage of being able to easily network with people you like as opposed to people you're only able to tolerate. In a compatible working culture, networking and finding mentors—both essential for your professional progress—will come naturally.

In my workshops, disgruntled ex-employees often blame their layoffs on their refusal to play "politics" or "brownnose." But I've noticed that people who work in a culture in which they feel comfortable do not view being considerate of their colleagues and managers as political—rather, it just comes naturally. It seems that when people are forced to be nice to people to whom they don't relate, they see it as brownnosing; but when they're nice to people they relate to, they see it simply as being a team player or just plain old considerate of others.

Of course, it can be more of a challenge to feel comfortable in a working environment when you are of a different race than the majority of the people in your business culture. Understandably, these coworkers will notice the difference as will you. But if the overall culture appeals to you, this may not be a big issue. If you allow yourself to be open and focus on the common work interests you share with your colleagues, you can establish a positive bond and develop strong working relationships.

Stepping Away from the Wrong Environment

If, despite your planning, you find yourself stuck in a work environment that goes against your grain, there are things you can do about it. You may be able to simply transfer your skills to a different industry as Naomi did; or you may decide to switch careers altogether as Claudia did.

Immediately after graduating from college, Naomi took a position with a company in the defense industry. The job was in purchasing, and she considered it an important one. After eighteen months, however, she realized that the industry and the attitudes inherent in this male-dominated militaristic environment conflicted with her basic nature. A lighthearted woman who functioned best in an unstructured environment, Naomi felt constricted by the serious personalities and rules and regulations of the industry.

The experience turned Naomi off in terms of her job and made her want to chuck her whole career, return to school, and start off in a new direction. But with the help of a career counselor, she figured out a way to transfer her skills to an industry that better fit her personality. She found a job in the purchasing department of a toy manufacturer and felt immediately at home in the company's more casual and fun environment.

Claudia had a similar experience, although her discomfort with her working environment compelled her to start over on an entirely new career path. After graduating with a Bachelor of Science degree, Claudia found an engineering job with an aerospace company. She thought the new job would give her a sense of accomplishment and that she would be satisfied with her career progress. But she wasn't. Naturally outgoing and sociable, Claudia found the quiet, structured life of the engineer stifling. However, because she had followed the engineering path to satisfy her parents' wish for her to have a career with a good future, she decided to stick it out.

After four years, she almost jumped for joy when the company decided to reduce its staff and presented her with an easy out. The layoff gave her the perfect opportunity to find a new path. Claudia met with a career counselor who pointed out that she would likely find greater satisfaction by combining her ability to handle details and follow through with her outstanding interpersonal skills. After agonizing over how a career change would disappoint her parents, Claudia did some networking with her friends and mentors and eventually elected to pursue a career in hotel management.

Through one of her networking contacts, she found a position as an assistant to the sales and marketing manager for a medium-size hotel. It didn't pay much, but it had the potential to lead to a position of responsibility within hotel management. It took only a few days on the job for Claudia to know that she had made the right decision. She felt absolutely at home in the more social atmosphere, amid the hustle and bustle of organizing conferences and banquets at the hotel. Within a few weeks, she had made the commitment to take a course in hotel management to prepare herself for career advancement.

Both Naomi and Claudia might have avoided landing in working cultures that did not suit them if they'd done more research before committing to their careers. Taking the time to do good research will help you better determine if you'll fit into a particular work environment. To get a sense of how a work culture will suit you, ask yourself:

- Am I comfortable with the people in the culture? Do we share some common interests? Do some of them have personalities similar to mine? Would we be likely to laugh at some of the same things?

- Would I be able to network easily with the people, or would I feel I was "brownnosing?" Could I be myself?

- Do I feel my race or gender will make a significant difference in my being successful within the culture?

WHAT EDUCATION OR TRAINING DO YOU NEED?

Once you've gotten a sense of the work culture, you'll have to figure out what practical skills you'll need to get there. Of course, we've all heard of those gifted people who, without the specific education or experience needed for their career goals, manage to soar gracefully and easily to the top of their fields solely on the basis of their talent, energy, and belief in themselves. If you're one of those fortunate few, blessed with a finely tuned talent that's ready-made for the present and future workplace, congratulations. The rest of us will have to commit to some level of formal training now, as well as later, to move forward in our professions.

Obviously, the ideal time to get formal training is before beginning a serious career trek, when you have fewer commitments and financial pressures. But for any number of reasons, that simply may not be possible. You may have started working before you had clearly identified a goal; you may not have had the money to attend school; or you may have majored in an area that does not support your current career goal. But once you've established your goal, don't let your concern over starting late deter you from getting the proper training and education. With commitment and motivation, you can attain the skills and knowledge you need and still achieve your goal.

"GET PREPARED"

∎

"I didn't have a lot of direction. Neither of my parents went to college, and I didn't have counselors directing me toward career goals and helping me to understand my options. Eventually, however, I fell into a career that matched my skill set." Like many people, Charsetta chose her college because she had friends there and she liked the location. She decided to work toward a degree in speech pathology and, after graduation, to become a teacher. Because she had several relatives who were teachers, this career choice seemed familiar and comfortable to her.

"It wasn't until my senior year that I realized that teaching wasn't for me because it was not stimulating enough. The school atmosphere was not what I wanted." Deciding that business would provide the challenge and stimulation she sought, Charsetta found an entry-level job in a corporation. At the same time, knowing she needed more education if she wanted to advance in a business career, she went back to school part-time and earned an M.B.A.

"My first job was in human resources. I enjoyed the people contact, which matched my skill set of language and verbal competence. I came in at a clerical level and worked my way up. I wouldn't recommend that path for a degreed person, though—it's hard to make the jump to the professional

ranks after having been labeled clerical because people don't automatically think of you as a candidate for professional positions. If you have some options, come in as a professional."

After seventeen years and four companies, Charsetta has progressed from clerk to her present position as manager. Now, positioning herself for a move to a director level, she continues to prepare herself by developing professional breadth and depth. By taking on human resource assignments, both at the plant and the corporate office, Charsetta has mastered all aspects of human resources management, including compensation, staffing, training, benefits, and equal employment opportunity. In the future, she plans to further broaden her skills by seeking assignments in management development, organizational development, and training. Meanwhile, she continues to prepare herself for future career advancement by teaching herself computer skills and taking classes to stay current with new software packages.

For Charsetta, the importance of taking responsibility for one's own professional growth cannot be understated. "Companies are not taking a strong involvement in helping people get ahead, so mentors and networking are becoming increasingly important," she says. "Competing will be difficult. Many of us are still in awe of whites because we have not interacted with them in schools, colleges, and in our social circles, so we hold back. Instead, we need to be more assertive, toot our own horns, and take responsibility for our own careers."

■

CHARSETTA HENDERSON
Black manager
Kraft Foods, Chicago, Illinois
Business: Human resources management

Options for Learning While Your Earning

Maria, a quality control inspector with a major electronics company, had tears in her eyes when she told me how much she wanted to be a software engineer. She had never been interested in the type of work she was currently doing, but with only a liberal arts degree and poor English skills, she was unprepared to pursue her dream. Although she was only 23, Maria thought she was getting a late start in going after the career she truly wanted. Still, being highly intelligent and very motivated, she ignored this worry and began to work to overcome her deficiencies. Though it was tough on her, she went to night school to enhance her English-speaking skills and to get the technical training she needed to become a software engineer.

If you're getting a late start on a career path you are truly driven to pursue, remember that you, like Maria, can work and get paid while gaining the experience and training you need. The only excuse for not doing so is lack of commitment. If you want more education but cannot pursue it in a traditional daytime program or at night school, you still have options:

A work-study program. Cooperative education integrates classroom theory with practical experience by enabling a student to combine specific periods of attendance at a college with specific periods of related employment. Programs and courses in all disciplines are available in many colleges and universities all over the country. Check with local colleges to see if work-study programs are available and in what areas of study they are offered.

Distance learning programs. There are thousands of telecourses and complete degree programs and certificates offered by two- and four-year colleges and universities, delivered to home or work via television, computer, or audiotape and/or videotape. Distance learning is a good option for people who need to study when and where they want to and around busy schedules.

If your action plan includes working and going to school, you'll want to focus on finding work with employers that will support your education and training needs. The best employers are those who are progressive in all their business practices, including employee education, and who offer tuition-reimbursement programs for classes, seminars, and workshops related to the industry. Some employers will even reimburse your education costs regardless of what type of degree you're pursuing.

Communication/Interpersonal Skills

To compete in the high-tech, multicultural, team-oriented global workplace of this and the coming century, you will need not only the experience and training required by your profession but also effective communication skills. Being able to interact with people of all races, cultures, and temperaments and to work well within any environment is just as important as having talent and a goal. In fact, a good part of any hiring decision will likely be based on "chemistry" and how well the employer thinks you'll fit into his team. He must feel confident that you can communicate well with all people, particularly those who are part of the business culture of your profession.

I recently observed an excellent example of very effective communication skills. As my colleague Ann, an Asian-American career counselor, and I walked out of a restaurant, we passed a table of hourly workers employed by one of Ann's client companies. The white, Hispanic, and black men were attending a seminar nearby. Away from their normal workday environment and dining in a somewhat elegant restaurant, they looked a little uncomfortable in their surroundings. Ann stopped at the table and asked how they were doing. Her queries were light and casual, mostly comments about the weather, but her smile and her manner communicated the universal language of warmth and caring. Her friendly, relaxed, and mostly nonverbal communication immediately put the group at ease.

Ann's interpersonal skills came to her naturally, but some of us have to work at building them. A long time ago, I discovered a technique (I'm sure it's not new) that helped me develop good interpersonal skills quickly and easily; it may also work for you. I found that once I stopped worrying about how I was coming across and made a point of just being considerate of others, the communication seemed to flow smoothly and naturally. I've also learned that the best way to understand and reach others is to imagine myself in their shoes.

When you find yourself in a difficult or strained situation with another person (for example, when a new manager comes in to oversee your department), ask yourself how you would feel or react if you were in the other person's shoes. Try to step back and observe the situation without judgment while being sensitive to the discomfort and challenges of the other person.

If you're in a new environment, especially one that is culturally diverse, and the people seem reticent, don't assume they're rejecting you. They may only be unsure about approaching you. Instead of waiting for them to make the first move, try opening up the lines of communication yourself. A warm smile and a friendly "hello" might be the only things needed to bridge the gap. Always be willing to extend your hand first—even to someone who holds a job or social position superior to yours. But be careful not to be too forceful or aggressive; it can make people uncomfortable. Overall, the recipe for good interpersonal skills is a balanced blend of warmth, self-confidence, modesty, empathy, and humor.

Computer/Technical Skills

As fundamental and essential as strong communication skills are, computer skills will be just as important in advancing your career in the current workplace. Computers are everywhere, doing everything, and being used by everybody. Bosses, secretaries, service people, delivery people—workers at all levels of business use the computer to get the job done: to develop reports; retrieve, track, and organize information; plan functions; diagnose diseases; develop blueprints; balance checkbooks; locate missing persons; and train employees, among other things. Without computers, most modern businesses could not function. And now, the Internet has taken computer technology to a whole new level, linking people around the world on one communication network and offering the ability to communicate easily and instantly, transfer documents and data, and operate businesses from thousands of miles away.

Naturally, the future work environment will depend even more on computers and electronic technology. There's no getting around the fact that we'll all need some level of computer skills no matter what profession we go into. So don't be surprised when an employer wants to know not only if you're computer literate but also in what software programs you're proficient.

If you've somehow missed out on the computer revolution and have little to no skills in this area, start learning them now. Before you enroll in a class, find out what software programs and computer systems you'll likely use in your field. Even if you're already computer literate, you may need to learn a new program or computer system to match the requirements of your career. There are a number of ways to brush up on computer skills, learn new programs, and explore the Internet:

- For a nominal fee, adult evening classes at a high school or community college offer basic knowledge of personal computers, common word processing and spreadsheet programs, and navigating the Internet.

- Computer training centers generally charge higher fees and offer more specialized and in-depth training at weekend seminars. (If you're working now, your company may pay for these classes.)

- Some computer stores rent out computers on a weekly or monthly basis. If you don't yet have a computer at home, this might be a good way to practice your skills or keep current with new technology.

USING THE SKILLS THAT FIT YOUR GOAL

A formal education will supply the necessary theory and technical tools to move you in the right career direction, but it's the application of these skills in a practical setting that will be your truest test and teacher. Not only will this hone your talent, but it will also bring your goal into clearer focus. Getting experience before you actually get a job will help you find out whether you have the temperament, along with the talent and skills, to work well in a given business culture and to make the sacrifices that may be required. Most important, it could prevent you from committing to something you later realize is not right for you.

In addition to gaining practical experience, taking advantage of opportunities to develop applicable skills will sharpen your focus. For instance, if you have a degree in finance, serving as an assistant (voluntary or for pay) to the controller of a community-based or nonprofit organization could prove to be the right opportunity for you to apply the techniques you've learned in school to authentic situations in a real-world environment in order to see how effective you really can be.

In a competitive climate where employers want employees to be productive as soon as possible, it pays to have actual experience to support your technical knowledge. Volunteer work and internships are excellent ways to get this experience (see Internships: Learning on the Job). And oftentimes, these experiences turn into real job opportunities—after you've demonstrated your value.

Volunteer Work

Probably one of the easiest and fastest ways to gain the experience needed to support your career goal is through volunteer work. You should consider a six- to nine-month volunteer project as part of your continuing education, an investment in laying the foundation for your career.

There are plenty of nonprofit organizations that would be happy to allow you to develop skills within their ranks. Numerous agencies in every community need help in areas such as accounting, public relations, newsletter writing, and managing other volunteers. Serving as a volunteer not only develops your skill and builds your confidence, but it also enhances your marketability. You can include transferable skills gained from volunteer work on your résumé, which you can then use when seeking positions for which you have no direct on-the-job experience.

INTERNSHIPS: LEARNING ON THE JOB

Beyond volunteering, an ideal way to gain on-the-job experience is through an internship. If you have sufficient education and training as well as some contacts, you may be able to get an apprenticeship through a school program or start as an assistant to a senior professional. Generally, companies hire interns to work at minimal pay (or sometimes at no pay) while learning and performing the duties of a particular job.

Although interns generally work in low-level positions—as administrative support or assistants, for example—an internship provides exposure and experience that are recognized by other companies and that often open up doors—perhaps right at the company where one's interning.

While internships can be found in every area of business, some industries are particularly well-known for using interns. *Internships 1997* (Peterson's) has detailed information on more than 35,000 paid and unpaid internships in the United States and abroad. Listings are organized by subject areas, including:

- Creative, performing, and fine arts
- Communications and media
- Human and social services
- Public affairs
- Government and law
- Environment
- Education
- Business and technology

Stephanie, a black professional who visualized herself directing a major community service effort, effectively parlayed her volunteer experience into a job. She had little practical experience in community services, and although she had a college degree, it wasn't related to community work. She had a day job at a bank and started volunteering her services in community efforts after work and sometimes on weekends. After doing this for several months, she wrote a program proposal for one of her community groups and requested funding through a local nonprofit agency. This proposal included a position for herself as project director. When the agency granted funding, Stephanie got the job and was on her way to meeting her goal.

Nonprofit agencies are not the only places to look for volunteer positions. Few people realize, for example, that some corporations will consider hiring people to work for them on a volunteer basis. Approach the human resources department of a company you'd like to work for and ask about doing some volunteer work in the area you're interested in. The action alone will certainly show that you are committed to your profession. And even if the company does not hire you, after a while you will have developed transferable skills and gained, most likely, an excellent reference that could help you get a job elsewhere.

Volunteering isn't limited to people just starting out; those well along their career track do it too. Maybe you've noticed that new community groups and nonprofit agencies often fill key positions with executives from companies in the community. In fact, many executives use volunteering as a transition to a new career. Volunteering allows them to demonstrate capability in the new area as well as make contacts for the future (see "Volunteer to Build Your Career"). If you pay attention, you may notice that after a high-profile community project has been successfully completed and then publicized, the key people in the project often end up being recruited by companies to take on similar responsibilities and duties on their behalf, but this time for pay. You should think of volunteering as something you'll do throughout your career to develop new skills and contacts, and contribute your time and talent to good causes.

"VOLUNTEER TO BUILD YOUR CAREER"

■

Bob's first job was as an engineer at TRW, but his vision for himself has always included helping others. His passion for volunteering has been instrumental to his professional success. "While at TRW, I volunteered to counsel at-risk high school students by bringing them to the company so they could see actual role models of black engineers and scientists. I also got some fellow peers to do the same thing. This led to the write-up in the Los Angeles Times, *which credited TRW for initiating the program. As a result, the company decided to institute a companywide social responsibility program."*

Managers offered Bob the job of heading this program. He took it and continued his volunteer efforts while at the corporate office—but in another direction. Volunteering at the Opportunities Industrialization Center, headquartered in Philadelphia, he taught welfare-dependent mothers and at-risk youths job skills for electronic assembly, as well as basic reading and math skills. "The beauty of that program was that we were able to incorporate the basic educational skills these people needed with job skills. The participants were motivated because they knew they'd have a job afterwards."

As part of his corporate responsibility position, he connected with an African-American printer who had a $10-million contract with TRW. This brought Bob to the attention of the Interracial Council for Business Opportunity, which recruited him from TRW to serve as the council's executive director. "My task was to spearhead an all-volunteer operation charged with assisting people of color in packaging their loans and business plans to obtain financial aid from financial institutions. I was also responsible for fund-raising." To meet the challenges of this position, Bob enrolled in night classes at UCLA in an executive program to learn about business and finances.

He went on to become a troubleshooter for the council, traveling to its different chapters and developing several branches around the country to work out financing and fund-raising problems. His activities captured the attention of another group, Opportunities Funding Corporation, which recruited Bob as its volunteer director and charged him with raising funds, including his own salary, for the organization.

Bob's participation in various volunteer projects throughout his career has culminated in the challenging position he now holds—heading the Los Angeles Community Development Bank. The agency was established to assist people of color in south-central Los Angeles in setting up and developing businesses.

Bob's volunteer efforts are directly in line with his vision of service. Through his efforts, he has developed a career that's enabled him to progress from helping people just survive to helping them grow and expand so they can, in turn, help others.

■

C. ROBERT KEMP
Black executive
President & CEO,
Los Angeles Community Development Bank
Business: Community development

FITTING YOUR SKILLS INTO THE WORKPLACE

Forward planning, knowledge of your various options, and an analysis of how well your action plan aligns with your life-career plan should be an integral part of determining the best places to seek work. For instance, if you want to work in corporate America, research several industries, not just one. That way, if one industry starts to go into a slump (as aerospace has recently done), you will already have an idea of where you could transfer your skills. In addition, being familiar with several industries will give you a broader perspective for making a good job selection.

To help bring your career planning into even sharper focus, you'll also need a clear sense of your economic responsibilities. You may have to plan on working at a full-time job doing what you want, supplemented by a part-time job to keep you afloat until you get on an even plateau with your career—just as an aspiring artist might work part-time as a clerk in an arts supply store while spending her free time in the studio.

Finally, the bottom line will be the number of jobs available. Resources like *Workforce 2000*, by Joseph H. Boyett and Henry P. Conn, offer valuable information on what to expect in the new workplace as well as the skills needed and the types of jobs that will be most plentiful as we move into a new century. If there are only a few jobs available in your field, you may have to look at changing your objectives in order to stay in the professional arena in which you think you'd be most comfortable. If, on the other hand, there are plenty of jobs or opportunities in your field, you need only to develop a strong accomplishment-oriented résumé, hone up on your marketing strategy, and go for it.

"MATCH YOUR SKILLS WITH MARKET NEEDS"

■

"My dream has always been to be an entrepreneur. Most of my male family members are self-employed or professionals with a business on the side, so even though I didn't know what kind of business I wanted, I knew that I wanted one."

When Jerry first started out in business, a combination of coincidence, luck, and timing helped him turn a small photography studio into a lucrative modeling agency. "I opened a storefront and taught myself photography, including darkroom work, and learned by trial and error. The first person who came into the studio was a model. During our photography sessions, she complained she was not getting a lot of work because no agency was really handling blacks. About that time, some guys came around selling services in a black directory, so I listed my business as a modeling agency and started getting calls for black models."

For a while, Jerry did well with his modeling agency. Eventually, however, he established himself in a related but more lucrative and diverse endeavor. He relocated from Chicago to Los Angeles, where he developed a niche market placing safety engineers in executive positions. He has built a successful business by continually meeting the sometimes impossible parameters set by his clients in filling their staffing needs.

Jerry learned quickly to focus on the real goal of his business, which is placing qualified people in executive positions, regardless of their ethnicity. He deals with a diverse candidate pool, including black, Hispanic, Asian-American, and white men and women. Basically, Jerry believes that to succeed, a person must be able to recognize opportunity and be adaptable enough to respond to it quickly.

■

JERRY MEDLEY
Black entrepreneur
Search Professionals, Los Angeles, California
Business: Executive selection

RESOURCES

Internships

Internships 1997 (Peterson's, 1996). This excellent resource lists over 35,000 opportunities (paid and unpaid, national and abroad). Lists hard-to-find positions from organizations like Procter & Gamble and Amnesty International to stints with BMW of North America. Listings are conveniently organized by subject areas and include descriptions of each organization, type and number of positions available, salary (if a paid internship), eligibility, and contact information.

Making the Most of Your Education

How to Make Use of A Useless Degree: Finding Your Place in the Postmodern Economy by Andrew Frothingham (Berkley Publishing Group, 1996). In this absolutely delightful book, Frothingham shows you how you can transfer the skills you learned in college to the professional world and how to turn degrees into meaningful work that pays money. For example, he explains how to transfer the writing skills that come from writing college term papers into a viable profession, such as freelance writing, advertising copywriting, PR writing, journalism, technical writing, and desktop publishing.

Work-Study/Cooperative Education

The College Directory of Cooperative Education, edited by Stewart B. Collins (Drexel University), is an excellent reference source for cooperative education programs in the United States and Canada.

Distance Learning Programs

Distance Learning (Peterson's, 1996). A complete sourcebook of accredited educational programs delivered electronically. The book includes a full range of degree and nondegree programs available from more than 700 American and Canadian colleges and universities. Information includes how distance education compares to more traditional programs, how programs are assessed to ensure quality, selecting the right program, the nuts and bolts of applying and registering, taking exams, transferring credits, interacting with professors and classmates, and how to locate financial aid.

Virtual College by Pam Dixon (Peterson's, 1996). A concise guide to what distance education is all about, the equipment and technology know-how you'll need, time commitment and costs, what it's like being a student without a classroom, and more. A good book to read before you look at the course directories or sign up for a class.

Tuition Reimbursement

The Best Companies for Minorities: Employers Across America Who Recruit, Train and Promote Minorities by Lawrence Otis Graham (Plume, 1993). This excellent resource provides a listing of companies that offer tuition reimbursement programs and includes guidance for evaluating a company's commitment to its employees.

The Future Workplace

The Great Jobs Ahead: Your Comprehensive Guide to Surviving and Prospering in the Coming Work Revolution, previously published as *Job Shock*, by Harry S. Dent Jr. (Hyperion, 1996). This book provides excellent, timely information on factors that are driving the current work revolution (e.g., strategic focus, being customer driven, focus teams, information systems). It includes information on new skills needed (e.g., problem-solving, people and integrative skills, business and information technology skills), new career paths for the specialized generalist and the generalized specialist, and the behavior patterns needed to fit in.

Networking

Encyclopedia of Associations (Gale Publishing, updated annually). Available in the reference section of your local library, this resource provides information on local and national associations of all types, including trade and professional organizations. Through these associations, you will be able to get information on trends, salaries, and other issues that may be relevant to your career path. If there is a local chapter of the association in your city, you can sit in on its meetings and network with others in your profession. This will help you determine if the culture and its requirements are right for you.

CHAPTER

JOB RESEARCH

I f you know you're committed to a goal, you may wonder whether it will matter if you take a "little" job outside your chosen professional area just to get by while you're working toward it. The answer is yes—it can matter a lot. In fact, it can ultimately be the first step on a path that you may later find very difficult, if not impossible, to get off of. We've all heard certain people talk wistfully about the career that got away, the one they'd always wanted, which is different from the one they have. Usually, circumstances evolved in such a way that never gave them a chance to realize their dreams. Often, these are the people who, ten, fifteen, or twenty years earlier, took that "little" job just to get by.

The laws of nature are such that the universe will not tolerate a void. If you need a job, then a void exists, and it will be filled. If you have a job, whether or not in your chosen profession, then opportunities will pass you by because no void exists. This means that you won't seek out opportunities, or you will fail to recognize them when they do appear. That's why it's so important to make smart choices early on, so that you fill that void in ways that advance your career and challenge your potential.

My friend John learned this lesson the hard way. He wanted to be an attorney, and everyone in his life knew of his ambition. In effect, all his friends were potential mentors—they could keep their ears open in their social and business networks for job opportunities and refer John when they heard of something appropriate.

After graduating from college, John looked for a job that would help pay his tuition while he went to law school. A friend told him about a new management training program at the restaurant where she worked. His degree easily qualified him for the position, which offered attractive benefits, including excellent pay and a tuition reimbursement program that would allow him to pursue his law degree. Meanwhile, however, another friend told John about a research position at a law firm. This job involved hard work at much lower pay, but the firm also offered a tuition reimbursement program and, just as important, the position was in line with John's career ambition.

In the end, John decided to pursue the management position at the restaurant. He reasoned that he could upgrade his lifestyle with the additional income, go to night school, and then transfer to a job in law after obtaining his degree. But things did not work out at all as he planned. Working hard at the new job, which turned out to be more demanding than he had expected, John progressed quickly in the organization and began to take on more and more responsibility. At the same time, he began dating someone seriously and, with all his energy going into the new job and the new relationship, he decided to put off law school for awhile.

Now, five years later, John manages several restaurants, is married, and has a second child on the way. Sometimes he thinks about his dream of being an attorney, but now it is just that—a dream. He has too much responsibility to think about quitting his job and, after dealing with the paperwork he brings home and helping his wife with the children, has no time or energy left to study law. Of course, he sometimes wonders where he would be now if he had started off by going after the research position in the law firm.

I have seen this kind of scenario repeated over and over with both genders more times than I can count. Don't make the same mistake—don't let yourself be distracted from your goal before starting the journey. Think of your first job in the same way that you would think of meeting someone important for the first time. Just as you'd want to establish, in the first meeting, a good foundation for a relationship with that person, you want to establish, with your first job, a solid foundation on which to build your chosen career.

You only get to start once, so make it a good start. That first step can put into motion a set of circumstances that can place you on an irreversible course—so it's essential to stay focused on your goal (see Are You on the Right Track With Your First Job?). When considering a position, ask yourself:

- How will this job move me closer to my goal?

- Am I being honest with myself about the possibilities I see in the option?

- Do I have other options that may be initially more demanding or less lucrative but that might advance my career to a greater degree than the position I'm considering?

AVOID STEREOTYPES

I've noticed in counseling people at all levels and in many fields that our decisions are influenced even more than we realize by other people and by society. We've all heard the stereotypes: Women don't make good truck drivers or police officers; Asian people should stick to hi-tech or numbers-oriented jobs; people with a scientific or technical leaning shouldn't take jobs that require strong interpersonal skills. And the list goes on. Don't let these kinds of stereotypes deter you from following a career path that fits your aspirations and talents.

When someone you respect or someone who holds a position superior to yours makes a recommendation about your career, you

ARE YOU ON THE RIGHT TRACK WITH YOUR FIRST JOB?

Your first job is important because it starts you on your career track. Whether you already have a job or you're just starting to look, you will fall into one of the following categories. The significance of where you fall is explained following the categories and will confirm that you are headed in the right direction or provide guidance in getting on track. Choose the one category that best fits your current status.

- I am looking for a position now, and I realize that I need to choose carefully. I am clear about the skills I want to develop to advance my career and will be seeking a job along those lines.
  (Excellent. You are on the right track.)

- I have already accepted a job and can see that it will be very beneficial to my skill development and in advancing my career.
  (Excellent. You are on the right track. Start planning now for your next job move, whether in your company or to another company.)

- I have accepted a job, but I am not sure that it will help my career in the long run. I plan to seek advice from a mentor, a career counselor, or a human resource professional at my company to determine if I am on the right path to reach my goal.
  (Very good. But don't delay seeking guidance to ensure that you are on track. The longer you wait, the harder it will be to make a change.)

- I accepted a position outside my career goal because it was readily available. I like what I am doing so much now that I want to rethink my career goal.
  (It is good that you recognize the need for reevaluation because you always need a plan based on a goal if you want to achieve success. Rethink your goal as soon as possible and set up a new career plan.)

- I accepted a position because I needed immediate money, but I am still looking for a job that will support my career goal, and I will not stop until I have secured one.
  (Do not delay in getting on track. Temporary jobs can turn into permanent delays where you end up feeling frustrated and unfulfilled many years later. If you have to accept another "temporary" job, try for something that will allow you to build skills or get exposure in your chosen profession.)

probably take it very seriously. In fact, your thinking may be strongly influenced by her advice. But now that you've accepted responsibility for your own career, you'll need to carefully evaluate these recommendations to determine how they align with your goal. If you find that the advice does not support the career path you've laid out for yourself, then you'll simply have to challenge it.

Begin by looking at where that person is coming from—in terms of background, age, culture, work history, and the like. An older person's recommendation, for example, may be tainted with an outdated cultural belief about gender roles. On the other hand, someone who's suffered through hard times might make recommendations based on survival issues rather than personal satisfaction. Then there are the people who claw their way up the ranks, taking any opportunity that comes their way, and feel lucky to have arrived at their current position; these people, who are motivated merely by need to secure a job and who have not developed their own careers, often place little value on choosing the right job—one that fits a career plan. Such people might suggest, for example, that you take a secretarial job only because it pays more than an analyst position, when the analyst position would, in fact, be more in line with your career aspirations. Or if you're being paid well as a foreman, they might encourage you to stay in this position rather than accept, say, an accounting position at a company where you'll have the opportunity to advance in management at a corporate level.

"I ORCHESTRATED MY CAREER"

■

Fannie started her career with a clear vision. "After doing some research at Louisiana State University in the food industry and receiving my master's in chemistry at Southern University in Baton Rouge, I left school with the goal of being a corporate quality manager. I didn't just fall into my current position—I orchestrated it."

Fannie began by doing some research, talking with people and professors who had worked in the industry. This helped her to take a realistic inventory of her talents, get a strong sense of the industry, and then successfully land a job. "When I first entered the workforce with Quaker Oats, it was on a trial basis. My alternate plan was to continue my education and to teach. With my first job, I was eager for the experience—it just so happened that the money was good, so I got a great two-in-one deal." Fannie remained with Quaker Oats for fourteen years, until the company started downsizing. At this point, she decided to leave rather than move into an area that did not interest her.

After relocating to California, she responded to an ad for a quality supervisor with Kraft. Within a month, she had the job. With her vision still intact, Fannie set out to develop the additional people skills she needed to move closer to her managerial goal. "I took on leadership roles in the church and in community activities wherever I could, and I continue to do so. I still like to teach, so I always find a way to use that skill—currently, I'm involved in the Adopt-A-School Program, as the principal."

As she continued to develop her leadership and interpersonal skills, Fannie wanted more opportunity to work with people, to guide and motivate them. Fortunately, her company recognized her abilities and offered her just such an opportunity. "I have always been interested in helping people grow and reach their highest potential—to perform to their full capacity. My job as plant manager came about because my boss saw in me that potential to lead and influence others to achieve. After handling a management position in an unfamiliar area, I was asked to interview for the job as plant manager."

Fannie's advice for people setting out on a career path is simple and to the point: "Take advantage of every opportunity there is to learn. Find a role model. Seek help wherever you can get it."

∎

FANNIE PICOU
Black manager
Kraft Foods, California
Business: Plant manager

If Fannie, a black plant manager for a major food company, had listened to one of her managers at the first company where she worked, she might never have set a management position as her goal (see "I Orchestrated My Career"). Claiming that scientists don't make good managers, the manager advised Fannie, who has a master's degree in chemistry, to stay on the technical side of the business. But Fannie had focused her sights on a quality management position in the food industry, and she believed that to make an impact in the business, she needed to combine her technical skills with working with people. Also, she knew she had the necessary interpersonal skills to work in management. By participating in church groups and community activities, she had gained confidence and experience in this area, not to mention transferable professional skills.

Fortunately, Fannie had the strength of mind to ignore the manager's advice. While working as a chemist, a division head observed her interacting with others and recognized her leadership ability. He recommended her for the first management position that came up—and she was ready to take on the new challenge. Because she remained on her path, she ultimately did combine her technical skills with her talent for managing people.

Fannie describes her evolution from technician to manager in this way: "I had decided to be a good manager from both the technical side and people-management side. In spite of the recommendation that I develop my career in the typical way—on the technical side—I orchestrated a move into management. When I got the plant manager position, everyone was surprised. The position had always been held by a male (all white, except for one Hispanic); it was not a typical role for a woman in the organization. I was the first and only black woman chosen for the job."

Of course, not all of us can carve out so straight a path. Carol's career was sidetracked after a family priority forced her to relocate. After holding progressively responsible management positions with a major electronics company, she found herself faced with starting over in a new city. Unable to find a position in her field, she accepted a temporary secretarial position on the recommendation of a family friend. She needed quick money and this was an easy solution.

The move proved to be a bad one, however, because it negatively impacted Carol's career in several ways. She did not seem credible as a manager to the people who knew her as a secretary, so they were not comfortable recommending her for managerial positions. Also, she could not establish viable networking contacts at the company where she worked because all her colleagues perceived her as a secretary, not a professional. Finally, making no reference on her résumé to the secretarial position (which lasted for eighteen months), she had a hard time explaining to prospective employees what she had been doing for that long stretch of time.

To avoid stereotypes in pursuing your first job, ask yourself these questions:

- Am I considering a job outside of my career path only because it's easy and I don't know how to get one that is relevant?

- Am I considering a job because it's available and it's one of the typical jobs that people of my culture or gender go into to get started—even though it doesn't relate to my goal?

- Am I allowing myself to be influenced to accept a position by someone I respect, even though it is inconsistent with my career goal?

YOUR FIRST PRIORITY: MONEY OR WORK?

There is a popular saying that if you do what you love, the money will follow (and a book of the same title by Marsha Sinetar). In an ideal world, we'd all be able to follow our bliss, unencumbered by any real concerns about money. We'd be free to go after our first job with no other thought than how it would help us reach our goal.

Well, this is not an ideal world. Sometimes circumstances—such as a family emergency, an unexpected layoff, or a relocation—will

PURSUING THE RIGHT JOB FOR YOUR NEEDS

Your career is part of your life-career plan; therefore, you need to consider the goals and circumstances surrounding that plan as you decide which jobs to pursue. The process outlined below will help you analyze your options, sort out issues that are important to you at this time, and make the best decision to meet your overall needs.

My career goal (where I am trying to get to) is:

_____

Responsibilities or factors that I have to consider at this time that will affect which option I choose (e.g., no car, sick relative, past-due debt, children):

_____

_____

_____

_____

_____

throw you off track, forcing you to make a detour in your plans. You may have to take a position for which you are overqualified, perhaps to pay the bills or, like Carol, to reestablish yourself in the workforce. But, even then, you should make the most of this detour, and seek out a position that will develop your skills and enhance your career—rather than getting stuck in a role that could set you up for future stereotyping. If your circumstances dictate that money be your top priority, strive for a compromise or secondary job that will allow you to meet those needs while still giving you some opportunity to build skills that will support your career goal (see Pursuing the Right Job for Your Needs).

PURSUING THE RIGHT JOB FOR YOUR NEEDS—*Continued*

Job options I am considering and their ability to advance my career goal and satisfy factors listed above:

	Pros	Cons
Option 1 _____	_____	_____
_____	_____	_____
_____	_____	_____
Option 2 _____	_____	_____
_____	_____	_____
_____	_____	_____
Option 3 _____	_____	_____
_____	_____	_____

The job option that best satisfies my priorities:

The job option that best satisfies my career goal:

The job option that will provide the best compromise (if different) to meet my priorities and advance my career:

Regardless of the circumstances that will ultimately influence your job choice, it's important to develop and implement an effective job search campaign that will help you meet your goals. First, establish a criteria you can use for evaluating all job options; write down all the factors that you can think of that would influence your decision. Then systematically evaluate all job options against your criteria and select the option that will best enable you to meet your responsibilities and life-career goals.

THE FUTURE WORKPLACE: WHERE WILL THE JOBS BE?

An important factor in your criteria for evaluating job options is knowing where jobs are likely to be available in the future. It is pointless to plan a career around an occupation that is going the way of the dinosaur.

Statistical trends show that in the future, opportunities will be plentiful in areas relating to computer technology and services that depend primarily on free-flowing interactions with other people. Of course, we can't all be systems analysts, home health-care providers, or day-care workers but being aware of these trends will help us in evaluating our job options.

How can you keep up on industry trends as an ongoing part of your job search? Read books—like *Workforce 2000*, by Joseph H. Boyett and Henry P. Conn—that offer insightful information about how growing trends will shape future jobs and possibly the career you have in mind. Browse through periodicals, news reports, and magazines for general information and to stay current on changes that could impact your profession. Those publications geared toward people of color add the additional dimension of viewing the information from our point of view, with our particular needs in mind. Go to your local library and review national magazines like *Hispanic Business, Black Enterprise, Fortune* (this offers a white perspective, but we need that viewpoint as well) and, if you're in a technical field, *Journal of the NTA* (National Technical Association) to start keeping yourself up to date on useful information.

Also, make it a daily practice to scan the front page and business section of your local newspaper. If you live in a major city, that paper will provide you with timely and relevant information on your professional focus. If you live in a small town, consider subscribing to a paper from a large city (especially from a city you might be interested in relocating to someday). Read the newspaper and trade journals not only to stay current on what's happening but also to keep an eye out for names of people you might contact for an informational interview. If you're ready to assert yourself, make a cold call; if not, write some letters to those contacts and request the information.

If you have a computer and a modem, go on-line to gather up-to-the-minute information from a host of excellent sources. Subscribe to relevant newsgroups on the Internet to find out what others in your field have to say about the industry or current trends.

And—always—network with other professionals. Join professional groups or participate in association activities to enhance your knowledge about trends and get real-world information about activities in which companies in your area are involved.

I know this might sound overwhelming. You're probably thinking that participating in all these activities would be so terribly time-consuming that you wouldn't even have time to look for a job—let alone work at your present one. But, I assure you, it's not that difficult to stay current—as long as you set aside some time to do it. For instance, try to read the newspaper every day, go to the library a couple of times a month to update yourself, and attend a professional group meeting at least once a month. Successful professionals are always looking for work—either within their company or somewhere else. Staying current on trends should be an integral part of your ongoing research and planning effort to establish and advance your career.

CHOOSING A GEOGRAPHIC LOCATION FOR WORK

In addition to professional or marketplace trends, you'll have to consider the locations of the economic centers of your profession (see Business Power Seats). For instance, if your career goal involves medical research, your action plan might include relocation to a city that would better support that goal. When evaluating location, consider the aspects of your lifestyle that you'd rather not change. If factors like climate, culture, nightlife, and the nearness of family and friends are important to your happiness, you'll need to determine how they would be affected by your career choice.

A couple of years ago, a fellow consultant woke up to the realities of her lifestyle preferences when she relocated from California to the East Coast. After six months, she returned home with the firm realization that she could never live anywhere but Los Angeles. She admitted that she had taken her lifestyle for granted and had not considered the dramatic changes that would be involved in such a move. You can avoid making a similar mistake by making a checklist of the aspects of your lifestyle that you consider necessary for your well-being. Then, look them over and determine whether relocating would force you to give them up.

The Chamber of Commerce in the city you're interested in is an excellent source for information about the location. A postcard or call requesting information will get you what you need.

SELECTING INDUSTRIES

As I mentioned in the last chapter, working in the right industry can be very important to starting your career off right. Again, you can go to your library for help in getting key information on various industries. For guidance in selecting the right industry on which to focus your search, look at these publications to get answers to the following questions. They are all listed in the reference section of your library.

What are the high-growth industries?
- *Directory of Industry Data Sources* (also lists company names, addresses, and phone numbers)

What are the salary levels in specific industries?
- *The American Almanac of Jobs and Salaries*
- *American Management Association Surveys* (this may not be available at the library; if not, contact the American Management Association directly).

BUSINESS POWER SEATS

City	Industries
Atlanta	Financial services, telecommunications
Austin	Medical research, computer software and hardware
Boston	Computer software and hardware, financial services, medical research
Branson	Tourism
Charlotte	Financial services
Chicago	Financial services, medical research, telecommunications
Denver	Computer software and hardware, telecommunications
Houston	Computer hardware, medical research
Las Vegas	Tourism
Los Angeles	Film and TV production, tourism
Miami	Tourism
Minneapolis	Computer software and hardware
New York	Film and TV production, financial services, medical research, telecommunications, tourism
Orlando	Computer hardware, film and TV production, tourism
Philadelphia	Telecommunications
Provo	Computer software
Portland	Computer software
Raleigh/Durham	Computer hardware and software, medical research
San Francisco	Computer software, film and TV production, financial services, telecommunications, tourism
San Jose	Computer hardware and software
Seattle	Computer software, medical research

Compiled from Fortune *magazine articles*

Who are the competitors in an industry?
- *Dun & Bradstreet's Million Dollar Directory*

What industries use specific types of professionals?
- *Encyclopedia of Associations*
- *The Career Guide: Dun's Employment Opportunities Directory*
- *Encyclopedia of Career and Vocational Guidance*
- *Occupational Outlook Handbook*
- *National Trade and Professional Associations of the United States*
- *Directory of U.S. Labor Organizations*

SELECTING COMPANIES

Once you've chosen the industries where you will market your skills, you'll want to make sure that you target companies within those industries that have practices supporting growth and advancement for people of color. *The Best Companies for Minorities* by Lawrence Otis Graham highlights employers across America who recruit, train, and promote people of color (see Where Can People of Color Get Ahead).

It's also important to know about the history of a company, its key players (especially if you decide to direct a letter to one of them), and its background. This will give you a sense of the company's philosophy and, possibly, an idea of the corporate culture. Such information will help you not only determine whether you'd fit into that culture and have the opportunity to advance within the environment but would also give you some ideas for how to focus your résumé and for questions you might ask if you're interviewed by the company.

The 90-Minute Interview Prep Book by Peggy Schmidt (see Resources) and a number of other recently published job search books encourage you to use the Web as part of your research. If you're not on-line yourself, you may be able to use a computer at your college or local public library to find out information about companies. Many large companies have their own Web sites, as do most companies whose business is technology. Usually, all you need to do to find a

WHERE CAN PEOPLE OF COLOR GET AHEAD?

Based on a nationwide survey, extensive interviews, and in-depth research, *The Best Companies for Minorities* by Lawrence Otis Graham offers criteria for people of color to evaluate companies. The book profiles Fortune 500 and other large companies that genuinely promote diversity in their employment practices, offer career advancement without glass ceilings, and put their money into charities, scholarships, and training programs supporting people of color. It spells out:

- Salary information
- Total number of people of color in management jobs and upper-level executive positions
- Affirmative action programs and ongoing recruitment of people of color
- Training/retraining programs, internships, and mentorships
- Social support systems and in-house organizations for people of color
- Corporate commitment to community programs, scholarships, and the use of businesses as suppliers that are owned by people of color
- Frank evaluations by current employees of color

particular Web site is to type http://www. followed by the company name or acronym and finally by .com, leaving out any apostrophes and spaces (for example, http://www.petersons.com). It's worth looking at the home pages of companies that interest you; you'll find plenty of information about the company (and sometimes even job listings). Keep in mind that since companies put together their own Web sites, you won't find anything other than a rosy picture there. Another option is to do a key word search (of the company or industry you're looking into) in the business news section of newspapers featured in commercial on-line services.

To round out your research, get information from other sources as well. Check out the following reference sources in your library for information on specific aspects of the companies you have in mind:

Products the company offers:
- Moody's Manuals
- Thomas Register
- U.S. Industrial Director
- Dun & Bradstreet's Million Dollar Directory
- Standard and Poor's Register of Corporations, Directors, and Executives
- Individual company annual reports—contact the company's public affairs department directly and ask the person there to send you a copy

Key people in the company and their backgrounds:
- Dun & Bradstreet's Reference Book of Corporate Managements

AVENUES TO THE JOBS

After you've established a job goal and have made a commitment to it, the next step is to develop ways to find the jobs that fit that goal. Ten years ago, professional-bound people could simply wait until recruiters came to their colleges and offered them jobs in their fields. Or after graduation, they could submit unsolicited résumés to a number of large companies; if they had good grades, relevant class work, and showed strong potential, their résumés were sure to generate interest from some of the companies contacted. A qualified candidate would often be invited for an interview and possibly get a job offer.

But times have changed, as we all know. Now many recent college grads spend months, even years, trying to land a job in their chosen profession. At the same time, professionals with experience and qualifications often find it very hard to get another job in their field after a layoff.

In the past, the business culture valued people who could be trained and cultivated for long-term employment. Today, however, downsizing and restructuring have created a very fast-paced work environment where there is high turnover and a focus on short-term projects that demand immediate skill sets and experiences. Because this environment does not allow for a long learning curve, employers want to hire people who can be quickly brought up to speed with minimal training. They therefore meet their staffing needs in a variety of ways, some quite different from those they used in the past. For instance, more employers than ever use outside contractors, consultants, and temporary workers. Some companies also outsource to service groups to meet, for example, their graphics and printing needs rather than have their own in-house groups.

All this makes it very important for you to use a variety of search strategies when you're job hunting.

The Internet

The Internet is the newest way to find out about job openings. It does not replace interacting with people (yet), but it is proving to be another valid way to find out about a large number of positions across the country and even around the world. Many companies have their own Web sites, where they provide information on their corporation and sometimes post job openings. There are some Web sites designed especially for job hunters, offering job search advice and lists of positions available in many companies, often sorted by field and by region (see below). Also, newspapers from around the country are listing their classified ads on-line.

The Internet is the worldwide network of computer networks, and the Web is only one of the networks on the Internet. An excellent source for using the Internet is *Hook Up, Get Hired!* by Joyce Lain Kennedy.

If you have a computer (or access to one) with a modem, you can easily go on-line to access jobs on the Net—as long as you know the right sites to go to. Otherwise, you can spend hours and run up high access charges searching, with no real results. I suggest you begin your search with the following sites; they focus only on job search:

- The Riley Guide—Directory of employment resources: http://www.jobtrak.com/jobguide/

- A meta-list of online job-services: http://www.careers.org/gen/all_gems.htm

- Job search and employment opportunities—Best bets from the Net: gopher://na.hh.lib.umich.edu:70/00/inetdirsstacks/

- The Black Collegian Job Assistance Selection Service: http://www.black-collegian.com/jobsg.html

- Career Mosaic: http://www.careermosaic.com

- Career Path: http://www.careerpath.com/

- The Monster Board: http://199.94.216.76:80/

- America's job bank (maintained by the U.S. Department of Labor): http://www.ajb.dni.us/

- Yahoo's listing of employment: http://www.yahoo.com/Business/Employment

- Department of Labor: http://www.careers.org/

Networking

Networking simply means using word of mouth to find out about jobs and let jobs find out about you! It means letting people in your life—friends, family members, neighbors, professional contacts, and anyone else you think might now or at some other time know or hear about a job—know that you're looking (see Six Steps to Effective Networking). It might include informational interviews, which are not interviews for a specific job—rather, they are less formal meetings, phone conversations, or even e-mail exchanges with people to find out about a type of job, a field, or even a company that you might be interested in. Ask people you know if they have contacts whom you can interview for more information about your chosen profession.

How Informational Interviewing Works

Sonya, a marketing graduate looking for a job in the competitive retail environment, needed help meeting prospective employers for informational interviews. She didn't know anyone in retail but did have a strong network of friends working in good jobs in other industries. She asked them for help in making contact with people who could give her an insider's point of view and tips on how to get into the retail business.

A friend put Sonya in touch with his mother, an attorney who had a good friend working as a marketing director for a major retail store in town. Sonya met with the woman, who was happy to help and impressed that she was doing her homework by researching the market before officially approaching an employer about a job. In the interview, Sonya learned what to expect in developing a marketing career in retail and what salary range would be reasonable for her. The marketing director also supplied her with three contacts in the industry, one of which led to an assistant marketing position with a medium-size store.

Some people believe that the concept of networking has worn thin because so many people are doing it and because the contacts you make through networking are not fooled when you say you're doing research and just want an informational interview. They know you want a job. That is probably true, but it's also true that if you're networking with people you know and people they introduce you to, then you'll probably be the person to get the recommendation for any open positions they hear about.

Ads

Contrary to what you may have heard—that no decent jobs are advertised—companies still use ads as a method of filling their positions. Many companies resist paying agency fees because they know they can access a pool of qualified people by advertising their positions.

SIX STEPS TO EFFECTIVE NETWORKING

Networking is a key way of meeting as many people as possible face-to-face and letting them know who you are and the skills you have to offer. These people then become agents for you and can lead you to contacts who may provide the link to a wonderful job opportunity. So, talk to people—everyone you know—about your goals.

1. Decide what kind of information you need from industry insiders to help with your job search: salary range, expected responsibilities, key things recruiters will look for on your résumé, questions most likely to be asked in interviews and examples you can give to demonstrate your skills, and contacts for getting into a particular industry or company.

2. Make a list of all the people you know. Decide what kind of information you will seek from each one. One person may provide better contacts than another; a different person may have a better focus on the market. Don't expect everyone to be able to provide the same information. If you restrict your contacts only to people in your own ethnic group, you'll sorely limit your opportunities. I have personally found that when I've networked with people of other races, I've been received very positively and felt that the other individual was very pleased that I would contact him or her for advice.

3. Have your résumé ready to show your contacts when discussing your job goals. Ask for feedback on your résumé. Don't worry about identifying a particular job in your conversations, but do be clear about the industry and/or companies you're interested in and the skills that you will be marketing.

4. Contact each person on the list (try to make personal contact) and ask them for names of others they recommend you contact. If you're not comfortable cold calling a new contact to whom you've been referred, ask your original contact if he or she would mind making the initial call for you.

5. Get information and guidance from contacts. If they have a job or know of one, they will tell you about it. Since your purpose for the networking session is to get information and contacts, do not discuss specific job openings—unless the contact brings it up first. If they do, then the networking meeting has turned into an interview, and you should respond in an interview format.

6. When you get your job, call the people you've networked with and thank them all for their help.

Of course, the fact that so many qualified people respond to a single ad can be a problem for you, the job seeker. Ads typically generate a large number of responses, so it's not unusual to be in competition with hundreds of applicants for a published opening, especially if it's a desirable position in a tight market—and it's advertised in the newspaper as well as on the Internet.

To get a leg up on the competition, keep these two important factors in mind when responding to ads:

- Do not be intimidated by the job requirements advertised if you honestly believe that you can do the job. An employer's hiring decision is not just based on how well an applicant meets the job requirements; one's motivation and personality are often just as important. That's why it's essential to indicate in some way in your résumé your motivational level as well as your positive character traits. When you do not have the specific on-the-job experience requested in the ad, you can highlight volunteer work or any other relevant experience that enables you to develop the transferable skills necessary to handle the job. Excellent examples of how to write out your transferable skills for a job can be found in *Perfect Résumé Strategies* (see Resources in chapter 5).

- In responding to ads, always include a cover letter, and make sure that both it and your résumé are targeted to the specific job opening for which you're applying. The primary purpose of the cover letter is to provide the person doing the screening (usually a human resource representative who may have to quickly scan hundreds of résumés) with enough succinct and relevant information to compel him to pass your résumé to the hiring manager instead of putting it in the "later" pile. The primary purpose of the résumé is to stimulate the curiosity of the hiring manager so that he wants to set up an interview. Neither the cover letter nor the résumé should be long, detailed accounts of all that you have done in life; instead, they should provide just enough information to generate interest and solicit a call from the employer to learn more about you. (See chapter 5 for guidance on developing résumés and cover letters.)

Agencies

Don't overlook agencies as an avenue to jobs. Signing up with a permanent or temporary employment agency or contacting a headhunter (or staffing consultant, as they now prefer to be called) can open up opportunities you may not have found on your own. The trick is understanding the different types of agencies out there and what they have to offer.

A retainer firm gets exclusive contracts with companies to fill specific positions. When a company retains an agency to handle a placement, it accepts applications for new openings only through that agency. A contingency agency does the same thing as a retainer agency, only without exclusivity or a contract; because of this, contingency agencies must compete with other agencies, as well as applicants, for the attention of the employer. Some agencies maintain retainer contracts with one or more companies while working on a contingency basis with others.

When choosing an agency, always ask whether it is a retainer or contingency firm. The biggest advantage of working with a retainer agency is that it is more selective in terms of the applicants it recommends for interviews. This means that if the agency gets you an interview with a firm, you won't have to compete with a herd of people from the same agency for the job. Also, a retainer agency can better prepare you for an interview by providing more comprehensive information on the background of the employer.

Don't limit yourself to permanent placement agencies, however, even if you are looking for a full-time permanent position. Temporary agencies can place people in professional as well as clerical and administrative jobs and, amazingly, are among the nation's top employers. Taking a temporary position is an excellent way to sample a company before seeking permanent employment with it. Similarly, companies often try out employees in temporary positions before extending a permanent offer. In fact, many companies regularly fill a certain percentage of their openings with short-term employees and sometimes will even advertise the position through an agency as "temp to perm."

Some guidelines to remember when working with agencies include:

- Deal only with agencies that are employer-fee paid. The best agencies are paid by employers to fill their positions, so you gain no advantage by paying an agency fee. Always ask the agency who pays the fee before dealing with it.

- Don't let yourself be pushed into a permanent or temporary situation unless it is a good fit for your career.

- Always maintain control of your own job search by telling the representative what you want to do and where you're willing to work.

- Tell permanent placement agencies in writing that you want to know in advance when they plan to forward your résumé for an opening. That way, if you've already contacted the company on your own, you'll avoid any conflict over the agency's fee. You could incur a similar problem by having a company receive your résumé from more than one agency.

- Agencies only get paid when they make a placement. So keep in mind that no matter how nice and helpful the representatives are, they are working for themselves and not for you.

Unsolicited Approach

It can sometimes be advantageous to approach a company with an unsolicited résumé—if you do some research and make sure your résumé and cover letter are tailored to the needs of the company. Address your résumé to the head of the department you want to work for, not the human resources department. Find out that person's name by networking or calling the company and asking the receptionist for the name and address of the head of, for example, the editorial, office services, or data processing department.

Be sure to target your unsolicited communication to a select number of appropriate companies. In most cases, you'll be wasting your time and money sending out a mass mailing. You'll find it more effective to send a few letters at a time and then follow up within a week with a phone call to determine whether your résumé met with any interest. You can't expect the companies to contact you.

Job Fairs

Job fairs are common, particularly in highly populated areas, because they offer a very efficient way for employers to connect with a large pool of applicants. They are held by a variety of groups—colleges and college alumni associations, career planning units of special interest groups (e.g., the *Los Angeles Times* in Los Angeles), urban social services centers—and announced through newsletters, the media, the Employment Development Department, posted notices, etc. They are held for college graduates, experienced workers, and sometimes teenagers.

Going to a job fair can be a very effective way to make contact with representatives from many companies. Go to the fair dressed to impress, with an attitude to match. Wear the same type of clothes you'd wear to an interview, pass out your résumés, collect business cards, be pleasant to everyone, and follow up with phone calls.

Professional Associations

As I've mentioned before, professional associations are an excellent source for networking, salary information, and making contacts. The members of these groups often know of openings, and some associations put out a regular publication that lists job openings. Check the *Encyclopedia of Associations* for chapters of appropriate professional groups in your area.

Before making a decision to join an association, attend one of its meetings. Some of these groups charge high membership fees, but you can probably attend one meeting or function for an affordable fee. Paying the fee and going to one or two meetings may be all you need to make some good contacts and get information that will help you later with your job search.

College Placement Centers

These are obviously an excellent source for the recent college graduate. Even after you've graduated, you can usually still use these placement

---

INDUSTRY CHECKLIST

Industry: _____

Standing: High, medium, low growth

Forecasts: _____

_____

_____

Factors contributing to potential changes in the industry: _____

_____

_____

_____

Growing trends: _____

_____

_____

_____

_____

Other pertinent information: _____

_____

_____

_____

_____

COMPANY CHECKLIST

This form can be used during an informational interview or when collecting data from print and on-line sources.

Name and address: _____

_____

_____

Contact name and phone number: _____

_____

History: _____

_____

_____

Size, growth rate: _____

_____

Profitability: _____

_____

_____

Product/services: _____

_____

_____

Financial history: _____

_____

_____

Major players:
  Names: _____
  Background: _____
  Average age: _____
  Philosophy: _____

Recent changes in company structure: _____

_____

_____

Changes in product lines or services: _____

_____

_____

SOURCES FOR FINDING WORK

Permanent placement agencies: _____
_____
_____
_____

Temporary agencies: _____
_____
_____
_____

Networking contacts (prepare one for each):
    Name: _____
    Address: _____
    Title: _____
    Phone number: _____

Newspapers, industry-related periodicals: _____
_____
_____

centers; most are available to alumni. They have directories and other information similar to what you might find in a public library, and they also post available positions that they receive from employers. Look at the postings carefully; if you see a position that's not in your field, take down the name of the contact person. Even if there are no immediate openings that match your skills, you can contact the companies and submit your résumé for consideration for future openings.

Government Placement Centers

The Employment Development Department (unemployment office) can be a resource for companies that are hiring (mostly for entry-level jobs) and for contact people at those companies (through the positions posted). Most EDD agencies have job clubs run by experienced people seeking work, and these people can sometimes be good contacts.

For federal government employment opportunities, contact: The U.S. Office of Personnel Management (1900 E Street NW, Washington, D.C.), which is responsible for nationwide recruiting for civil service positions at GS levels 1–15. It maintains a network of federal job information centers in major metropolitan areas. The telephone numbers are listed in the *White Pages* under U.S. Government, Office of Personnel Management.

KEEPING RECORDS AND REEVALUATING YOUR OPTIONS

You can avoid confusion and assess your job search information quickly if you keep it organized in a standard format. This will make your job search a lot easier because you'll have pertinent information at your fingertips to help target your résumés and letters as well as prepare for interviews. The forms here will help you with this process.

RESOURCES

The Internet

Hook Up, Get Hired!: The Internet Job Search Revolution by Joyce Lain Kennedy (John Wiley & Son, 1995). This book is a good resource for using the Internet and showing the advantages of being able to use the Net across town, across the continent, and around the world.

Networking

It's Who You Know: Career Strategies for Making Personal Contacts by Cynthia Chin-Lee (Pfeiffer, 1993). If you're hesitant about even talking with people you know about your job search, this book is an excellent resource to help you with networking. Easy to read and with clear explanations, it describes all the processes and avenues for effective networking. I believe this book would be particularly helpful for shy people who may resist networking, but it could also provide some insight to others.

Employment Agencies

The Directory of Executive Recruiters (Kennedy Publications, 1996) is an excellent source for agencies that handle permanent placement. The information is organized both alphabetically and functionally. The directory has a listing of over 4,100 offices nationwide, representing almost 3,000 contingency and retainer search firms.

The Directory of Executive Temporary Placement Firms (Kennedy Publications) is one of the newer and more valuable employment directories, which lists more than 225 firms that place executives in short-term positions.

General Job Market

Where the Jobs Are by Joyce Hadley (Career Press, 1995) provides information on salary levels, skills, and education required, as well as the largest employers in the field and advancement opportunities.

Nontraditional Job Search Methods

303 Off-the-Wall Ways To Get A Job by Brandon Toropov (Career Press, 1995). When you cannot seem to get to the right job no matter how much you try with traditional methods, then it's time to be creative. This book offers real methods used by real people who've obtained real results by using all kinds of methods to get that right job—from cornering decision makers during plane flights to making a name for themselves in the organization by working for free. One approach I liked was to find out who got the job you went after and ask that person about the leads they didn't follow through on. Obviously, the innovative approach you try has to be something that fits your personality, but the book may give you some ideas.

Reference Material
(available at libraries and career centers)

- *Dun & Bradstreet's Reference Book of Corporate Management*
- *Dun & Bradstreet's Million Dollar Directory*
- *Encyclopedia of Associations*
- *Moody's Manuals*
- *Directory of Industry Data Sources*
- *The American Almanac of Jobs and Salaries*
- *National Trade and Professional Associations of the United States*
- *Directory of U.S. Labor Organizations*
- *The Career Guide: Dun's Employment Opportunities Directory*
- *Encyclopedia of Career and Vocational Guidance*
- *Occupational Outlook Handbook*
- *U.S. Industrial Directory*
- *Thomas Register*
- *Standard and Poor's Register of Corporations, Directors, and Executives*

JOB SEARCH

All the preparation you've gone through thus far has been for one purpose—to get a job you want. Always be in a state of readiness during your job search because you never know when or through whom that great job is going to come. Being ready starts with truly believing that you can have the job you want—actually visualizing yourself in the position and carrying out its responsibilities. With such an attitude, you'll project an image to the world that fits your career goal. If your dream is to be a successful manager, then you must project yourself as a self-assured, organized leader. That image will be reinforced by others, who, sensing your confidence and belief in yourself, will feel that you are well-suited for such a career. At the very least, they'll affirm that with your positive attitude, you'll likely accomplish what you set out to do.

A good friend of mine wanted to be a psychiatrist and, even from an early age, projected quite naturally an image of someone who'd be good at psychiatry. In one-on-one conversations and in groups, he was always willing to listen to the problems of others. He knew how to probe for information without being offensive and could usually figure out what might be the cause of someone's trouble. Not surprisingly, people often made comments like: "You know, you'd be perfect as a psychiatrist"; "Have you ever thought about psychiatry as a career?"; or "I bet people tell you all the time that you're good at helping people sort things out."

Of course, he found comments like these very encouraging because they affirmed his career choice. Just as important, I am certain the perception that I and others had of him gave him confidence, and this good sense of himself was later apparent to prospective employers. This helped him, I am sure, because any aspiring psychiatrist looking for a job would need to show his skills as convincingly in person as he did on paper.

Achieving your dream begins with projecting an image and living your life in accordance with your life-career goals; this is important for any job in any industry. You'll be able to do this best if you've taken time to develop a solid goal based on your capabilities. However, this is only the first step. The next step to turning a goal into the reality of an actual job is to create effective résumés that are targeted to the needs of the prospective employer. Most employers won't have the benefit of meeting you in person until after they've seen your résumé, so it's essential that you develop résumés and cover letters that reflect on paper the same image that you project in person. Think of your résumé as an advertisement—a brief piece of information targeted to the reader's interest and geared to getting you an interview.

ORGANIZING AND MANAGING YOUR JOB SEARCH

Start your job search by getting organized. Create a separate file for each company you research and each job you apply for and include in it all pertinent information related to the job or company:

- Company information, contact names, and phone numbers, plus external contacts who can provide information about the company, interviewer, job, and industry

- The position description as advertised (if you're applying for a posted position)

- The appropriate salary range for the position; if none is listed, do your research and come up with one yourself, in case you're asked to give one during the interview

- A copy of the résumé and cover letter you developed specifically in response to the ad or, if you sent an unsolicited résumé, based on your knowledge of the company or industry

The information in your files will be your guide for targeting and tracking résumés and letters you develop. And you can refer to these information files when companies call you to set up interviews. Use an answering machine to screen your calls (make sure it has a professional-sounding message on it) so you won't be caught off guard when someone responds to your job search. You'll have time to reacquaint yourself with pertinent information in the file before returning the call. This is especially important when it comes to salary; a company representative may ask about your salary requirements over the phone if you did not give a specific figure or range in your cover letter.

Also, be sure to have a pad ready to take notes when you're called. Try to avoid letting the phone call become a complete interview by emphasizing how much you'd like an opportunity to meet in person. If you go into the company for the interview, document all the pertinent information you remember after the interview, including the names, titles, and phone numbers of the persons you met with (ask for their cards), and add it to your file. This way, you'll be on a firmer footing if you're asked to come back for a second interview. Also, you can use this information for your follow-up letter.

"WHAT WILL YOU BRING TO THE PARTY?"

■

Leslie offers career advice from two perspectives: as manager for her fifteen-person department and as recruitment manager for the company. In these two roles, she's seen countless résumés cross her desk. A good résumé, she says, clearly presents the applicant as having a focused direction and a solid understanding of what he or she wants from a job and what he or she can offer a company.

For Leslie, this sense of purpose can be more important than experience. "I've interviewed candidates right out of school who I feel can offer more than someone with experience. For instance, I'm impressed with people who have held internships and summer jobs relevant to their goals because that shows they have real focus. I see a lot of young people who want to get ahead and who have a philosophical drive for excellence, but they don't have a direction yet."

In addition to identifying and clarifying their goals, Leslie encourages job seekers to prepare a résumé that sells them. "It's not often that I see a résumé that is accomplishment-based, yet those are the résumés that I'm most impressed by. Even people who are just out of school or have been working for only a couple of years should be able to find one or two things they are proud of and that they feel have been successful in.

"I look for résumés that sell the applicant—but how do you sell yourself if you are not sure what you bring to the party? During an interview, I'll ask someone why he wants the job and what he has to offer. If he can't sell himself and doesn't know what he wants to do, then all I can do is explain what we have to offer. I tell him that he needs to figure out where his skills might fit in and if what we have is in the direction he wants want to go."

■

Leslie White
Recruitment manager
Walt Disney Feature Animation
Burbank, California

TURN YOUR RÉSUMÉ AND COVER LETTERS INTO SALES TOOLS

The résumé is usually the first piece of information the employer sees about you. For this reason, it needs to be concise and compelling (see "What Will You Bring to the Party?"). Besides piquing the employer's interest so that you get invited for an interview, the résumé can also have an influence on the position you're eventually offered and final salary and benefits negotiations.

In my twenty years as a career counselor, I've seen every type of résumé cross my desk—from typo-ridden coffee-stained messes to highly professional, polished masterpieces. Each résumé told a different story about the person behind it and gave a clear indication about whether or not he or she would be right for the job. Here are some examples of disappointing résumés I received while working as staffing manager for a Fortune 100 company. Each is followed by points to remember so that you can avoid making the same mistake.

Who Wrote This?

I received a beautifully printed, eloquently worded, two-page résumé detailing the applicant's numerous accomplishments, which might have convinced almost any reader that this person was a real professional who would add inestimable value to their organization. Unfortunately, the cover letter that came with the résumé destroyed that impression—it was written in pencil on college-ruled notebook paper and stapled to the résumé. I guess the sender didn't want to spend the extra bucks to have whoever wrote the résumé also write the cover letter. Or maybe he was just too young and inexperienced to know any better.

Point one: Your résumé is a reflection of your skills and your personality. As a good résumé writer, you will make sure to retain your voice and your style. Most likely, this applicant had his résumé created by a professional résumé writer who did not take the time to ensure that the polished document matched the voice or style of the client—or to coach him in the basics of writing his cover letters. It's all right to have someone critique your résumé—actually, it's a very good idea because it will usually help you make it more focused and more reflective of your personality and voice—but always, always make sure that the language and voice are yours. Make sure to use the same types of words and tone in your résumé as you would speaking in person.

Point two: Your cover letter and résumé should always be printed on the same type of paper and have matching styles (e.g., fonts, voice, overall look). The cover letter should always be typed, and it, as well as each page of your résumé (keep it to one page if possible but no more than two), should have your name on it. Your cover letter should be printed on letterhead that includes your address and phone number.

Are You Applying for a Security Clearance!?

I loved the five-page résumé that could have served as an application for a security clearance. The woman accounted for every moment of her adult life. She even volunteered explanations for the times when she wasn't working, giving specific dates and pointing out that she had stopped working during those periods to raise children. Character-affirming behavior, to be sure, but not information likely to inspire an employer to call her for an interview; in fact, such details might raise a concern in the employer's mind that the woman would have a high absenteeism because she would have to take care of the children.

Point one: You need only include information on the résumé that is relevant to the job opening; don't bare your soul. For example, you are not required to list dates, except on an application form, which a résumé is not. Also, you are not expected to account for all your time between high school graduation and the present.

Point two: Never, ever supply information that might raise a negative concern in the employer's mind. To make sure you don't, have someone critique your résumé for impact before you submit it.

He Actually Sent a Sample?

Another priceless example was the résumé accompanied by a piece of pipe with a bolt on it, pictures of the pipe, and copies of certificates (no doubt from where the person had attended pipe school). He was a draftsman and wanted to provide a sample of what he had worked on. Also, the résumé he submitted went into extensive detail—too much, in fact. Obviously, both the résumé and the sample were the applicant's way of trying to establish without a doubt that he was qualified for a draftsman position.

Point one: Résumés should not have attachments. Samples may be brought to the interview to be shown if and when it seems appropriate.

Point two: No matter how well-written or how detailed it is, a résumé will not get you a job. At best, it can only stimulate an interview. Remember, the résumé is only the hors d'oeuvre—the interview is the meal.

And What Happened Next?

Another example of an overly long and detailed résumé came from an applicant who explained in full detail—on seven pages—all the responsibilities for each one of his jobs. Yawn. He not only outlined his accomplishments (an effective way to market yourself on a résumé), he gave detailed explanations for how he had obtained the results. His writing aptly exemplified communicating the who, what, when, where, and why of an activity. Yawn. Yawn. Yawn.

Point one: Use the KISS, TELL, SELL method. KISS—keep it short and simple. Tell—give a summary at the beginning. Sell—list accomplishments to support the summary and include information on where you've worked and the titles you held, if appropriate.

Point two: Always try to list examples of having carried out a duty rather than listing the actual overall responsibilities of the job. For example, "Trained 300 sales representatives at four locations within 90 days" tells more about your actual skills than "Manager of Sales Training, responsible for developing sales material, coordinating training activities, scheduling, etc., etc., etc."

Glad You're Not Sick Anymore

Another résumé certainly worth mentioning is the one on which the applicant stated, under personal information: "Health excellent, three successful bypass operations." My God! All I could think was my company probably wouldn't want to be responsible for him having a fourth successful bypass operation.

With some things, you can't win. If your health is excellent, why mention it? It's not the type of thing one should try to prove. On the other hand, if you've suffered from some injury or illness, what good will it do to tell a potential employer?

Point one: If you have an illness, injury, or disability that affects your ability to carry out the essential functions of the job, then you are required to admit that to a prospective employer. If not, don't mention health.

Point two: Generally, it's best to leave out personal information. But if you have hobbies or other activities that your research shows would be well received by the interviewer, include them. This may be the very information that would get you an interview. For instance, if you know that the prospective employer is a minister, then he or she will likely be impressed by the fact that you attend church regularly, teach Sunday school, or sing in the choir.

The Truth and Nothing but . . .

I could go on and on, but I'll end with the example of a programmer who believed in being absolutely truthful on his résumé. Also, he wanted to be recognized for his many years of experience—thirty-six in all. So he emphasized the total years worked as part of his summary statement, which started, "Programmer with over 36 years experience in—" He also used a chronological résumé with actual dates (months and years), listing every job he ever had, as well as his entire salary history. The résumé was four detailed pages long. This approach did not get him an interview. Too much, too soon.

Point one: No company is obligated to pay you for your seniority in life. Employers are only willing to pay the industry standard for the position they've advertised. Communicating your age does show experience, but that can be overshadowed by the fact that it shows your age and could be opening you up to age discrimination. Also, to employers, an emphasis on age and seniority probably implies a high salary expectation.

Point two: Never include your salary history in the cover letter or the résumé—even if it's specifically requested in the job description. Generally, employers don't expect to get it. If a company does ask for this information and you feel compelled to comply, give only a salary range based on what your research has shown would be appropriate for the job you're applying for.

CREATING AN EFFECTIVE RÉSUMÉ

Now that you know some of the things you absolutely should not do when developing your résumé, let's look at things that you should do—how to create a résumé that will be a strong self-marketing tool and set the stage for an interview that will be to your advantage.

Consider the Employer's Point of View— Target the Résumé

Let the situation dictate the information you include on the résumé. If you're responding to an ad, every piece of information and every statement on the résumé should support your objective and be targeted to a prospective employer's needs to convince the employer that you have the skills, motivation, and personality for the job. If you have a job description, read the information in the description, sentence by sentence, and target the summary statement and accomplishments to respond to the job requirements. If you're sending a unsolicited résumé (doing a cold mailing) or one as part of a networking follow-up and you are not asking to be considered for a specific position that you know is open, the information should be tailored to the industry or the company. Be guided in developing your résumé by the research you did on the company (see chapter 4).

A good résumé is geared toward an objective, which may or may not be stated on the résumé. If you do not state an objective, you should still have an objective in mind to serve as an unseen guide to help clarify the information on the résumé. If it is actually stated on the résumé, position it right below your name and address. The objective should not be some grand-sounding statement but, instead, tailored to the job described in the ad or to a position you're interested in. For example, if the ad is for a sales trainee with retail experience, an appropriate objective might read: "Seeking a position in which I can apply my retail experience as a salesperson to help meet the company's profit goal." It should not read: "Seeking a progressive position with a major company where I will be able to advance and achieve my goals in management." The employer wants to know how you are going to bring value (the popular term today) to the company and help meet its goals—not how the company is going to meet yours. What's more, the second one really doesn't say anything; it's vague.

The rest of the information on the résumé, such as accomplishments and job history, should be tailored to support the objective. Because each position will have unique requirements, you may have to revise your résumé every time you apply for a job. For this reason, it would be a good idea to keep your résumé on disk and have access to a computer and laser printer so that you can easily and quickly amend it.

Do KISS and TELL

As I mentioned earlier, keep the résumé short and simple. Do not write long paragraphs filled with highfalutin words and detailed information about the duties and responsibilities for each job. Instead, summarize your background and experience in a few concise sentences (keep it to about six to eight lines); follow this summary with a bulleted listing of accomplishments (preferably about one sentence long for each); and, if appropriate, list the names of the companies where you've worked, your title for each position, and the dates (month and year) you worked. Include equivalent education (e.g., ten years experience plus a number of college-level courses and a certificate in a specialty instead of a business degree) as well as transferable experience (e.g., experience gained in relevant volunteer activities).

Include Only Positive Information

To create an overall positive impact, consider these tips:

- Include dates only if they enhance your chances (e.g., long-term employment with a company) and leave them off if they hurt your chances (e.g., a series of short-term positions; large gaps in employment).

- Don't include any demotions. (List department headings or functional titles rather than your actual titles so there is no emphasis on the demotion).

If you know you want a job exactly like the last one you had, use a chronological format—listing the jobs you've held in chronological order, starting with your most recent position first. For everything else (e.g., making a career change or summarizing a lot of experience) use a functional format. For example, if your background includes experience in various types of industries working in management, sales, and administration, list your accomplishments under those functional headings. You may also include separately on the second page a list of companies, your titles, and dates you worked there.

Do the Right Thing with Paper and Type

Use only white or off-white paper for both the résumé and cover letter, and use the same stock for both. Some companies use computer scanners to read and sort résumés, and most scanners don't pick up well from colored paper. For the same reason, do not use underlining or italics. Also, do not capitalize words to add emphasis (even if they are important words to you), and do not include any blocks of information more than three lines long—except the summary statement, which generally appears right after your heading and may be six to eight lines long.

The purpose of the cover letter is to get your résumé read. In developing the cover letter, you should be guided by the same KISS and TELL principles used in developing a winning résumé. You need only write three paragraphs for an effective cover letter. The first paragraph should state what job you are applying for, which would be the job advertised, or a need you hope to address within the company.

The second paragraph should show how your qualifications match the needs of the company or the job. Here is where you can reemphasize the points made in the résumé, but use different examples to do this—don't repeat the same ones you've included in your résumé. The third paragraph should express your interest in setting up an interview and your willingness to supply the employer with references.

THE INTERVIEW

I once heard someone tell a salesperson who had just given a presentation to a group of potential customers that her appearance and presence spoke so loudly about who she was that she hadn't needed to say a word. She looked successful—and the people in the group were sold on her product because they were sold on her. She had achieved this effect through planning, research, and careful execution. By studying her client base, she knew how to appeal to it and, because of this preparation, felt confident in her ability to communicate to the group.

You have within your control the ability to walk into an interview and do the exact same thing this salesperson did—if you lay a firm foundation before getting to the interview. Establishing that founda-

MORE JOB SEARCH ADVICE

For more about résumés and interviewing, take a look at chapter 10: Changing Companies. While it addresses résumés and other job search tools particularly for people who've been working for some time, it has some advice that novices will find very useful, particularly the boxes Oops! Avoiding Résumé Bloopers and Check It Out!: Selecting and Evaluating Companies as well as the section Preparing for Interviews.

tion begins long before the actual interview. Peggy Schmidt has more help for you here. Her *The 90-Minute Interview Prep Book* is an excellent resource for preparing for and successfully executing the interview. It's as easy to follow as her résumé book.

Actually, the interview is the fifth step in a nine-step process to getting the job you want (see Nine Steps to a Successful Interview: The Essential Job Search Chain). The steps form an interlocking chain, so if a link is weak or left out, it will impact negatively on the effectiveness of the entire chain. Proper planning requires knowing what you want to do, something about the industry and company, the right salary to ask for, and projecting an image that fits the job.

All of this leads to putting your best foot forward in the job interview. And the interview is, simply put, a conversation between you and one or more individuals within a company who want to find out if you have skills and experience and the right "chemistry" to make a good "marriage." If they find that you have best components (i.e., better than the other applicants), you will receive an offer. Then ideally you'll be in a position to negotiate for a good salary and benefits, which, combined with the job, will help you move forward on your career track.

What If You Think There's Discrimination?

What I've described is what you can expect if all things are equal. But often they're not. As a person of color, you need to know that discrimination might rear its ugly head and affect the hiring decision. It may happen before you even get to the interview. I've heard of situations where the interviewer mysteriously disappeared when it was time for a scheduled interview. In one case, the interviewers were looking out the window when the black man drove up. He waited for a couple of hours but was never interviewed.

Discrimination may show through in a comment or question that is made outside the formal interview. An Asian woman told me that an interviewer seemed shocked by who she was—the fact that she was Asian. Her name on the résumé had not revealed this fact. The

NINE STEPS TO A SUCCESSFUL INTERVIEW: THE ESSENTIAL JOB SEARCH CHAIN

The Link . . .	If It's Weak . . .	If It's Strong . . .
Goal Setting	Unfocused search. Poor résumé. Vague answers in the interview. Looking for any old job.	Productive search. Winning résumé. Clear responses in the interview. Job on the right career track.
Research	Unfocused search. Generic résumé. No information to prepare for interviewing. No idea of appropriate salary to quote.	Focused search. Productive résumé. Confident, two-way interview. Successful salary negotiations.
Multiple Strategies	Limited opportunities. Longer search.	Expanded search. Mentors. Shorter, more successful search.
Résumé	Untargeted. Takes longer to get interviews. Interviews for jobs you don't truly want.	Targeted. Significantly increases chances to get interviews for jobs you want. Sets parameters for the interviews. Position in line with career objective.
Interviews	Poor preparation. Poor result.	With a solid foundation of steps (links), this will be a piece of cake. Prior practice will enhance result.
Offers	Probably only one or none.	Most likely one that will fit well with your career goal.
Negotiation	Not likely.	Absolutely. Job first. Then salary. Then benefits.
Acceptance of offer	A job.	A career with a future.
Future outlook	Poor unless the process is improved.	Excellent. Plan your next move and repeat the prior steps.

interview was very awkward; the interviewer seemed uncomfortable, and the conversation was strained. Discrimination may surface when you're greeted in the waiting area, while at lunch with the interviewer, when you say good-bye ("How did you happen to apply to this company?").

While the employer may consider any such remarks "off the record," the Equal Employment Opportunity Commission may not. So if you believe that you have been discriminated against under the law, immediately contact: The U.S. Equal Employment Opportunity Commission; 2401 E Street NW, Washington, D.C. 20507 or call 800-USA-EEOC (the TDD number is 202-634-7057) to contact an EEOC field office.

Here's Looking at You Kid

You should always go to an interview looking like you fit the job you want to fill. You can't expect to command an $85,000 salary with a $35,000 image. On the other hand, you don't want to go to an interview for a $40,000 job dressed in a Chanel suit. Or interview with a law firm dressed in a loose flowery skirt and sandals or a bright jacket and a wild tie. Get the idea?

The best approach, when in doubt, is to dress conservatively— especially when you're not sure about how people dress in that culture. This is definitely not the time to wear an outfit from your "cultural uniform." Only something consistent with your "business uniform" is acceptable here. I know the navy blue suit is a boring idea, but it still works. It's part of the "business uniform." I've never seen a person yet who didn't look businesslike in a navy blue suit—something about it just says "professional." Even children recognize the navy blue suit as the uniform of a business person. Once, I walked past a group of kids wearing my navy blue suit, and one of them told me I looked "business-y."

This conservative approach should follow through in the rest of your attire: conservative hairdo, moderate makeup, discreet jewelry. No strong perfumes or aftershave. The idea is to keep the interviewer's attention on your sterling qualifications and sparkling personality rather than some distracting element that might cost you the job.

QUESTIONS YOU SHOULDN'T BE ASKED

Federal law does not expressly prohibit inquiries concerning an applicant's race, color, religion, sex, national origin, or physical or mental disabilities; however, such inquiries must directly relate to a *Bona Fide Occupational Qualification* (BFOQ). A BFOQ is a qualification reasonably related to the essential job requirements in circumstances in which the needs of the group adversely affected by the qualification cannot be accommodated without undue hardship on the part of the employer.

BFOQ has been narrowly construed by the Equal Employment Opportunity Commission and the courts, so the employer must be sure that any qualifications imposed are significantly related to successful job performance. In other words, an employer had better have a very, very good reason for asking any of the following questions. And if such inquiries are made by a potential employer, you should ask how the information relates to the job.

- Are there any holidays other than those usually observed that would require you to be absent from work?
- What are the nationalities of your parents?
- Would you like to be called Miss, Ms., or Mrs.?
- Are you single, married, or divorced?
- Do you plan to have a family?
- Do you have any disability?
- How severe is your disability?
- Have you ever been arrested?
- What was your maiden name?
- Where were you born?
- Of what country are you a citizen?
- What is your native language?
- Whom should we notify in case of an emergency?
- To what clubs, societies, or organizations do you belong?
- What kind of discharge did you receive from the military?
- Can you read well enough to take this test?

Don't One-Up the Boss

I've known people to lose an opportunity because they appeared not to need the job or they one-upped the interviewer with their image. According to a high-level executive I know, an applicant should never project an image beyond his or her job level—and certainly not beyond the boss's level.

I hate to say it this way, but you'll be dealing with human beings—not perfect beings—which means you'll be dealing with people who have egos. The sad truth is some interviewers don't want to hire someone who seems more prosperous than they. Maybe you don't want to work for anyone like that (and I can surely understand that feeling); however, if you're aware of this potential obstacle up front, you have the option of toning down your image—if you choose to. Who knows, the job may be so appealing that it will be worth making any minor adjustments.

For example, if you're being considered for an entry-level job and you drive a Lexus or a Mercedes to the interview, it may appear as if you don't need the job. If that's all you have in terms of an automobile, try and be discreet about it by parking in a low-profile place in the parking lot.

Somebody's Watching You

Whenever you drive onto the company's parking lot for an interview, there is a chance that you are being observed by someone at the company—possibly even the person who'll be conducting the interview. So be on your best behavior: Make sure that your car is clean, inside and out; don't make unseemly adjustments to your clothes while walking into the building; and carry yourself gracefully and with an air of confidence.

Be nice to everyone—beginning with the parking attendant or the doorman—everywhere, all the time, even in the restroom. You never know who has the boss's ear. An informal procedure at some companies is to ask the receptionist what they thought of the applicants—in terms of how they presented themselves at the reception area, how they acted when they were waiting for their interviewer, and so forth. In fact, more and more companies are now making this a part of their formal screening process. So keep in mind that the person you may be inclined to ignore may be someone who will have a significant influence in the final selection.

In Case the Interviewer Doesn't Know How to Interview

It's hard to believe when it actually happens, but there will be times when you will have done everything you're supposed to do in preparation for that very important interview and then end up with a person who doesn't know how to interview. The best way to deal with this is to prepare some questions ahead of time so you can guide the interview and sell yourself. I suggest that you consider beforehand what issues would be of concern to you and have questions in mind that you can ask concerning them. For instance, if you're a creative person and most productive when given free rein to accomplish an assignment, you'd want to know how much freedom you would have in carrying out your responsibilities.

You're more likely to get a true assessment of the situation by asking a series of open-ended questions, such as:

- How are projects assigned?

- How are they monitored?

- How do company managers like to work with the staff (e.g., with a teamwork approach or specifically assigned duties)?

- Which project management style has proven to be most successful in the company?

Equally important is how you ask the questions. Always use an open, nonjudgmental, noncondescending tone. Never, ever give the impression that you think the interviewer does not have his or her act together.

The Top-Ten-Plus Interview Questions

An employer might ask any number of questions to find out whether or not you have the skills to confront the challenges of the position, the motivation to work through any problems that arise, and the personality to fit into the work culture. If you can handle the following frequently asked questions, you should be able to handle any interview with confidence.

- **Tell me about yourself.** Keep your answer short, to the point, and under 2 minutes. I would give a brief career overview, point to a couple of accomplishments that demonstrate your skills and that align with the job responsibilities, and then mention why you are interested in the job. If you developed your skills doing community work or are just out of school, mention the activities you've been involved with that demonstrate skills related to the job. (*The 90-Minute Interview Prep Book* provides great examples of how to answer questions if you're a recent college graduate.) It's best to avoid discussions about your spouse, children, or personal issues, because it may work against you later, even if the interviewer expresses a positive attitude about it at the time.

- **Why are you leaving your current company?** Separate your job search action from any action your former company has taken that has caused you to look for a job. Try an answer like "The company is restructuring, and I've decided to seek a new challenge." Never, ever say you've been fired or laid off, because it lends a negative air to the conversation. By the same token, if you've quit a job because of intolerable working conditions, don't speak negatively about the experience or the company. Simply say that you felt it was time to move on and challenge yourself in new areas.

- **What are your strengths?** This question could be posed in a variety of ways, such as: Why should we hire you? How do you see your skills enhancing the department? What would your supervisor (or peers) say about you? When responding, give examples that align with the job requirements. For instance, as a financial analyst applicant you might say "I've always been complimented by my managers for my analytical ability. I even received a bonus for discovering an error that would have caused the company several million dollars."

Or as a public relations applicant, you might answer: "I was asked to head up a special community project by a company that contacted me on the recommendation of several community groups, so I believe one of my strengths is that I'm respected within the community." You can prepare for this question by researching the job, company, and interviewer (through networking) to get a clear idea of the specific skills and strengths the employer is looking for.

- **What are your weaknesses?** This question might also be posed in a variety of ways, including: In which areas do you need to develop? Or, tell me about a failure you've had and what you learned from it. Rather than pointing to an obvious flaw or making up an answer, focus on the overuse of a strength that you have a handle on. For instance, you can say something like "I know that I tend to be a perfectionist, and sometimes that causes me to put in extra time on a project to satisfy my need for perfection and meet the project deadline." Of course, only say something like this if it's absolutely true.

- **What are your goals?** Only discuss goals that are attainable within that company, preferably that particular department. It's always a worthwhile goal to say you want to grow professionally. Don't assert or even hint that your goal is to one day get the interviewer's job—the statement is passé and could be frightening in the current downsizing environment.

- **What did you like best about your present/former manager?** Whatever you say, let it be positive because the answer reflects more on you than on the manager. If you felt overburdened with work in your present/former situation, think of it this way—it afforded you an opportunity to grow professionally.

Therefore, you could say, "He/she challenged me to develop my skills and take on more responsibility" or something to this effect.

- **What was it like working at your former company?** Your answer here also needs to be positive. Even if the interviewer has something negative to say about the company, don't allow yourself to be trapped into agreeing with a negative comment. If the interviewer mentions something negative, don't argue with him or her, just express, in a nondefensive manner, that you had a more positive experience—and let it go.

- **The psychological questions.** Questions along this line may or may not occur, but if they do, there is no way to anticipate what kind of question might be asked. While some companies use psychological tests to evaluate candidates, more often interviewers will pose pointed questions to get a sense of a person's outlook and psychological makeup.

  Some of the psychological questions that I have heard asked include: If you were a tree, what kind of tree would you be? What would you take with you to the afterlife? What animal would you choose to be? There are no right or wrong answers to these types of questions. They are usually posed as a way of determining how you would fit into that company's culture. Take the questions seriously and take your time to answer them as honestly as you can.

- **The situational question.** Here, an interviewer might ask you to imagine yourself in a situation likely to come up in the job and describe how you would deal with it. Whatever your answer is, always remember that on the job you'd be expected to get the job done, so make sure your answer ends with that kind of conclusion.

- **The difficult question.** Generally, these are questions unique to your situation or background that you probably would prefer not to answer. Usually, they refer to something on your résumé or in your background that stands out or is inconsistent and they generally address such issues as, for example, the fact that you have no degree, your erratic work history, job gaps in your work history, and, subtly (or not so subtly), your age. If you ask someone to review your résumé prior to your job search, they will likely spot any issue that might give rise to a difficult question. This way, you'll have time to think about how you might best answer and be better prepared when it comes up in an interview.

- **What kind of salary are you looking for?** For each job that you go after, have a salary range in mind that is consistent with the industry standard in your geographic location. A little networking with friends, peers in your professional association, or placement agency representatives who specialize in your area of expertise should help you arrive at an average for your locality. Keep in mind, however, that you should only provide this information when you feel you must. When you are first asked in person about salary requirements, your initial response should be that you're open on the question of compensation and that it would depend on the job requirements. If the employer asks again, then state the salary range that you're research shows is appropriate for the job and area. If he or she continues to press and asks specifically what your last salary was, give a range that aligns with the industry standard. Never give an exact salary because it does not allow you room to negotiate later.

Don't Leave Without It

At the end of the interview, find out what the next step will be. Then, based on the response, ask if it's okay for you to follow up. For instance, if you're told a decision will be made in a couple of weeks or the next stage of interviews will be in two weeks, you might say, "Why don't I check back with you then?" On the other hand, if the interviewer clearly states that you will be contacted within a week, one way or another, then wait for someone from the company to call you; if you haven't heard from anyone by that time, then follow up with a call.

Take That Extra Step

Be sure to write that thank-you letter—it only takes a few minutes. Most people don't follow up, so doing so will help you stand out. The note should be typed, brief, and well-written, with a professional, not casual, tone. If you interviewed with several people, it's all right to send the letter to the primary interviewer and extend a thank-you to the other interviewers in the same letter.

A VARIETY OF INTERVIEW TYPES

Essentially, an interview is a conversation we have with someone to determine how we might fit with some purpose he or she has in mind. That conversation could occur anywhere, anytime, and in a variety of circumstances. Overall, the keys to a successful interview conversation are knowledge of self (your goal and skills) and the company (when being interviewed by a company representative), preparation (knowing what to expect), and practice (knowing what to say). Properly armed, you'll be able to handle any one of the following types of interviews:

Over the Back Fence

I don't believe that any conversation is casual when it centers around getting a job, even though the tone might be. For instance, a conversation about jobs with a neighbor over the back fence (who happens to be employed by a major electronics firm, for instance) could turn into a subtle screening interview or even a decision interview, depending on the person's job level at the company. Whether they take place over the fence, at the supermarket, or at your kid's soccer match, I'd take these conversations seriously. Give responses consistent with your goals and present yourself in a positive light.

Phone Interview

One of the first things I noticed when I started working out of my home was that when I answer the phone, my tone is often dictated by what I'm wearing and, sometimes, the position I'm in when answering. I soon figured out that the best way to answer the phone during business hours is when I am in a business mode. By that I mean fully dressed, made up, and my hair in place (i.e., not lounging around barefoot in a T-shirt and sweats) and sitting upright and alert, preferably at my desk.

I've also found a couple of other approaches that help convey a businesslike tone. First, I always keep my answering machine on. That way, if I'm not in a position to answer with the proper tone (i.e., at my desk and in a business mode), I have time to get organized before returning the call. Also, while talking to a potential employer, it can sometimes be helpful to stand facing a mirror and smiling while talking because it conveys better energy.

If you already have a job, determine whether it will be all right to receive calls from potential employers. This is usually acceptable when your current employer knows that you are leaving. Otherwise, when a potential employer calls you at your place of work, ask to call him or her right back, then go to a quiet place where you can return the call in private.

Informal Interview

A client once told me about an interviewer who had set up a meeting with him, saying that the interview would be informal and conducted on a Saturday. My client arrived at the "informal" interview wearing a very casual suit, only to find the interviewer dressed in a regular business suit. Surprised at my client's attire, the interviewer commented, "Oh, I see you decided to dress casually."

I've learned that interviews are never really informal, even if the company's culture is. The interview is always serious business, so always put your best foot forward—even if the interviewer says the interview will be informal. But, if the interviewer specifically tells you to dress casually, then do. If you're not sure what "casual" means, ask for clarification. For instance: "Slacks and no jacket?" Or "No tie?"

Over a Meal

By the same token, an interview is not the time for an "if it's not all over the place, it shouldn't be in your face" burger—and it definitely is not the time for any drink stronger than coffee or a soft drink. The suggestion that you have a chat over lunch or dinner does not take away from the intensity of the interview; rather, it adds to it. Do not be so relaxed that you're unable to stay on point. Also, I suggest always ordering something easy to eat—like soup. Stay away from pasta dishes, finger foods, or salads, especially the ones with the cherry tomatoes, which tend to slide off the plate when you're trying to cut them.

An interview is usually stressful at best, so it makes sense to keep everything as simple as possible. A complicated and difficult lunch only adds to the stress. Most important, in an over-a-meal interview, mind your manners—the interviewer may be evaluating your social graces. Be kind to the waiters, don't talk with your mouth full, and eat slowly and with moderation.

Light Conversation with the Receptionist

Once, my friend Paul arrived early for an interview and started a "light" conversation with a person at the front desk whom he thought was the receptionist. After about 10 minutes of conversation, she let him know she was the personnel manager and proceeded to escort him back to her office to finish the interview. Luckily, he had not said anything that could have damaged his chances for the job, but he might have, just because he assumed she was the receptionist and that he could relax.

Even with the receptionist, it's not a good idea to relax to the point of not putting that best foot forward. Many receptionists have the ear of the boss and, therefore, may have significant influence in the selection of the final candidate for the job.

Stress Interview

This type of interview normally will not occur unless there is a lot of stress in the job and the interviewer needs to determine how you will handle it. The stressors applied will usually be something that a person in that job would be expected to be able to manage. For instance, a candidate for a training manager's position might be asked to make a short presentation to a group of peers and/or members of the upper-management team. You can prepare for this type of interview by role-playing with friends, pretending you are in a stressful situation similar to something you might encounter on the job. Then, ask your friend for feedback on how well you handled it.

Panel Interview

Some people consider this type of interview as being similar to a stress interview. Panel interviews have become very popular in this era of self-directed work teams because greater consideration is given to everyone being able to work together effectively. A panel could consist of between three and five members and be composed of any combination of people, including a manager, a human resources representative, peers, and an upper manager.

One-on-One Boss Interview

Eventually, at some point in the interview process, you'll be interviewing one-on-one with the person who will be supervising you. In some cases, especially at a smaller company, this will be your first and only interview. The one-on-one interview with the boss has definite pros and cons. On one hand, you're closer to the power with this interview—therefore, if you make a good impression here, you'll more likely get the job. On the other hand, it gives you no room to recoup after you've made a mistake or to develop allies who could help prepare you for the big interview, as is possible when interviews are set up progressively.

Prior research is going to be very important before this interview. One of the best sources for information is networking. Usually the more confident (not cocky) and spontaneous you are in these interviews, the better. One client was stumped when the head of an accounting firm snapped, as his first question, "Why should I hire you?" She stammered and couldn't come up with an answer. She told me that if she had been prepared and not thrown off balance, she would have replied, "Because

I get along well with all the key people in the department and with people in three of the top companies you represent." Certainly, that answer would have been preferable to the "no answer" she gave, especially since it would have been a natural response.

Progressive Interviews

This is probably still the most common interview process. You interview with a human resources representative first or a search agency representative followed by a human resources representative; then you meet with your prospective manager and then interview with the manager at the next level up. If you "make it" at one level, you will be prepped for the next interviewer. If the interviewer is inexperienced and does not do this, be sure to ask what you can expect and how you should prepare for the next interview.

GETTING OFFERS AND NEGOTIATING JOB AND SALARY

When the interviewer asks "How much money would it take to get you here and when can you start?", does it mean you've been made a definite offer? No, it doesn't. That question is probably asked of all candidates interviewed. An offer is not a question—it is a statement consisting of a starting date, salary, and title.

Any negotiation should start first with the job responsibilities and accountability because that will be the basis for any salary offer and negotiation. Preferably, issues relating to the job, such as duties and title, should be negotiated before a salary offer is made. When you receive an offer, find out when a response is expected and set a date then and there to get together to discuss your acceptance.

Be sensitive to how much negotiation is possible (follow your gut on this one). You need to be able to recognize when negotiations have gone as far as they will go. You should not negotiate an offer if you have discussed every facet of the job during a series of interviews and there has been some give-and-take on both sides. In this case, you've actually been involved informally in the negotiation process all along. By the time the offer is extended, it is just a formality (or should be). To try to negotiate at that point is inappropriate, and the employer might think you're playing games and withdraw the offer.

I've known this to happen before. I've seen offers withdrawn when the candidate got greedy or misread the interviewer and overplayed his or her hand. There is no need to negotiate an offer that you know is fair. If you've done your research, then you should know the appropriate salary range for your skills and for the job.

I recommend taking the following approach in handling any offers:

- Know your absolute bottom line—what you must get from the job in terms of salary, title, perks, etc. I believe in making sure the company meets your most important (nonnegotiable) expectations before going forward with any other negotiations. After they've met these considerations, you can think about the factors that would be nice to have (e.g., a reserved parking space, a membership to a health club). Because every issue cannot have equal importance, you must prioritize your needs. You might have to give up something, so you need to know ahead of time where you're willing to make adjustments.

- Next, consider how the position will help advance your career. If it does not, you may want to ask for additional responsibilities to accomplish that goal. Even if you don't get more money for taking on additional responsibilities right away, the added experience will ultimately pay off.

- Ask for a salary that aligns with your newly negotiated job. If the employer is not willing to meet your salary expectation right away, suggest you be given a performance review in three months and ask if the issue can be revisited at that time. If you do not wish to make a commitment to permanent employment without the salary you believe is fair, ask for a three-month trial period, after which they could agree to meet your original sum or, at least, renegotiate. (Realize, though, that by this time, you may have made an intellectual and emotional commitment to the job and believe that it is a good choice for you, or the employer may recognize the added value you bring and be able to flex a bit on the salary. At any rate, these approaches bring up the issues without backing you or the employer into a corner.)

- Finally, have a list of benefits or other perks that you'd like. Ask for these last. But be prepared to give in on these items, unless one of these is a nonnegotiable item for you, in which case you should have found out if you could get this item before proceeding to this point.

- After you've reached agreement, put everything you've negotiated in an acceptance letter to the employer. It can be simply stated. For instance:

Dear _____,

Per our conversation on (date) I will start working on (date) as (title) for $_____ annually. We agreed to the following: (list everything you agreed to during your negotiation meeting).

If you receive more than one offer and the company you prefer makes the first offer, you should thank the second person and say that you have an offer on the table you're considering. If your second choice makes the first offer, ask for at least two days to respond, then let your first choice know that you have a serious offer on the table and, if they are interested, you will need an offer from them within 24 hours. Sometimes this will make your first choice step up the hiring process; sometimes it won't.

I've known people to accept an offer then get a better one and leave right away to take the second offer. There may be no serious consequences to this kind of action, but it concerns me. It's a small world, and burning bridges like this can possibly damage your reputation.

Whatever your decision, receiving and accepting your first offer is a major accomplishment in your career. Congratulations. Now, exhale, take a deep breath, and get ready for the real world of work.

RESOURCES

Overall Job-Search Help

101 Great Answers to the Toughest Job Search Problems by Ollie Stevenson (Career Press, 1995). There are times when you will follow all the proper steps in your job search and nothing seems to work—because you have a unique situation or problem. I wrote this book to help with those problems in any area of the job search. It addresses such dilemmas as being too old, too young, underqualified, overqualified, race, gender, salary, relocation, handicaps, etc.

Résumés

The New 90-Minute Résumé by Peggy Schmidt (Peterson's, 1996) is excellent. It provides good résumé models, plus easy-to-follow steps for getting there. The book also includes a Résumé Tool Kit on disk, job-related Web sites, and before-and-after résumé samples. This is the easiest-to-follow, best résumé development book I've seen.

Perfect Résumé Strategies by Tom Jackson and Ellen Jackson (Doubleday, 1990). For transferring skills, this book is great. It highlights seventy-five success stories of real people in times of change, including the résumés, cover letters, and strategies they used. The book offers good examples of transferring skills learned in volunteer work and developing targeted functional résumés that appeal to employees.

The Résumé Catalog: 200 Damn Good Examples by Yana Parker (Ten Speed Press, 1988) is another superb résumé. In addition to providing a range of résumé samples and styles, this book also deals with how to address some of the problems that would be revealed in the résumé.

Résumés That Mean Business by David R. Eyler (Random House, 1992) is another book I like. It provides seventy-five model résumés, as well as cover letters, and gives an explanation for each point made in the different samples. The book also addresses the issue of electronic résumés and using on-line services for job searches.

Cover Letters

There are a number of books on the market that address cover letters but, quite frankly, I recommend only one style of cover letter for everyone—one paragraph indicating what you're applying for, a second succinct paragraph responding to the company needs and highlighting your qualifications, followed by one paragraph stating your interest in the position and in setting up an interview. A sample of this style, as well as several variations of it, can be found in *Cover Letters That Knock 'Em Dead* by Martin Yate (Adams, 1995).

Interviewing Tips

Interview Power: Selling Yourself Face to Face by Tom Washington (Mount Vernon Press, 1995) lists eighty-nine tough questions with answers and provides good suggestions for salary negotiation.

The 90-Minute Interview Prep Book by Peggy Schmidt (Peterson's, 1996) is an excellent companion to her résumé book. If you're like me, you don't like to waste time and will appreciate the efficiency of this book.

60 Seconds & You're Hired by Robin Ryan (Impact Publications, 1994) has suggested answers plus employers' reasoning behind seventy of the toughest questions that could be asked during the interview. It also includes tough questions for college students and new grads and gives examples of illegal questions.

CHAPTER

EARLY ON-THE-JOB SUCCESS

To be effective and successful in a job, you need to have a thorough understanding of what makes the organization tick and what your real job priorities are. To do this, you've got to learn the work culture, the processes for getting things done, the people, and the criteria for advancement. When you join a company, you must adjust your general business mind-set to one specific to that particular company.

Realize that when you start a new job, you'll be at the beginning of another stage of your career. Expect to experience the discomfort and awkwardness that goes with starting something new. You will be going through a transition as you adapt to fit the objective and working styles of your new employer. It matters not whether you've just graduated from school, you're starting your first career job, or you're changing jobs. Wherever you came from, there was a standard that went with it, and you probably developed a level of security and confidence working within that framework. Now your comfort will be challenged. To make a successful transition into your new job, you'll have to approach it with an open mind, ready to learn a different way of doing things.

MAKING A SMOOTH TRANSITION

What kind of differences might you face as you adjust to your new environment? Let's say that at your former company, everyone dressed casually, the executives interacted very informally with the staff, and it was perfectly acceptable for you or any of your coworkers to join the president at lunch in the cafeteria and bring up any concerns or suggestions. Now, in your new company, you quickly find that everything is much more formal, much larger, and the executives maintain a certain amount of distance from the staff. In this new environment, if you approached the president with an issue without first discussing it with your boss and your boss's boss, you probably would be considered out of line. Two different companies, two different mind-sets.

The transition from college to the business arena can be even more dramatic. In his book *The New Professional*, Ed Holton offers wise advice for newly hired college graduates in their first year of work. His advice is also appropriate for anyone wanting to make a good start in a new situation. Here are some of his tips:

- Get comfortable with being new.

- Be the best inexperienced new employee you possibly can.

- Make good first impressions so you will get the chance to really show your stuff later.

- Don't try to do more in your first few months than you should; set realistic goals.

- Look for a chance to get on the success spiral; most of all, don't let a college mentality keep you off the spiral.

- Remember that you, and only you, are responsible for your success.

- Transition means adapting, changing, and learning: Be prepared.

- Have realistic expectations, which means looking past what you learned from the recruiting process.

- Focus on being a great new professional, and don't get ahead of yourself.

- Make learning breaking-in skills your first priority.

Get Off to a Good Start

Rodney Gee, a black staffing manager, has found through his years at Motorola that getting a mentor and learning the boss's expectations are important parts of the first-step process. "Once on the job, it's critical to get a mentor, figure out the ground rules, and get a clear sense of your manager's expectations," he says. "The best way to get a mentor is to perform. Let someone see that being connected with you is a positive thing. Be flexible—learn from anyone. Your mentor does not have to be the same race or the same sex. He or she will help you know where the traps and land mines are; and knowing that will enable you to run better," explains Gee.

"As a new employee you should figure out the company's unwritten ground rules in the first thirty days on the job, and make sure that you and the manager have the same expectation level regarding success and failure," he points out. "It may take two or three meetings to get this information, but it's worth it because twelve months later, you'll want the manager to be happy with you. So find out what's in her head, not just what is on paper."

Your race will be the added factor that you'll need to consider—both from a positive and negative prospective. Even with the greater diversity in the workplace today, you are likely to be in a minority in your company. Everything you do will probably be magnified through the lens of the majority group. This can have its advantages and its disadvantages (see "Working with the System"). Either way, it will place an extra burden on you to connect with the other team members, but you have to get to know them to become an accepted part of the culture. You may have to be the one to extend yourself first because some of your coworkers may be unsure about how to approach you. This extra burden can be offset by the fact that others will notice your work more easily simply because you are different from the majority.

"WORKING WITH THE SYSTEM"
■

Judy followed an ideal model to get her job with Hughes Delco. First, she worked for the company during the summer while attending school. Then, after she obtained her Bachelor of Science degree in electrical engineering from California State University, Chico, Hughes Delco management asked Judy to join the company as a full-time employee.

"I started as an associate engineer and worked my way up to a project manager within a three-year period," she says. "I have to admit, though, that it's twice as difficult for a woman engineer to succeed, because it takes longer to be taken seriously. Many times, people thought I was the secretary coming into meetings. But I did my homework and studied everything, often working until 10 or 11 at night. I proved I was just as good as the men, and after that I was able to ease up."

Part of Judy's success has come from learning how to deal effectively with people, especially her bosses. "I like to learn about people and what makes them tick. I learn the preferences of people and then I adjust accordingly," she explains. "For example, I had a supervisor who liked one-on-one interaction; a written report meant nothing to him, but if I explained the issue to him in person he was very impressed. Another supervisor was just the opposite, so for him I would write a report."

Judy has experienced some of the downsides of being a woman in a male-dominated profession. "I've had to deal with men coming on to me, especially powerful men who are customers. I've also had to deal with the jealousy of peers, especially other women. I've even been verbally attacked and ridiculed in meetings. At first, I would ignore incidents like this, hoping they would stop. When they didn't, I knew I had to confront them. Before doing so, I always did my research, making sure I knew my area of work and that of the person who was attacking me so that I could respond knowledgeably to the person's comments."

While Judy believes that the disadvantage of being a woman may initially mean not being taken seriously, it's outweighed by the advantage of standing out and being noticed. This, she says, can help in your career progress—as long as you're willing to prove you're competent. "My advice to a person coming out of college is to give it your all. The first year is extremely important. Work 16 hours a day if you need to in order to establish a good reputation. After that, you can relax a bit."

■

JUDITH SCHULTE
Hispanic-American engineer
Hughes Delco Electronics
Santa Barbara, California

The bottom line? You need to be willing to make the necessary adjustments to achieve early success on the job. If you adjust your mind-set and proceed with a positive, open attitude and a willingness to learn and work hard, you will be on your way to achieving the success you desire.

HOW TO ACHIEVE EARLY SUCCESS IN ANY JOB SITUATION

Get a Mentor
A knowledgeable mentor is like an excellent attorney, financial adviser, or doctor. He or she can provide key information that may

literally save your professional life. Find one mentor or two. The mentor you hook up with should be someone who has been with the company for a while, who knows his or her way around the organization, and who is known and highly respected. Mentors can come from any organizational level—they don't necessarily have to be top managers or executives. Once you find a mentor, stick with him or her and make the effort to learn all you can: Your mentor can serve as your guide and teacher and help you reach your career goal.

"MENTORS: A KEY FACTOR TO SUCCESS"

■

With a twenty-five-year career that has culminated in a key position at Chevron, it's safe to say that Gregory knows how to achieve on-the-job success. "People think it's all about working hard and being competent," he says. "Of course, that's essential, but having mentors has been instrumental for me. I was fortunate—when I first came to work, I found a mentor who advised me to get things done within the context of how the company wanted things done and to get a grip on how to deal with the office politics."

Throughout his career, Gregory has relied on mentors to help him handle difficult situations. "The EEOC guy became a haven for me—I could go to him and scream and then go back to work. He was very helpful in discussing strategies and options for getting around a situation so it wouldn't happen again. He made me realize that I faced the same obstacles as everyone—color was not the issue. If there was a 9-foot hurdle, I needed to be able to jump 11 feet or make someone think I could."

Realizing early that he needed a plan to make his success happen, Gregory was willing to follow any positive role model—no matter what that person's color. One of his early mentors was a white supervisor who offered to teach him what it took to be successful. Later, Gregory found mentors in two managers who had faith in his ability to get the job done. "I was very lucky. I worked for an organization whose vice president was using visionary principles and optimizing human resources before it was popular to do so. Ultimately, I worked for two guys who did not see it as a risk to put me, a black man, in a management role—because if I didn't cut the muster I would have been replaced just like anyone else," Gregory explains.

"One of the issues that people of color need to deal with is that the bottom line in corporate America is to make money. I have found that if I can help the company be more profitable, they don't care what color I am. They may have had some issue initially about how I would compare with the white male, but that was overcome when I was able to show my competency in reducing tax costs."

■

GREGORY REDMOND
Black manager
Chevron Corporation
Business: Tax planning and coordination

Understand the Significance of the Company's Mission

Know and understand the company's mission: its purpose, the reason it exists. Many companies have a formal mission statement that appears in its employee handbook, its annual report, or its long-range plan. Some promote their mission in slogans and advertisements. A mission statement may be a single phrase or several sentences or paragraphs. Get to understand and accept it so that you can incorporate it into your job. For instance, if a company's mission is to upgrade the physical quality of people's lives through its products and services, it wants to project a healthy image of itself and its employees. For you this may mean not only doing good work but also participating in walkathons and campaigns to ban smoking or to develop healthy eating.

Understand the Culture

The company's culture is its personality. People who are most successful within a culture are those who are compatible with its personality. Observe how the greatest number of people behave in the organization; how things get done; how people talk, dress, and interact with one another. These clues will show you the behavior and values that will be rewarded in the company. Your mentor can guide you in developing an understanding of the company's culture. He or she can help you form a positive relationship with the company by giving you information that will save you from making mistakes or wasting your time in unnecessary or unrewarding actions.

Project a Great Attitude

Learn to cultivate a great attitude no matter what the circumstances. Approach tasks with a "can-do" attitude; changes with a "flexible" attitude; disappointments with a "mature" attitude; projects with a "team" attitude; and disagreeable people with a "pleasant" attitude. The right attitude in all circumstances will be a tremendous aid in being successful careerwise. Luckily, this is another area where you can gather the resolve of your cultural mind-set to help you endure the challenges of maintaining an even and pleasant disposition under any circumstances.

Get Along with Your Boss

Develop an understanding of your boss, your boss's boss (to the extent you can), and the rest of the corporate hierarchy. Don't judge your boss; that's not your job but someone else's. No boss is perfect, just as no person is perfect. A lot of what your boss asks you to do will be dictated by his boss, who, in turn, is following directives from her boss, and so on and so on. Make the effort to understand your boss and find out what he needs to have done to make his work life easier—then do it.

Get Along with the Other People on the Job

Get along with the other people on the job—peers, subordinates, and support staff. Remember that everyone has his own cultural mind-set, just as you do, so there are bound to be different points of view and approaches to dealing with tasks and issues. Understand that the organization has a collective voice that is made up of bits and pieces of all its people. If you want to be included in that voice and respected for the part you contribute, learn early to respect and get along with others.

Learn How to Get Credit for What You Do

Also, keep in mind that you and your peers are all in competition for promotions, top jobs, the boss's approval, whatever. So, balance friendliness, helpfulness, and team play with a sense of responsibility for taking care of your own career. If you have been clearly designated as the primary person on a project that turns out well, don't worry about tooting your horn, because everyone will already be aware of your role in the project's success. But if you support one of your colleagues on an important project and she takes the credit, make sure that the right people know of your contribution. The best way to do this is to subtly communicate your achievement to the people who matter. For instance, if you have not received credit for a project, ask your mentor what you should do to avoid that situation in the future. His advice will help you later; at the same time, you'll be alerting someone else in the company of your contribution to the project. Another approach might be to mention your involvement during lunchtime conversations with your peers or to include your final contributions in your regular status report to your manager.

Make the Most of Meetings

I used to think meetings were a waste of time (when I was younger and in more of a hurry), but I've grown to appreciate the benefits of a good meeting: The synergy produces some good ideas and allows you to reality test your own concepts. Meetings provide an arena where you can express ideas, observe other styles of management and problem solving, and learn who in the organization has clout and who doesn't. A lot can be said about meetings, and in *I Went to College for This?* (Peterson's, 1994) Garrett Soden offers a charming and humorous slant on them. He describes a variety of meetings, presents a pretty accurate view of what is actually going on at them, and suggests how to prepare for each type. For instance, when it's a show-and-tell meeting, make sure you have something to show; at a brainstorming meeting, let loose and contribute your ideas if the meeting is truthfully set up for that purpose (your idea may be the winning one and score big points). Be aware, though, that people sometimes set up brainstorming meetings simply as a forum to get their message out, in which case it's a fake meeting and you'll be wasting your time if you try to contribute.

Stay in the Right Mind-Set for Business

Evaluate the things that happen on the job against your business mind-set and not your cultural mind-set. As an example, if your cultural mind-set values status and titles and a department reorganization causes you to change positions from, say, manager to project leader, you might have an immediate negative reaction from your cultural viewpoint. You may feel embarrassed to tell your friends because you expect them to think you've failed or lost face. But in evaluating the change from your business mind-set and with your goals in mind, you need to ask yourself if that's really the case. Will this position actually advance your career in the long run? Are the responsibilities ones you would enjoy handling? How critical is the project to the company? If your answers are positive, then accept the position for the good opportunity that it is and forget about losing your old title.

Follow the Social Rules for Business

Whether at work or in a social setting, when you interact with colleagues you're still, in a sense, "at work." You are being watched and evaluated—especially if you are a person of color. Because of this, the one absolute no-no is to hang out with your boss or peers and to drink or participate in any kind of unacceptable behavior. I've seen several careers derailed because of this. Drinking with your boss is as bad as drinking during an interview. It should never be done. On occasion, of course, you will attend social functions (e.g., the office party) with your boss and your peers where alcohol is served. But remember that a party with your coworkers is still an extension of work. I avoid alcohol, and that is never a problem since a lot of people, like myself, don't drink for health reasons. An occasional drink or glass of wine is probably fine, but it is never a good idea under any circumstances to get tipsy.

Know That Every Level Has Its Price

Accept that the business arena is a tough, competitive environment where you will have to start at the bottom doing grunt work and carrying out "gofer" duties until you work your way up the ladder. Everybody has to go through this; it's called paying your dues. The reality is that every time you join a new organization or move to another division or job in a company, you'll have to go through a process of paying your dues, to some degree. Also, understand that as you move up the ladder, the price will be progressively stiffer at each level. So, as you consider your moves forward, carefully evaluate each one against your whole life-career plan to make sure that the price is worth the sacrifices that you may have to make.

STARTING A NEW JOB AT A NEW COMPANY

It's very possible (maybe even probable) that the responsibilities of the job you interviewed for will change when you come on board. One of the first things you'll have to do is adjust the expectations you originally had about the job to fit the realities you find after starting. No matter what you anticipated the job and the company would be like, both will be different—they may be better or they may be worse, but they will definitely be different from what you expected. So look around, take an inventory, and compare what you expected to what you actually got; then you can begin to get an idea of what you'll actually be dealing with on a day-to-day basis.

Once you have a clear picture of the realities of the job, you'll need to clarify and reaffirm the information you received in the interview. For a variety of reasons, a job description may change somewhat between your interview and the start date. Any number of circumstances can lead to a modification from the original description: for instance, the person who was to have trained you has since left the company (and took the training materials); the company may have undergone a major redirection; your department may have agreed to take on a new, unexpected project; or a new supervisor may have taken over in your department.

Whatever the case, you start the job only to find that you won't be doing what you thought you would be—at least not right away. If this occurs, you might want to give the situation a couple of weeks, then discuss it with a mentor and sit down with your manager to clarify the modified responsibilities, accountabilities, reporting relationships, projects, and priorities. If you find, after talking with her, that there exists a serious discrepancy between your original understanding of the job and the new parameters, what should you do? You may want to ask your manager if you can have a couple of days to consider the impact of the change. Then, after thinking it over, get back to her to discuss and resolve your concerns and present any modifications you feel are appropriate.

If it looks like your modifications will not be accepted, you may want to consider changing jobs (perhaps within the company). But, first, evaluate the job at hand and its potential against your goal. Even though it is not what you bargained for, would succeeding at it help advance your career? If so, then it may be wise to stick with it. If you don't want to do this or the job doesn't support your career, it may still be best to stick with it for at least a year, because leaving so soon might not look good on your résumé. You might find it worthwhile to bide your time until a change comes about. The boss may change, the job may change, or you may find a temporary or volunteer way to do more of what you want to do outside of the job, which would then increase your value to the company or at least to your résumé.

THE REAL WORLD VS. THE IDEAL

Once, while working on consulting assignments for several companies, I had an opportunity to meet two newly hired marketing representatives—Pam and Kurt—who were both going through the process of adjusting their expectations for their new jobs to the realities of what they found. Pam had been recruited by one of my client companies to fill a junior marketing role; Kurt had been hired by another company for a senior marketing position. They were both in the same profession but at completely different places in their careers: While Kurt brought thirty years of business experience to his new job, Pam had only been out of college a few years.

NEW JOB REALITY CHECKLIST

The following checklist will help you to objectively evaluate your new job and identify areas that are different from what you expected and that could affect advancement of your career plan. Once you've pinpointed these areas, you can then discuss ways to gain the skills and experience you need with your manager, determine if you want to alter your plan and follow a new career direction, or decide if you want to look for another job in a year.

Whom did I expect to report to?

Whom will I actually be reporting to?

What kind of people did I expect to be working with?

What kind of people am I actually working with?

What hours did I anticipate working and what responsibilities did I expect to be accountable for?

What hours am I working, and what responsibilities am I actually accountable for?

What kind of working culture did I expect?

What is the culture like?

In what ways did I expect the job to impact my career path?

In what ways do I now see it affecting my overall career path?

Overall, is the job different but better?

If so, has that caused me to want to change my career path to fit this new discovery?

Interestingly, Kurt's prior business experience didn't seem to give him any edge in adjusting to his new work environment. With his experience and seniority, he expected the same special consideration he had received at his former company. Instead, the managers and executives treated him as they did any other new employee. They did not immediately recognize capabilities that Kurt considered obvious, and he felt insulted by the oversight.

Pam faced similar difficulty in adjusting to her new job. In her junior marketing role, she had expected to be meeting with clients from day one. Instead, for the first few months on the job, she functioned primarily in a clerical role. She complained angrily to me that she had not been hired to be a clerk.

After I counseled with them, both Kurt and Pam decided to stick it out and try to make a go of their jobs. Eventually, they both made friends within the company who were very supportive of them. These colleagues helped them over the initial hurdles and encouraged them to keep plugging away until they had established their reputations and niches within the companies. Both Pam and Kurt did adjust to their situations. They let go of their original expectations, accepted the reality of their jobs, and figured out how to make the most of them.

You can do the same by understanding that adjustments take time and by accepting these basic realities:

- No matter who we are, where we come from, or how much experience we have, we all have to prove ourselves in a new setting. Whether you are a novice or an experienced professional, you are still an unknown entity to a new employer and the people in the company. You have to prove yourself within the framework of values that exist in the department and conform to the culture. Not to worry, though—cream always rises to the top. If you're good at what you do and sincerely want to do a good job, your value and commitment to the company will be recognized by the people who matter.

- You have to accept your place in the pecking order of whatever group you're in. One of the best examples of this that I've seen was a new vice president bringing coffee and otherwise catering to the company president. Since they were both white, race was not an issue. Rather, the vice president simply recognized that as the new person in the group, he would need to go through a type of initiation to be accepted in the new culture.

- Even if everyone in the group has the same job title, the person who's been there longest, is the highest producer, or in some other way shines above the rest will always be higher up the ladder. It may be subtle, but an invisible pecking order exists in every company. It's always a challenge being the person at the bottom of the pecking order, but remember, it won't last forever. It will get easier—I assure you—once another new person joins the organization and you advance a rung.

- It's essential, when joining a new company, to become part of the team. You won't automatically be accepted as a team member because of the authority implied by your job title. No matter what your position, you will have to earn that acceptance by sincerely pitching in, doing your part, and then helping others in the group who need it. You need to emphasize "we" and not "I" in your attitude and actions—being quick to compliment others for their contributions rather than seeking compliments for your own.

SETTING THE STAGE FOR PROGRESS

You have a perfect opportunity to start setting the stage for progress in your first weeks on the new job, as you start to have informal conversations or lunch with peers and management. People will be curious about you; they'll wonder what you're about and what you have to offer. This curiosity is usually more pronounced for a person of color—especially if you're the only one in the group. In a way, those first several weeks will be like a mass interview. Some of your new colleagues may ask questions about your background or comment about it in relation to the department's needs. Often this dialogue is just an effort to be polite and welcoming, but it does provide an opportunity to let people know about your capabilities and your goals.

Let's say you're a financial analyst with a volunteer background in social services. During lunch one day, a new colleague might say, "The department manager mentioned that you've done some work with underprivileged children." Keeping a friendly and conversational tone, you might respond by describing the volunteer work you did for a social services organization, where, as part of the finance committee, you helped develop a budget and set up an accounting system. Then, if it seems appropriate, you might mention, still in a casual tone, how much you enjoyed doing that kind of work and that you'd like to do more if time permits.

Now you've left your colleague with a clue about something that interests you for the future. He might later be the one to suggest your name for a human services role, simply because you planted that seed early on. Of course, having a specific goal in mind will help you maximize these opportunities.

A key opportunity to lay a foundation for career development comes when you sit down to talk with your supervisor about goals. During your initial conversation after joining the company, you probably talked about goals in general. After the first three or six months in the job, many managers review new employees' job performances, and they usually do it regularly about once a year after that. If a review doesn't happen within the first year, I'd ask for a meeting to synchronize your expectations with the manager's goals for the job. At the meeting, keep the conversation low-key as you ask questions. Focus on getting a clear understanding of what the manager expects of you first before making comments about your future goals. Part of establishing a reputation as a team player means performing well at the job for which you've been hired, and not just using it as a stepping-stone to the next opportunity.

Beyond this, informal exchanges with your peers will help you lay a foundation for working with them by giving you a sense of what they expect from you and how they see you fitting with their team. For instance, you may find out that your presence in the department is stepping on someone's toes. Armed with this information, you'll be prepared to deal with a potentially problematic individual and handle any conflicts that may arise. Also, in talking with your colleagues, you'll likely find out how your predecessor performed on the job. If he or she handled some aspects poorly, then you can avoid making the same mistakes.

AVOIDING LAND MINES

Based on the situations I've experienced and observed, I believe that the tasks associated with performing the job are usually easy compared to the challenge of dealing with the people. Unfortunately, office politics and dealing with various personalities and styles are unavoidable in any work environment. Often, I'll hear people say they want no involvement with politics on the job—all they want is to do their work. By refusing to get involved, however, these people are hurting themselves. They're hampering their effectiveness and perhaps jeopardizing their chances of advancing to more responsible positions. I think it's impossible to function in a job without being involved with others, especially in a team-oriented environment; and if we're involved with others at all, then we're involved with office politics.

In dealing with people in the workplace, I have found that three key factors will help you avoid any land mines:

1. Work at a job that aligns with the goal in your soul. If you do work that you respect and enjoy, you'll be in an environment that's a comfortable fit, with people in tune with you. Your shared interests will make it easier for you and your coworkers to bond and work harmoniously—reducing the potential for uncomfortable conflicts or stressful office politics.

2. Treat others the way you want to be treated. Really, this is just a matter of showing consideration and having good manners. Acts of consideration are like planting positive seeds—they will surely bear the fruit of returned consideration from the people to whom you show kindness, as well as from others who observe your behavior.

But be sensitive about this because not everyone wants the same treatment. What may be respectful behavior in one culture may not be respectful in another.

3. Avoid situations that are potential land mines. Avoiding land mines requires sensitivity to the impact of subtle nuances and changes in your environment (for instance, being sensitive to the fact that two people who are key players in the organization have stopped communicating with one another). At the same time, it's important to understand that people have personal issues they may be dealing with, and that any negative behavior toward you may be a result of those issues.

While the first two points are self-explanatory, the last point begs discussion. The ability to sense and avoid land mines may ultimately determine whether you succeed in a given position—and whether you are happy in it. One of the most challenging consulting contracts I've ever had was with a company whose complex, volatile politics made interacting with the decision makers seem like dancing with an octopus. As soon as I got a handle on the arm of one problem area, I would be encircled by another. The situation challenged me on many levels, but I came out of it with a better ability to recognize and deal with the political nuances of any office environment.

The ability to stay effective when working among land mines takes time to develop, so as you're gaining it, it's best to walk softly, maintain a pleasant attitude, and keep your eyes open and your mouth shut. While you can't possibly anticipate or avoid every situation that might possibly arise, here are some common ones that could cause a big ripple in your plans. Know how to handle them:

Power Shifts

Power shifts occur when the person you report to maintains the title, the responsibility, and the office but has been replaced in power by someone else from behind the scenes, whom you may or may not know. In this situation, your boss is a lame duck; he doesn't have any clout.

When someone else at your boss's level or higher starts showing authority toward you or your department, you can assume that a power shift has occurred.

Sometimes a power shift is not so obvious. Instead, it may be evident in the lack of action or decision making shown by your boss in instances where you would normally expect him to take action. Even though you realize this is occurring, continue to treat your boss with the same respect and deference you always have. Respect the authority that goes with the position, even if the person in the position has lost his power.

Me, Not Thee

You might discover, after starting your new job, that someone else in the department wanted the job you were hired to perform. Now, unfortunately, you find yourself working side by side with a resentful, possibly bitter, coworker. This can be a real challenge because even if she behaves badly and refuses to cooperate fully, she may have the sympathy of the other people in the department. After all, people more often identify with the underdog.

To handle these potentially volatile situations, do your best to work with such individuals. If they refuse to cooperate, however, don't try to do them in. Instead, just step back and let them do it to themselves, or let someone else in the department call them on their behavior. You can only survive and win in this character-building situation by taking the high road in every instance. The person will either have to meet you at that place or leave when you refuse to stoop to her level.

The Emperor Has No Clothes

Sometimes, a supervisor will form an emotional attachment with someone in the department or the company and let that person manipulate her decisions and actions. Everyone in the department may know about this "shadow boss," but no one will risk being beheaded by talking about it. This person has the boss's ear and uses that power to pull strings in the shadows. Unlike a power shift, where upper management knows who is really in charge, upper-level personnel in this situation usually have no inkling that a "shadow boss" is manipulating the power.

Some of these "shadow bosses" can get cocky with power. I remember one such woman who approached me in the ladies' room and asked me what job I wanted in the department; she informed me that all she had to do was speak to the head of the department and the job would be mine. I couldn't decide whether she was overcome with her own power or so disliked in the department that she was looking for an ally. Probably, it was a bit of both. I avoided her offer by saying that I didn't know what job I wanted and I'd have to think about it.

It's not up to you to blow the cover off the boss or advantageous to get into a confrontation with the "shadow" boss. Treat them both with respect, and wait for the situation to blow over. It will. If it appears, however, that this situation will significantly block your progress in the company, then start looking for another job. You will lose if you try to fight, and you might damage your reputation during the process.

Who Did You Say You Were?

Another potential land mine might occur when you walk into work one morning soon after starting your new job only to find that your boss has been replaced—with no warning—by someone else. You're in trouble if this new boss is someone who would not have chosen you for the job and for whom you would not have chosen to work. What should you do? Be cool, cooperate, and, if you find this person impossible to work for, immediately start looking for another job. In the meantime, congratulate her on the job and say that you look forward to working with her. (Practice before doing this, and try to do it with sincerity!)

The Come On

It is possible for true love to occur at the office—and it's such a rare find that I would not tell anyone to refuse it, no matter when or where they found it. Just realize that every person who pursues you romantically is not necessarily motivated by love (especially if they're married). If you're being pursued by someone at the office, mention casually to some of your coworkers that a particular person has been very nice and friendly. Keep your tone light and casual, and do not make any judgments about the person's behavior. Your coworkers' responses will help you determine the intentions—and the reputation—of the person pursuing you.

If he or she is the wolf of the department (in plenty of instances, women do the pursuing), you'll want to steer clear of any involvement. A casual fling is not worth losing your reputation or credibility over. Of course, if the person is your boss or has become relentless, vulgar, or otherwise inappropriate in his or her behavior, then you're dealing with sexual harassment. Address the situation immediately with the appropriate people in your human resources department.

Birds of a Feather

Be courteous to everyone, but stay focused on the job that has to be done. Unfortunately, in this superficial world of ours we are often judged by the people with whom we spend time. I learned this lesson years ago, when I submitted an application to lease an apartment and mentioned that my friend, a former tenant, could serve as a personal reference. The manager looked at me oddly for a moment and then said she would rent it to me in spite of this connection. Apparently, my reference never paid her rent on time, although she appeared to me to be a very credible person.

MORE EDUCATION, TRAINING, AND SKILL DEVELOPMENT

It's a given that no matter how much you already know and how much training and experience you brought to your present job, there will be something new you'll need to know and some new skills to acquire as you move ahead in your career. I remember once asking a wise minister how long it takes to learn everything we need to learn so that it all comes together. Forever, he told me; we keep learning as long as we keep living. This is especially true on the job. New people join the company, bringing different perspectives, ideas, and approaches. The company restructures and takes a new direction. A key person moves on and we have to adjust and learn how to deal with new leadership—and on and on.

I find it easier to make adjustments if I feel I have some control over the when, where, and what. If you agree, take the initiative to assess the people, processes, and systems that support your new job. Determine the additional skills, education, and training you need, and then make a plan to acquire that knowledge. You can gain a sense of control by considering the following:

Systems Skills

Almost every department in medium and large corporations is computerized. Even though you may be familiar with computers, you might need to learn the software systems being used within your company. Most companies use standard packages, but some have software programs designed specifically for their operation.

Don't assume that just because you're familiar with personal computers you will automatically understand the company's computer programs. Instead, plan to find out about those systems and learn them right away. If you are not computer literate, take some night classes—you cannot afford to be out of the mainstream of communication and efficiency. The sooner you get up and running on a company's computer system, the better you'll be able to perform your new job and advance to the next step.

One of my clients, Janet, found this out the hard way in her new job as a college recruiter. Unable to format her own documents or go on-line, she had to wait for administrative support from the department secretary and others to format her work and perform research on the Internet. After showing up at several meetings with poorly prepared or late assignments, she lost her boss's sympathy. The boss expected her to take the initiative to learn the system. (Since most bosses do their own typing and computer work these days, they expect the same of their staffs.)

Process Skills

No matter how you learned to do something in school or at your former job, you're at a new company now. Learn how to do things right—their way. Do it their way for a while, and then, if you see a more efficient way that you could do it, begin to make suggestions for improving the process. These suggestions are likely to be better received if you've been a team player and tried the systems first in the way they've been established.

Communication Skills

If you don't speak well in front of groups, join Toastmaster's International or some other organization that will provide you with an opportunity to develop your speaking skills. You will definitely need this skill for presentations (formal or informal). Writing skills are equally important. Since you'll probably be writing for yourself and possibly for your boss as well, you'll need to be able to compose clear and concise letters and memos, as well as organized, well-written reports. Get prepared. If you know you have weak writing skills, take a business writing and/or English composition class to bring them up to speed.

Interpersonal Skills

Getting along with others is a must, especially in the new team environment. Most jobs are now interdependent, and the new style of project work demands that we have the flexibility to change roles. In the new culture, it's possible to be a project member on one project and project leader on another at the same time. Joining a professional group, preferably one where you'll be able to work on committees, will allow you to develop professional interpersonal skills in a safe environment. The people in these groups represent the norm in business, and the way they interact as part of the committee mirrors how people interact in the profession. I've gained a tremendous amount of knowledge just by observing others in these committees and then adopting successful approaches I've seen them using.

State-of-the-Art Knowledge

It's important to know about the latest whistles, terms, concepts, trends, gadgets, gurus, and books relevant to your business and your field. You should read at least two or three trade or business magazines regularly so that you're conversant and up-to-date on current ideas and innovations. For general business information, I like *Fortune* magazine, but I also recommend subscribing to a technical publication that specifically addresses your professional area.

KEEP YOURSELF FLEXIBLE AND OPEN TO POSSIBILITIES

Accept the fact that it may take you a while to figure out the realities of the job. Throughout the process, be sure to stay flexible and don't rush into making any rash decisions. Keeping a flexible and open mind helped Harry, a former client of mine, switch directions and get into a career that was much more satisfying for him. At first, Harry joined a large company as an accountant, with the intent of gaining experience so that he could start his own accounting business within five to seven years. He believed that owning a business would ultimately provide more variety and personal satisfaction than working for a company. Within three months on the new job, however, he had changed his mind.

Drawn to the auditing function at his company, Harry decided that the travel and cross-divisional interaction within that position would provide him with as much variety as he wanted. Plus, he realized that he liked the security and benefits the company offered. After refocusing and settling on a new career path as an auditor, he set about getting mentors to help him achieve his new goal.

Harry found his mentors not by asking for their help but by asking for information about auditing and the types of assignments he should request to prepare himself for an opportunity when it arose. He made every person he talked with aware of the fact that he wanted to move into auditing; in this way, he made them potential mentors. He clicked with a couple of those people in a special way, and they offered to help him.

"STARTING OVER"

■

At 26, Adnane received a Ph.D. in physics from the University of Paris, making him one of the youngest non-French people to receive a degree at that level. While his degree guaranteed him a job with status and a smooth career path in Paris, outside of France he had to struggle to make his mark.

"I had a career in France planned, but a family illness forced a move to the United States," he remembers. "With no job and no connections, I faced a lot of problems here. People were not familiar with what I had done, and I did not have a degree from the United States."

Adnane solved both the job and the education dilemma when he made a cold call to the head of the physics department at University of California, Santa Barbara (UCSB). He explained that he had his Ph.D. and had been doing some of the same work they had been doing. In his first interview, Adnane impressed the department head by clearly stating what he wanted from a job with UCSB and by showing his confidence in his abilities to achieve it. He got the job and, while working at the university, obtained a master's degree in nuclear engineering.

Interrupting his career in the United States, Adnane returned to his home country, Algeria, to complete a military commitment; when he returned to the United States, he found himself, once again, starting from scratch. "My wife suggested that I give training classes at Delco, since they were planning to send people to the Middle East. I had a knowledge of the culture, which could help with business transactions, so I approached management with the idea and started at the company on a contract basis. The training contract led to a full-time position as a senior process engineer."

In addition to training, Adnane also worked with the marketing group, serving as liaison between customers and management. Eventually, moving another step away from physics teacher, he became a business development manager.

How does Adnane align his original career goal in physics with what he does now? "Physics is almost metaphysical for me," he says. "It's my continuing goal, to study how the universe was created. But at heart, I'm an *entrepreneur—all the jobs along the way have presented a challenge to me. And I love what I am doing. That's 50 percent of what it takes to succeed. The rest is hard work."*

■

ADNANE BOUMEDIENE
Algerian manager
Hughes-Delco Systems Operation
Business: Business development for Middle East

Planning a Career Path

A couple of months after you've settled into your new job, take some time to reevaluate your career path and determine if it is still the one you want. By then, you have a sense of the job, the company, the culture, and the people. You may also be aware of some alternative options that strike you as more desirable than your original plan. Always be alert to new options or possibilities along the way, and be flexible enough to change your plan accordingly.

Once the realities of the job and your role become clear, you can start thinking about what adjustments (if any) you'll need to make so that you can continue to advance. For example, you may realize that you'll need more training in order to develop new skills to succeed in your new position and/or get to the next level. It may be as simple as learning a new computer program or as challenging as learning to function under an entirely different management approach.

At the same time, you may want to reevaluate your overall career plan to get a sense of where this job will ultimately take you, now that you know its realities. You may decide that it's exactly the right move to propel you on the career path you initially planned. On the other hand, you may determine that it could lead you in a different, though equally or even more rewarding, direction than your original goal, in which case you'll have to change your plan. Within three months, however, if you find that the reality is so far off from your expectations that the job will be a negative career move, then you need to cut your losses and start looking for a new job immediately. If you can find one soon enough, you won't even have to show your current job on your résumé. But if you stay where you're at longer than six months, you're running into time that will have to be accounted for; in this case, it's probably best to stay with the present job for at least a year so your résumé reflects that you're a stable person and not a job-hopper.

JOBS THAT LEAD TO OTHER JOBS

Even with a well-thought-out career plan, it's possible to end up in a job that seems to be a total deviation from your original plan (see "Starting Over"). This can happen, for example, when company managers recognize that a very pronounced technical or administrative ability of yours would fit well in a specific job that differs significantly from anything you've ever done. This happened to Steve, who was asked by the high-tech pharmaceutical company he worked for to take on the role of technical recruiter; his firm was having trouble identifying and recruiting the talent it needed. Steve's background as a chemist, combined with his outgoing personality, enabled him to identify and bring in several strong candidates to fill the company's needs.

For Rick, a career switch arose completely out of the blue from an entirely unexpected opportunity. An aspiring engineer, his career plan was moving along technical lines. One evening he went with some friends to a network meeting for the marketing of a health supplement, and although the meeting and the product had nothing to do with Rick's job, he found himself intrigued with the product and the sales process. He could not stop thinking about the presentation or talking about it with his friends. You can guess the rest. He got involved with marketing the product on the side and within nine months, he quit his engineering job and went to work for the health supplement distributor. Within a few years Rick had advanced to a high level within the organization and is earning a very good salary.

Rick's story shows how important it is to always be open to new opportunities and interests because doing so can lead to unexpected rewards. Regardless of how an opportunity surfaces, when it does, be willing to examine it for the potential it offers. I believe that opportunities are not accidents—they come when we are ready for them and when we have developed the skills to handle them.

RESOURCES

People Smarts: Bending the Golden Rule to Give Others What They Want by Tony Alessandra and Michael J. O'Connor, with Janice Van Dyke (Pfeiffer & Company, 1994). This book shows how to understand your style strengths and weaknesses, identify the styles of others quickly, and then adjust your behavior to make all kinds of people more at ease with you and you with them. An easy read and a neat book—you can read it all in one night or refer to it for a quick reference when you have an immediate problem.

The Workplace Survival Guide: Tools, Tips, and Techniques for Succeeding on the Job by George Fuller (Prentice Hall, 1995) gives very practical guidance on how to survive in a changing workplace. It includes information on how to read signs when your job is at risk, create opportunities and get yourself promoted, deal with the politics in your office, and more. Excellent practical advice.

Winning Office Politics: DuBrin's New Guide for the '90s by Andrew DuBrin (Prentice Hall, 1990) provides real-life examples of office politics, along with the courses of action and solutions used in each scenario. It also includes a test for measuring your political tendencies.

PART 2

MOVING FORWARD

Have you attained the success you want at your job and in your profession? Are you satisfied that you have challenged your skills and talents to their fullest capacity? Or is there more that you can and want to do?

Maybe you're now wondering what it takes to move up to the next success step. If you've been asking these questions, you're probably ready to refocus your goal and reassess your plan so that you can continue moving forward. Significant changes may have occurred in your life and on your job since setting your original goal. You'll need to take the time to evaluate any new internal and external factors relevant to your career and incorporate them into your plan.

After doing this, you may decide you're right on track and basically need only to continue implementing your original plan. But, if you're like most career-minded people, you'll recognize you've got some work to do, either personally or professionally, in order to reach your full potential. This may mean discarding some strategies and adopting some new ones, improving your image, widening your professional circle, or, at the very least, getting more specialized training or education.

Part 2 will address the issues that are likely to impact continued career growth. It provides tips and methods for reevaluating skills and clarifying or setting new goals. It highlights the significant factors contributing to *successfully advancing to the next level of achievement, and it looks at how to advance within your company or by changing companies. These next five chapters explore the full cycle of career growth, including the added dimension of sharing knowledge and insights with others who are less experienced than you.*

■

CHAPTER

PUTTING THE DREAM
IN FOCUS

J ust where are you along your life-career track now? Are you where you want to be? If so, great. But even if you're happy with your job and the direction you're headed, it's still a good idea to take some time to take an objective look at yourself.

If you're moving as you expected you would, where do you want to be in six months? In a year? Do you have a plan to get there? Perhaps you've reached a career plateau. Is it the right place for you—or have you more or less settled for what you have?

Perhaps you're not really where you'd hoped you'd be by now. If so, you're in good company. Many people reach a point in their careers when they feel just as you do, for all sorts of reasons. What's yours? Are you stuck in a dead-end or stagnant position? Maybe you've maxed out with your present skills and can't move ahead without more training. Or maybe you began working without ever really committing to a career, and now you're longing for the satisfaction and meaning that comes from making that true commitment.

If you're pretty content for now, then the first section of this chapter, Staying on Track, will help you explore your short- and long-term goals so that you can continue to enjoy a career plateau for now without cutting off future opportunities for advancement—or keep advancing at your present pace. If you are not completely happy with your progress, the second section, Jump-Starting Your Career, will help you get focused and moving onward and upward.

STAYING ON TRACK

Time waits for no man—or woman. As time passes, subtle changes and seemingly minor circumstances occur in all people's lives that can have a long-reaching impact on their life-career plan.

Both Joyce and Craig let this happen to them. For Craig, a company restructuring turned his life upside down. Although he'd heard rumors for three years that the company was going to be downsized, Craig did not worry or explore alternative options because he felt secure in his job. He had a good track record in facilities planning, and his career plan, which he had geared to the company, was right on track. So when a cost-cutting effort to support the downsizing eliminated both his department and his job, Craig was shocked and caught without any options. For Joyce, it was divorce that set her life spinning. Suddenly having to manage on only one income, she realized that while her career gave her a reasonable salary, it was insufficient to support her lifestyle plus care for herself and her children.

Joyce and Craig would probably have fared better at these critical junctures in their lives if they'd made sure to always have a strong backup plan ready to help them through an unexpected circumstance. Part of the responsibility of maintaining your career is always making sure you have options and alternatives that are not tied to just one company, as Craig's were. Just as important, it's a good idea to continually update and expand your skills so that you always have something useful to offer. You should also keep an eye on industry trends and developments so that you have some sense of where you can redirect your skills, where the jobs are, and when a company might be ripe for a downsizing.

Alfredo Arguello, a marketing manager for GE Medical Systems, offers some good advice: "The first step is to understand your goals. Review and update them every six to twelve months, and ask for participation from others so that you can uncover areas in your career where you can develop new skills and grow personally. The second step is to manage job performance daily. Look in the mirror every morning and ask, 'How am I doing?' Also, develop your communication skills and develop outside of the job through extracurricular activities, then make the tie-in to career objectives."

Some of Alfredo's other suggestions include doing everything with the purpose of achieving results related to work. For instance, he sees lunching with colleagues as a powerful tool to gain knowledge or skills for achieving what is necessary on the job. He also believes in stretching beyond one's comfort level. "One way to do this is to take assignments outside of your job requirements. For example, learn how to use the Internet and make it a useful tool within your company, or look at special problems and participate in their solution."

Following Alfredo's advice, along with the steps below, will help you keep your career alive and on track.

- Be sensitive to ways you may have changed in the last few years. You might have new psychological needs that you need to address and incorporate into your plan. (See Recognizing New Psychological Needs, later in this chapter).

- Stay current on the company research you gathered before starting your current job so that you will know where other opportunities exist. Develop contacts with at least two other companies where you can market your skills. If you did no research before you got your job, reread chapter 4.

- Stay current on your industry so that you have a good sense of where you can transfer your skills and still keep your career on track.

- Be sensitive to changes within your company. Most rumors have merit. Respond to any issues that could impact your company—and thereby affect your career—by revising and updating your plan accordingly.

- Stay active in a formal professional group or be part of informal social activities with people from a variety of companies. This will help keep you current with industry trends.

- Subscribe to (and read) at least two professional magazines a month. Watch for trends you need to plan for.

- Meet regularly with your mentor(s), either formally or informally, to stay connected, gain knowledge about company/industry activities, and seek feedback on the progress toward your goals.

- Research the additional education or training that you need. (Reread chapter 3 for sources, if necessary.)

- Review your career goal annually against your life-career plan to be sure that your career plans harmonize with and support your life goals.

- Keep old copies of your action plan (in chapter 3) and use it to chart the progress you've made and keep you on course.

JUMP-STARTING YOUR CAREER

Do you have a job but feel dissatisfied? Do you feel you ought to be more successful? At a point in my career, after working several years, I still felt a certain discontent. It surprised me, because I remember as a teenager thinking that if I could ever make a certain amount of money a month, I'd be in heaven; I'd know for sure that I was successful. It wasn't that I planned to measure my success by the money I made, but the money was my way of keeping score. Years later, however, when I had achieved many of my goals and was finally making that amount a week, the feeling of success was only fleeting. By that time I had grown and changed; other needs had surfaced and become priorities, replacing old goals and expectations.

Perhaps you've felt this way, too, at times. Maybe you're where you wanted to go but now you're not sure it's where you want to be. Do you find yourself experiencing a need for more—something different, something to bring back the excitement of meeting new challenges? Do you feel that your values have changed and are not in line with the work you are doing? Maybe since developing your original career plan, you have discovered new strengths (and weaknesses) that were not apparent when you first started out. Do you feel a need for new professional challenge and growth that are not part of your job now?

Possibly, your lifestyle and responsibilities have changed in the past few years as well; if so, a career that no longer meets your needs will only cause frustration. The circumstances surrounding your life may have changed enough since you made your original plan to warrant a change in your career objectives.

No doubt, if you've been working for five or ten years at the same company, in the same job, or on the same career path, and you're feeling dissatisfied or like there's something missing, it may be time to reassess your original dream and bring it into sharper focus—to look at whether you need to change your career path or revitalize the one you now have, either at your present company or somewhere else.

CLARIFYING YOUR GOAL

After working for many years, I decided to take a six-month leave. I thought I would be happy not working, but I was wrong. I was bored to death. During that extended time off, I realized that vacations are more fun when they are squeezed in between a busy schedule. I missed being part of a business enterprise, and I missed the mental stimulation of creating solutions for challenging problems and interacting with people with similar talents and goals. My biggest revelation was discovering that, as fulfilling as my family life was, it left a void that was only satisfied by working at something I felt was worthwhile. At that point, I knew I would always work and that I needed to make a commitment to developing my career.

Before my leave, I had been working for a few years in human resources positions and had allowed my career to unfold solely by responding to opportunities that presented themselves to me, without any thought to following a logical sequence of steps to reach a goal. I did not consider the specific education or training I might need to advance or the specific jobs I should go after to build a set of marketable skills.

Up to that time, I'd had a series of jobs with no plan for working beyond the time needed to satisfy certain financial goals. Part of the reason for my passive, go-with-the-flow approach was cultural—I was reluctant to advance past the males in my race—and part of it was a lack of role models in my circle of friends. Besides this, I only had a vague goal of "working with people and doing something in the area of human resources"; eventually I realized that if I was ever going to get anywhere, I had to spend time clarifying what that vague goal meant to me.

Perhaps my story sounds familiar to you. After working for five or ten years, maybe you have come to a realization that you've never actually committed to a career. And maybe now, for the first time, you're ready to establish a goal, based on your dreams, skills, and strengths—and commit to it. During the process, you may discover that you're happy on your current path but that you need to define your expectations, make specific plans for advancement, and search for new challenges and opportunities. On the other hand, establishing a goal at this point may mean switching directions and committing to an entirely new career.

If you're just coming to this book now after some years of working, you may want to read chapters 2 and 3 and apply the processes outlined there on goal-setting and job research to help you identify your goal. In going through this self-assessment process now, after you've been working for awhile, you have an advantage over a person just starting out: You can analyze the activities and accomplishments you've enjoyed on the job thus far to help find your success pattern (see A Road Map to Success).

It's a safe bet that you're working toward the right career goal if you would still do what you're doing without getting paid or at least some parts of what you're doing without getting paid. But you may still need to refocus your goal if you're dissatisfied with some aspects of what you do or the circumstances surrounding your work. For instance: You enjoy training but also want to design training programs; you like sales but would prefer not to travel extensively; you enjoy leading a group but dislike being accountable for hiring, firing, and performance reviews.

TIME FOR A CAREER CHANGE?

A good indication that you need to consider a career change is if you like the skills you use but dislike the culture where those skills are applied. For example, you might feel strongly about developing social programs for those in need but do not enjoy working directly with the recipients of the programs. In this case, you would probably be more effective in a corporate environment developing the programs and/or involved in the fund-raising—and turning over the hands-on work to someone else. Or if you enjoy the work but hate the surrounding politics, you may find that changing to a smaller company or starting your own company may be the answer, as it was for Barbara.

It was her divorce that started Barbara thinking about where she was going with her life. At 33, after eight years of mediocre performance as a personnel assistant with a major electronics company, she decided it was time to start looking for more from a job than just getting by, time for her to commit to developing a career. Money was not an issue, because the company paid her well. Rather, she was motivated by boredom and the sharp realization that even if a prince came into her life to take her away from it all, she would no doubt have to help him buy the horse as well as polish his armor! And she realized she wanted to do more than just work; she wanted to be truly productive. To this end, Barbara decided to seek guidance outside of her company on how to redirect her professional path.

An officer in one of her professional groups helped Barbara target a career goal based on the skills she enjoyed using. She realized that her

A ROAD MAP TO SUCCESS

Sometimes it's difficult to identify a career goal simply by naming a specific profession. Combining the activities that interest you with the skills and knowledge you enjoy using will help you to identify a profession where those skills will fit. When you use the same skills over and over, consider them strengths and use them as a basis on which to establish a career goal. The following steps will help you discover the group of skills on which you can set a career goal to which you can commit.

1. List at least fifteen accomplishments you've had on the job or in extracurricular activities. These accomplishments should be examples of how you've carried out responsibilities. They should start with an action verb and show a result when possible.

    For example: led a team in setting up an accounting system; coached a girls' softball team to first place; elected president of condominium association; developed a training manual and conducted classes on new accounting process.

2. Alongside each accomplishment, list the skills/functional knowledge that it reveals. Focus on people and administrative and technical skills. Do this for each one even if the same skills are repeated several times.

    For example: led a team in setting up an accounting system. Skills: leadership, problem solving, selling, motivating.

3. After analyzing each accomplishment, circle the skills you see repeated several times. These skills are the first component of your success pattern.

4. Determine if there are common themes running through all the accomplishments. You may need help doing this, so get someone to review your list of accomplishments and indicate what he or she sees as common themes.

    For example: Most of the accomplishments focus on creating, initiating something new, solving problems, implementing processes, etc. This is the second component of your success pattern.

5. Develop a list of interests—those things you enjoy, extracurricular activities, things you read about, hobbies, or an avocation.

6. Combine your success pattern (predominant skills with common themes) with your interests and knowledge to develop a career goal you can commit to and enjoy.

Example: Discovering Your Success Pattern

ACCOMPLISHMENT	SKILLS/ KNOWLEDGE
Worked with the systems group to develop a new process for conducting market research; program implemented companywide.	Analytical Conceptualizer Team player Marketing savvy
Initiated a cross-functional market-support team that helped develop a new marketing strategy with sales projections exceeding $10 million for the first year.	Leadership Conceptualizer Marketing savvy
Convinced upper management to establish a new product line in a unique location, which increased national sales by 17% in three months.	Communication Marketing savvy Implementer
Appointed to head a special task force for the city to uncover problems in major planning projects.	Leadership Analytical

Common Themes
- Creativity (develop, initiate, establish, uncover)
- Leadership (worked with group, developed team, convinced management, headed task force)
- Marketing savvy (market research, marketing support, product line)

Outside Interests
- Politics (supported various initiatives)
- Social causes (served on the boards of organizations to help children and people with disabilities)
- Fitness buff (ride a motorcycle, work out three times a week, scuba dive, play tennis)

Possible Jobs
- Marketing position in the fitness industry
- Fund-raiser for a social organization
- Fund-raiser for a political party

current job did not draw on her strong points; as a personnel assistant, she spent a great deal of time alone, interpreting and processing detailed benefit information to prepare long, intricate reports. Working in so much isolation and handling so many details left her feeling uninspired and unmotivated. Actually, she thrived best working around a lot of people in a fast-paced environment.

Over the years, Barbara had met those needs by working on committees with professional groups to which she belonged. While she had been relatively nonproductive at work, as a volunteer for professional and community-based organizations she played an active and dynamic role. These extracurricular activities gave her the sense of challenge and satisfaction that was missing in her job, so much so that Barbara decided to focus on a career in the area of community and public relations. Her years as a volunteer had enabled her to develop and refine her organizational, communication, and leadership skills, which in turn gave her a head start along her new career track.

Realizing that she could achieve her goal at the electronics company where she already had eight years of contacts and experience, Barbara decided to focus her efforts on seeking a promotion to the company's community affairs or public relations department. Her mentor recommended that she get a list of available openings within these departments and start networking with the appropriate people to let them know of her interest. She also advised Barbara to point out to them the extracurricular activities in which she had been involved that had allowed her to develop some relevant skills.

As she networked within the company and made her ambitions known, Barbara quickly found out that she had two major obstacles to overcome. Her poor attitude about her job had preceded her, so she had to establish a new positive image. She started that process by asking supervisors and managers in the public relations and community affairs departments for help in changing her image. The fact that Barbara had taken the initiative to seek advice demonstrated her desire for self-improvement, which impressed company managers; as a result, her image began to change for the better. Still, she had a second obstacle to overcome: education.

Although she had an undergraduate degree in psychology, her company expected managers to have M.B.A.'s. So she enrolled in a night school to start working toward an advanced degree. This combined effort at improving her image and going back to school for an advanced degree resulted, within seven months, in Barbara's promotion to an entry-level management position in the community affairs department.

RECOGNIZING NEW PSYCHOLOGICAL NEEDS

You may have reached a point in your career where you're bored with duties and responsibilities that once motivated you, and you're anxious to take on new challenges and explore new interests. If you're feeling this way, there's probably a simple explanation: You've changed—you're no longer the person you were when you first started out.

For instance, early in your career you may have been satisfied sitting back and following someone else's lead, even if you didn't completely agree with his or her approach. Lately, however, you've been speaking up. You've observed the inefficiency of certain processes and want to revise the processes so they will be more efficient. You've become curious about certain roles and wonder what it would be like to function in another role.

These needs you're expressing may not even be new; they may have been lingering for years but were more or less ignored. If you don't address them, though, they could sabotage your job performance, as they did for Edith, a financial analyst at an insurance company. Ignoring her needs for creativity and leadership caused Edith to develop a serious performance problem at work (see "Build a Solid Foundation"). Like Barbara, she participated in many outside community activities and, because she felt bored and unchallenged in her work, spent most of her time on the job handling extracurricular projects. At the same time, she actively promoted her volunteer causes and sought support from others in the company.

CAREER GOAL CHECKLIST

If you're not sure where you are in terms of your career—whether it's time to redefine your goal or switch directions—take a look at the checklist below. An analysis of your responses to the statements in it should help you in clarifying your career goal.

Ten years ago my career goal was (or I had no specific goal, but my objective for work was):

_____

_____

I am involved in the following social, professional, academic, or other activities to support that goal (or just because I enjoy them):

_____

_____

The above activities appeal to me because they satisfy my need for (leadership? creativity? skill development? autonomy? service? challenge? fun? friendship?):

_____

_____

During the past five or ten years, I've developed the following skills that I enjoy using, which I wasn't aware of when I was planning my career (see A Road Map to Success):

_____

_____

My interests, plus the new skills I've developed and past skills I enjoy using, are an indication to me that my original career goal is (good/not good and needs changing to a different goal) because:

_____

_____

Based on these considerations, my career plan (is on target/has changed). I will now be pursuing a career as/or move my present career forward by:

_____

_____

Before long, word spread throughout the organization about Edith's activities. A performance evaluation, calling her to the carpet for her inappropriate use of company time, forced Edith to admit that she had no real interest in her job and that she was only hanging on because she was afraid to change. Finally acknowledging her frustration, she set about developing a new career goal that would motivate her. Eventually, she left her corporate job to take a position where she felt she could make a worthwhile contribution—working for one of her state senators, whose views she sympathized with.

Unlike Edith, Bruce managed to satisfy his psychological needs while still performing well in his primary job as a systems engineer. He did this by working two jobs for twelve years. In addition to working full-time as a systems engineer, Bruce also owned and operated various businesses. His primary job provided benefits and financial security for him and his wife and their five children, while the three businesses that he owned over the years satisfied his strong entrepreneurial urges. For awhile, the arrangement worked out fine, but at a certain point, Bruce became frustrated—and tired—of walking two paths. Just about this time, his employer restructured and offered employees a severance package to reduce staff.

After calculating the financial risk, Bruce decided that his need to be creative and control his own destiny was now a higher priority than financial security. He had long lost interest in his "day" job and, like Edith, found himself spending more and more time on that job handling work for his own business. The severance package proved to be the catalyst that forced him to address his frustration and finally go into business for himself full-time.

"BUILD A SOLID FOUNDATION"

■

Being uncertain about your career goal or spending time on non-job-related activities while at work can have far-reaching effects beyond your immediate position. For example, poor performance can give you a bad reputation—one that might precede you when you are looking for another job. In a company like GE Medical Systems, which emphasizes employee development, poor performance on the part of an employee or a potential applicant would be hard to hide and difficult to overlook.

"At GE, when we have an opening, we work with the manager to develop the qualifications needed for the job. For candidates, we first look at employees within the company up to a certain job rank, and then we look at candidates from outside the company," says Marc Saperstein, global resources manager. "We do midmanagement-level recruiting at agencies, and the agencies do a lot of networking within companies to fill positions." If a person has a reputation for mediocre performance, the word could easily spread within the company or through the network of corporations and agencies with which GE networks.

If you're unhappy with a job, it's better to cut your losses early and move on, rather than risk developing a negative profile, Marc advises. "You may be concerned about projecting a lack of stability by changing companies, but this shouldn't be a problem as long as you have the necessary experience and don't change companies continually. Here at GE, we look for what's in a person's background. In reviewing résumés, we look for clear, concise accomplishments that are easy to read. It doesn't matter if a résumé reveals someone's age—we expect someone with a lot of experience to be older. Job gaps might be a problem, but if they've got the experience, we'd address the employment gaps in the interview."

Even so, Marc thinks too much fluctuation in a career—in other words, a number of different jobs or repeated layoffs—might signal a problem. If you do decide to change jobs, make sure that you've identified your goal very clearly and have chosen a path that you'll be able to stay on for awhile. "If a person has been laid off from five or six companies, that may tell you something. They should have either switched careers or changed their approach. After all, results don't lie."

■

Marc Saperstein
White manager
GE Medical Systems
Fairfield, Connecticut
Business: Global human resources

HAVE YOUR NEEDS CHANGED?

Sometimes it's difficult to recognize your own psychological needs, especially in the early stages when they may simply present themselves as vague yearnings. If you ignore them, you may very well find that they grow and fester, affecting your attitude, your performance, and your sense of self-worth and well-being. To explore your own feelings and see if you've developed new psychological needs in the past few years, take a couple of minutes to answer these questions:

Ten years ago, if I were part of an informal team gathered to complete a project, I would tend to take on the role of (leader, follower, mediator, scribe):

Today, I would take on the role of: _____

Ten years ago, I felt challenged by the process of moving up the corporate ladder because: _____
_____

Today I would feel challenged by: _____

Because: _____

The greatest need (desire) I had ten years ago was: _____
_____

The greatest need (desire) I have today is: _____
_____

My current career goal of _____ (satisfies, does not satisfy) my greatest need.

The career I (intend/will continue) to pursue is: _____

It will satisfy my needs for: _____
_____
_____

WHAT PRIORITY DO YOU GIVE YOUR CAREER?

As you progress through your career, time, circumstances, and experience will cause you to develop new values and priorities. The priority you give your career will be relative to its importance in carrying out the other priorities of your overall life goals. For example, if you value a secure, comfortable, and stress-free existence above anything and are not concerned about earning a great deal of money, then you probably won't give your career a very high priority. You may be satisfied with a nice job as long as it offers reasonable security and is stress-free.

On the other hand, if you place a high value on personal freedom and living well, you will need to earn a good amount of money to support these ideals. Because a successful career will be the means toward that end, you will have to give your career a high priority. Ultimately, then, the more you see your career as a means to achieve high goals, the greater priority it will have in your life and the more committed to it you will be.

This is why it's important to identify and understand your current nonnegotiable values and how they are supported by or in conflict with your career goal.

Paul's priority had always been to develop a solid financial base that would support his and his intended wife's lifestyle and give them the time and freedom to travel. To achieve this, he decided to use financial and business skills as an independent businessperson. After graduating from college, he took over the family's car repair business and spent five years overseeing the operation. The business, however, proved to be more demanding than Paul had expected. Spending almost all his waking hours either involved in car repairs or in managing the administrative details of the business, he had no time for a social life which caused strain on his relationship. When his fiancee gave him an ultimatum, he decided he had better make a career change or risk losing her.

Paul decided to rearrange his priorities. He sold the family business and, using his alumni contacts from college, got an accounting position with a major company. The discipline he had developed in managing his own business served him well in his new position, and within three years he had advanced several levels and accumulated enough capital to collaborate with other entrepreneurs to start financing small real estate projects. These investments helped secure a future for Paul and his wife. After several years, he was earning enough income from the real estate holdings that he was able to cut back to a part-time position and finally begin to enjoy the freedom and travel that had always been his first priority.

What priority do you give your career? Consider which of the following statements best reflects your position:

- I am only working to pay my bills or to upgrade my lifestyle a little bit. I would not have a problem giving up my career when my finances improve.

- My job is not part of a career plan; I just "fell into it" as a result of convenience. I wouldn't work if I didn't have to.

- If I did not have my career, my life would be different because I would have to find another way to get the same psychological needs met.

- Because of my career, I have improved as a person, and it helps provide a boost to my self-esteem.

RESOURCES

Build Your Own Rainbow—A Workbook for Career and Life Management by Barrie Hopson and Mike Scally (Pfeiffer & Company, 1995) guides you through a personal inventory to determine your present level of satisfaction and shows you how to achieve and maintain a sense of fulfillment throughout your life.

Do What You Are—Discover the Perfect Career for You Through the Secrets of Personality Type by Paul D. Tieger and Barbara Barron-Tieger (Little Brown, 1995). This book is especially good for people with very pronounced personality traits, traits that would be detrimental to them if they were in the wrong job or environment. After taking you through a process to determine your personality type, this book offers suggested careers for each one of them.

Going to Plan B—How You Can Cope, Regroup and Start Your Life on a New Path by Nancy K. Schlossberg and Susan Porter Robinson (Fireside, 1996) shows what to do when nothing happened but everything changed. Deals with how to recast your career goals to accommodate today's radically changed workplace and how to reconcile an unrealistic self-image and find inner peace. Also deals with letting go of old ideas and dreams and reshaping the dream.

For copies or information about the *Professional Planning and Development Guide*, contact GE Medical Systems, Fax 414-544-3384.

ADVANCING YOUR CAREER

Moving forward with your career means more than just reviewing your plan and refocusing your dream. It means adding to your skills and knowledge, expanding positive character traits while minimizing negative ones, and being more self-directed and willing to take calculated risks to move past obstacles. It means being willing to make the sacrifices necessary to move your career forward.

No matter what stage you're at in your career, there's always room to advance. Keep your dream before you as a guide. Regularly reevaluate all things concerned with your career against that dream. Use it to energize you to make changes or even switch directions if need be. All you need to do is keep in mind that whatever you can conceive, you can achieve.

Every endeavor always begins with a dream. But making it into a reality takes a plan and the necessary character strengths and skills to get there. At this point in your career, you may have had some successes and from them gained the confidence that more success is possible. Hopefully, by this juncture you've passed the point of *can't* (if you were ever there) and all your energy can be focused on *how*.

DO YOU HAVE WHAT IT TAKES TO REACH YOUR GOAL?

If you've chosen your career goal well, it will be something that you're good at, interested in, and enjoy doing and that you think is worthwhile. It will be something for which you are willing to work and make sacrifices. Now you're ready to look at what else you may need to reach your goal.

Here are fundamental personal qualities that can go a long way toward ensuring success in your career journey. I believe that, to some degree, everyone needs all of these in order to reach their goals.

Faith

You have to believe that the dream you dream has been given to you to accomplish. You have to believe that you have the skills and talents (which may need developing) to achieve your dream. If you believe this, it will be evident in your behavior, and if you don't, it will also be evident. A positive belief will surround your actions with an air of confidence that will draw people to you who can help you accomplish your goals. Also, your positive mental attitude will help you to recognize and grasp opportunities in every situation, which can bring you closer to achieving your objectives. When you discuss your goal with others, you will refer to it with the anticipation of succeeding, speaking in terms of *when* you accomplish your goal, not *if* you accomplish it.

A Plan

How does a person eat an elephant? One bite at a time. Turning a dream into a reality can seem as insurmountable as eating an elephant—if you look at it as something that you must accomplish all at once. But the task is not as daunting if you take it one step at a time. Break down your dream into sequential steps, make those steps your objectives, and then develop a plan for each objective while keeping your overall goal in mind.

Remember Barbara in chapter 7? She set a goal to develop a career in public affairs and community relations but had two obstacles that she had to address before she could accomplish it. She had to overcome a poor professional image that came from years of mediocre performance as a personnel assistant, and she needed to go back to school to get an M.B.A. She began by adjusting her attitude so that instead of seeing these things as obstacles, she approached them as objectives. Then she set about tackling both objectives simultaneously.

First, she let management and other people who could mentor her know that she had enrolled in school and the reasons she had taken this action. At the same time, she asked for advice on how she could change her professional image. Then, in response to this advice, she started getting to work on time and performing to the best of her ability. She changed her attitude from surly indifference to one of positive energy and dedication. When her managers and colleagues recognized that she was serious about achieving her goal, Barbara's plan paid off and she started moving forward with her career.

Time

Implementing a plan and developing a career takes time. Often those "overnight successes" you hear about or see on television accepting awards as bright new talents spent years preparing to get to that point. I recently met a 30-year-old man who was frustrated at his lack of ability to get a decent job. Then he came to terms with his dilemma and accepted the fact that it would take time and work to get his career on track. "It looks like I am going to have to change my career direction," he told me. "I think I'd like to be an engineer, so I'll need to go back to school. I realize I'll be 35 when I finish, but if I don't start now and put in the time, I'll just be 35 without a career instead of 35 with a career." A wise man, he realized that time passes no matter what we do with it. If we use time constructively and patiently go after a goal, then we will find ourselves a few months or years from now that much closer to achieving that goal—if we haven't already—instead of stuck in the same unsatisfying job.

Self-Discipline

No one is going to hold your hand and remind you to do the things you need to do to make a satisfying career for yourself. This is your career, and you're on your own. You have to make up your mind to do something and then not let anything get in the way of doing it (see The Art of Selfishness). Still, that's easier said than done.

I realize how challenging it can be to cultivate self-discipline because I had to work hard on it myself. I've always had a strong pleasure principle that is easily activated—it doesn't take much to make me want to drop everything to have fun. So in establishing my career, I had to learn to discipline myself to stay on track with my plan. At first, I found it a real challenge, but it became easier as I gained new pleasure from setting and achieving my goals. By exercising self-discipline, I developed more self-confidence in my ability to get important things done.

Perseverance

As you work toward your goal, you will undoubtedly experience setbacks and you will have to overcome unforeseen obstacles. All these things are part of life—part of the character-building process we all have to go through. You will find that you have more perseverance in a career that you truly enjoy than you would in a job you just tolerate.

Patience

Do you have the ability to endure, wait, and persevere without whining? Then you have the patience necessary to succeed. Attaining your goal is going to be difficult. If you accept that this is true for everyone, then you won't be expecting sympathy along the way—empathy maybe, from others like yourself who are also on the path, but never sympathy.

THE ART OF SELFISHNESS

Sometimes a simple phrase, a comment based in ageless wisdom, or a short little story with a strong moral will be just the impetus to get you unstuck and moving forward again with enthusiasm. This little book by David Seabury does that for me, as I hope it will for you. Below are some excerpts.

The Habit of Success

". . . Write a biography of the way you wish your next ten years to go. You cannot, of course, make the future come to pass merely by wanting it. But there is magic in wanting. Somehow, knowing what you want, defining your purposes, seems to start a chain reaction. Write the story not only of what you wish, but of how you intend to overcome some of the odds of destiny . . . Get ready to win and you will not lose. . . ."

Control Your Enemies

". . . Don't fight for the sake of fighting. Don't fight to inflate your ego. Don't fight to exalt your pride. Don't fight to overcome your adversary or to punish him. Fight only to win a larger end, and fight without fighting—incongruous as that seems. Strive for the positive force, the impelling power that will be invincible in overcoming your trouble . . . by this method you win by yielding."

The Wisdom of Life

". . . Unless all your associates are happy, easy, adaptable natures, it's foolish to expect them to consistently respond to your ideas. It is wiser to approach any plan you have to suggest by first speaking of the opposite values and contradictory facts. If you believe a certain course should be taken, discuss the risks of doing so and criticize the idea. Let your listener be the one to suggest that after all such a plan is needed. Then go along with him. . . ."

Which Way Happiness?

". . . The question of living life well is not one of wisdom only, but of daring. You may have intelligence enough to see a practical solution. Have you the nerve to follow it? If not, you might as well be stupid. . . . There is no right and wrong for you, therefore, in the handling of your problems until you decide what you mean by right: either adherence to the stereotype, or obedience to cosmic law. . . ."

Reprinted with permission of Pocket Books, a division of Simon & Schuster, from The Art of Selfishness by David Seabury and Aaron Sussman, © 1937 by David Seabury, © 1965 by Evelyn Lewis.

I find that it is easier to be patient when I can achieve little successes along the way toward a bigger goal rather than wait for the one end goal. If you set your career plan up so that each objective represents a milestone, however small, then accomplishing each one will give you cause for celebration. This will help you remain patient and continue until you meet the next objective; pretty soon you will have reached the winner's circle.

Flexibility

Absolutely nothing is ever going to go exactly as planned. That's a guarantee. At best, your career plan will be an excellent guide. The training and skill development that comes from handling a series of related positions and the mentoring (more about this in chapter 9) you receive will lead you on a steady path to your goal in spite of some obstacles. At the very least, your plan will be a point of departure. You may follow all the rules to make it work, only to discover part way through that it's not what you want at all. A disappointment, to be sure, but now you know what you *don't* want. You will then have to exercise a lot of flexibility to make a change to a new direction.

Remember Judy in chapter 3, who dreamed of owning her own realty company? Flexibility enabled her to keep herself on track when she discovered that being an independent real estate agent was not what she wanted to do. She redirected her interests and, using some of the same skills and knowledge, got a job managing the office for a large real estate firm.

Commitment

To me, being committed means that not accomplishing the goal is not an option. It's just that simple.

Self-Motivation

Your goal needs to be compelling enough that it instills in you a deep and abiding desire to go after it. If you're self-motivated, you'll take the initiative to reach out and do or learn the things you need to in order to move through your objectives. This includes taking any necessary steps to correct personal deficiencies that stand in your way.

Objectivity

Objectivity enables you to make the most of suggestions and even of criticism from others regarding your professional strengths and weaknesses. If you can listen with an objective and open mind, then you can consider others' ideas rationally and decide whether or not to follow their advice. Even if you think you know it all—as many of us so often do—you can usually benefit from picking up even one significant piece of information that can help you move a step closer to your goal.

Resourcefulness

A measure of resourcefulness can go a long way toward making the process of achieving your goal easier. Resourcefulness is closely tied to creativity, which is a natural talent for some people. It means being able to take any problem and draw on your abilities and available resources to find a creative workable solution. If you find that this is not one of your strengths, then spend more time with people who are good at being resourceful. By bouncing your ideas off people who can instinctively come up with workable solutions to problems, you'll probably discover new ways to overcome obstacles. Most likely, the more you work with such people, the more you'll learn to tap into your own creativity, trust your instincts, and draw on your resources for solving problems.

Take a few moments now to reflect on whether you have the characteristics and personality traits you need to move ahead. Think about activities or situations that have required you to give an extra measure of yourself and which traits surfaced prominently to enable you to do that. Think about the positive comments that people make about you and what traits they point out. If you receive written performance reviews at your job, they will probably emphasize certain characteristics you've demonstrated that coincide with these.

"WISDOM IS KNOWING YOURSELF— AND YOUR IMPACT"

■

"My ancestry defined my identity," says Sam Chan, whose mother is of mixed white-European heritage and whose father is Chinese and Mongolian. "I was raised in a traditional Chinese culture, but, because of my mother, with her Midwestern roots, I felt at home in mainstream American culture. From her, I inherited a gift for gab and an ease in being entertaining and publicly visible. From my father, I got the traits of humility, hard work, and sacrifice. My paternal grandmother, who must have anticipated the challenges I would face with my mixed heritage, gave me two Chinese middle names that mean 'patience' and 'anything possible.'"

As a biracial child of the fifties, Sam learned early how to harmoniously blend his diverse personality traits. That kind of blending carried forth into both his studies and his work, and it allowed him to advance rapidly in his profession. He currently manages two major and complex programs: a youth and family services consortium and a diversity consultation and training program. Both programs focus on ethnically diverse populations in underserved communities. "As an administrator, I continue to look for the new and different, while working to bring people together without conflict," he explains.

The lessons learned early in managing the conflict of his double heritage serve Sam well today in his relations with others. "I do not try to exacerbate conflict and I don't run away from it either. I view conflict as a gift of energy, and I direct it somewhere for the good. After all, some energy is better than no energy, and having it is an opportunity to create something positive—for example, bringing about harmony between Asians and blacks, who are often pitted against each other."

Part of Sam's self-refinement comes from expanding beyond his field and placing himself in new environments, where he encounters new challenges, people, and ideas. For him, this continual stretching beyond the familiar and comfortable brings personal growth. He says this has increased his appreciation of shared efforts. "In encounters with others, I appreciate the *blending of personality traits to achieve a group voice. This group voice is something different than each individual brings to the table and is owned by everyone there. I believe this is the value of sharing versus an individual competitive interest, because shared work leads to a group investment."*

And in sharing, he believes the most important thing he can give is himself. "My knowledge is your knowledge," Sam asserts. "The most important source of power is information, and wisdom is knowing clearly about yourself and who you are and your impact upon other people. As one of the Zen masters says, 'The greatest gift one can give is the essence of one's self.'"

■

SAM CHAN, PH.D.
White and Asian-American executive
Director, Professional Services Center
California School of Professional Psychology, Los Angeles, California

REFINING YOUR PERSONALITY TRAITS

The older we get, the more we become who we are. Or, as one of my accounting teachers once said, "People don't change—they intensify." The problem is that this sometimes means that the very traits that are our strengths can also be our downfall—if they are carried too far or become too intense. For example, detail-oriented perfectionists might focus so much on the little parts of a project that they lose sight of the big picture—and drive others crazy in the process. People who like to talk and interact with people might let socializing get in the way of their job performance.

To avoid allowing a personality trait to become a liability, you need to be sure to keep it in check. And here's where you can use objectivity to help you stay on track. If you make it a regular habit to seek feedback about your personality style, especially as you take on

191

positions of responsibility over others, you'll be able to curb extreme traits or flaws and develop strategies to ensure that they do not cause your downfall.

Take a look at the following extremes that we'd all be better off avoiding:

The Wall

Many times over the course of my career, I've met professionals who are absolutely inflexible. They follow the policy book to the letter. This behavior might be expected and even desirable in a security guard but not in a person managing or working with people as part of a team. Wall types usually come across as very rational and logical in their communications. They present themselves as balanced, fair, and open to hearing what others have to say. They may even encourage employees to express their ideas and to offer suggestions for resolving problems. Then they reject everything. After this happens a few times, they leave coworkers and staff members feeling discouraged and, ultimately, unmotivated. Wall types completely stifle creativity because they're driven by their emotions. They're afraid. And in most cases, they're afraid of making a mistake.

You cannot advance without some risk, because there is no safe and secure path for anyone. It's human nature to be apprehensive when trying something new, but when apprehension develops into irrational fear that immobilizes you, it can be detrimental to your career growth. If you recognize behavior in yourself that might define you as a Wall type, then you need to develop relationships with people at your level or higher whom you trust, respect, and can seek advice from. Bouncing ideas off these people and getting input on your decisions may help minimize the risk of failure. Since you will probably be more comfortable connecting with someone outside your company, seek such relationships in professional associations and social groups.

The Nitpicker

I know, I know. The only reason you're so careful about everything is that you want it to be perfect. Nitpickers are fascinated with and involved in every detail of a project. Not only that, they're also involved with perfecting everyone and everyone's role in the project. They think they have their finger on the pulse of what is happening, when actually they're so caught up in details that they may be missing the big picture.

These people come off as condescending (after all, no one can do it quite as well as they can), and they immobilize and demoralize people who report to them. After they correct and change everything that is done, they leave their coworkers feeling as if there is no point in creating anything, because the Nitpicker will only change it. This personality trait is often combined with a blazing wit sprinkled with liberal portions of sarcasm, both of which impede the development of confidence in others and are not conducive to effective team-building. Overall, the actions of Nitpickers discourage initiative and growth.

If you recognize this trait as part of your personality, you can keep it in check by seeking feedback (from peers and subordinates—or both if you dare) and allowing room in your planning to encourage initiative in others. In planning a project, you should include as part of your outline those elements that you have determined must be included and a description of the format in which they should be developed. After that, allow others some creativity and freedom in developing the aspects for which they are responsible, as long as their ideas are consistent with the overall goal and timelines. Then, accept their approaches and suggestions if they meet the bill, even if it's not exactly the way you would have done it.

The Philosopher
Philosopher types see all and know all, so much so that they have a hard time getting anything done because they are more interested in talking about a project than doing it. Seemingly very astute about everything (and everyone) in the department, they often cannot be pinned down to carry out in a timely manner very specific tasks for which they are directly responsible.

Philosopher types tend to create a great deal of frustration among their coworkers because they often deviate from the issues at hand and take up a lot of unnecessary time dealing with peripheral issues surrounding a project. For instance, if a philosopher type were planning a series of meetings to discuss a certain issue, he or she, during the planning stages, might go off on tangents about how people behave in meetings, the difficulties of organizing such meetings, and other points totally irrelevant to the main issue.

If this behavior sounds familiar, you can work toward correcting it by writing out very specific interim objectives with a time schedule—which you must follow on a daily basis—to enable you to meet overall goals by keeping focused on *doing* rather than *thinking*.

The Super Expediter

The extreme opposite of philosophers, super expediters are action-oriented and do everything quickly. They may even ride roughshod over the feelings of others without meaning to. They just don't make the time to take those feelings into consideration because they are so focused on accomplishing their objective. Their extreme independence can leave people feeling breathless and uncared for, as if their input on a project were not important.

If you've demonstrated behavior similar to this, you need to factor in extra time to accomplish each objective—you should focus not just on getting the job done but on taking the time to ask for and listen to input from others who are involved in your projects. They may share some information that will make the outcome even better than you anticipated.

Take an Objective Look, Then Act on What You See

Now that you have some idea of personality traits that can block your success, take an objective look at your personality and working style. Also, since most of us have a blind side that prevents us from knowing completely the personality traits that we show to the world, input from others will help us gain that objective view. Get input from people you know—friends, peers, mentors, your boss—about the personality strengths and weaknesses they see. The more objective and detailed these people are, the more helpful their comments will be to you.

A friend once asked me for such a critique and then laughingly added, "I've buried all the sharp instruments, so I won't hurt myself after you give me your opinion. So go ahead, I'm ready to hear the truth." You need someone whom you trust to be honest with you in order for it to be meaningful. Once you have the information (i.e., your self-critique plus feedback from others), then you can develop a plan for modifying some of your more extreme personality traits.

UPGRADING AND EXPANDING YOUR SKILLS

As you move ahead toward your goal, you will face new challenges and different demands at every level of professional growth. For example, you may have to deal with unfamiliar technical or business information, master a new technology, or learn to effectively supervise people. The wise professional will take the initiative to gain an understanding of what is needed and seek out the appropriate means for securing this skill and knowledge.

Bob Kemp in chapter 4 provides an excellent example of someone who recognized a deficiency in his skill base and then set about correcting it. When he achieved a leadership position at a financial institution, he knew that his engineering background was not sufficient for the task, so he enrolled in school to secure a degree in business. Charsetta in chapter 3 is another good example; she obtained her M.B.A. in order to advance in the human resources field.

Your next job may not require returning to school for a full course of study, but it probably will require additional education or training on some level. As a matter of fact, you should expect that at each higher job level you'll need some new skills—ones you may be able to acquire right on the job or through outside training courses. To determine what new skills you may need for a job you might like to advance into, do a bit of research. Get a job description if you can and talk with two or three people who hold a position similar to the one you're interested in. Find out what additional training they required and also what skills or training they already had that proved helpful in the position.

Then sign up for courses or classes to upgrade your skills in those areas as necessary. (Refer back to the information in chapter 3 on education and training for resources and ideas.) Additionally, if you work in a larger organization, you can ask someone from the human resources department to provide information on training programs they recommend.

Even if you find that you do not need to upgrade your specific technical or business knowledge, you'll no doubt have to upgrade your peripheral skills. For instance, you may have to take a class on business and report writing or upgrade your computer knowledge in order to develop and produce effective business reports. Also, in most business environments, you will be expected to make oral presentations. The higher you go, the more likely it is that you will be speaking in public—at conventions and seminars, for example—so you can certainly benefit from training in this area at any point in your career. (Consider joining Toastmasters International, a professional organization established to help people develop and build confidence in their public speaking skills. It has hundreds of member groups all over the world.)

Without a doubt, you'll also want to develop your people skills; specifically for the twenty-first century, you'll need to be effective at guiding and motivating others and building productive, self-directed work teams. Fannie's story in chapter 4 offers good examples of some ways to develop these leadership skills. Now might be the time to step forward and volunteer to head up one of those committees in your professional organization or any other social or professional group that you belong to. Another excellent way to get personalized and customized support in moving to the next career level is through an executive coach (see An Executive Coach—Your Invisible Mentor).

AN EXECUTIVE COACH—YOUR INVISIBLE MENTOR

Coaching is designed to assist technically proficient professionals and executives in maximizing their strengths and identities and in overcoming personal barriers to success. Using a coach is an excellent option when other more traditional forms of employee development are either unavailable or do not address your individual development needs. You can hire a personal coach on your own (and pay for it) or get your company to hire a business coach to work with you.

The following interview with Diane Sanders, senior partner in Corporate Coaching International, LLC, Los Angeles, provides more highlights on coaching.

What is business coaching?

"Just as a sports coach gives his or her players ongoing feedback about how to maximize their strengths and overcome obstacles to success, business coaches work with technically proficient men and women who encounter difficulty along their career paths. The job of a coach is to help employees understand how their behaviors may be going out of bounds and to illuminate appropriate alternative behaviors that will ensure long-term success.

"No matter how talented a person may be, unspoken success factors such as the ability to build positive workplace relationships, work effectively as a member of a team, and the willingness to go the extra mile can and do affect career mobility. Good coaches have the courage to speak the unspoken, whereas a staff member's own manager may be hesitant or lack the skills to help the person develop."

Who should use a coach?

"Traditionally, coaching has been confined to senior managers and high-potential fast-track managers who are being groomed to move up in the hierarchy. With the rapid changes occurring in the new corporate environment, development tools, including coaching, are being used

Continued

now by some mid-level managers as well because of their added responsibility and authority to affect decisions. Coaching provides an opportunity for the company as a whole, and for each individual to better understand the perceived environmental factors that may affect their future success."

How do business coaches know what's needed within a particular culture?

"Good coaches have often worked in more than one corporate or business environment and understand what it takes to succeed. Capable coaches work in partnership with the organization, the employee, and the employee's management."

Can you give me an example of a coaching situation?

"I coached Jack, a highly competent industrial engineer who worked for a large oil company. Jack's technical competence was great and the company did not want to lose him, but his interpersonal behavior was so out of bounds that no one could work with him, and the company had nowhere else to move him. Jack's manager explained that Jack appeared to have mood swings; he'd lash out at his peers and his customers at inappropriate times. Jack was described as a technically proficient 'loose cannon.' When Jack and I discussed the feedback he got from his assessment and his management's concerns, he admitted that he always tried to do perfect work but his peers and often his customers were just too unsophisticated to understand what he was trying to explain; he'd respond by exploding in frustration and anger.

"As part of the coaching process Jack began to see that it wasn't his peers or his customers who were at fault, he was. When he understood and accepted his responsibility for the problem, he realized that what he was really experiencing was burnout because he always had to do perfect work. He also acknowledged that the company's structure had changed to a more team-oriented environment and that he no longer fit in; he worked better as an individual contributor.

"When he reached these conclusions on his own, he could then specifically ask for help to move out of the company in order to start his own consulting practice where his technical competence and ability to work on his own would be of value. He worked with the company to develop a plan to provide consulting services rather than stay in a traditional employer/employee relationship. Both Jack and his company benefited in the end."

What information does the coach share with the company?

"The coaching relationship is a confidential one. Coaches share only information directly related to helping employees achieve specific behavioral goals. Coaches do not reveal any information obtained from interviews, meetings with employees, or feedback instruments."

How much time does coaching take?

"Once the assessment phase of the coaching process has been completed and goals and objectives have been outlined, the coaching process, with follow up, may take anywhere from three to six months to, in some cases, a year."

How does a person know if having a coach is right for her?

"If a person wishes to further develop her leadership, interpersonal, or communication skills and is flexible about making changes, open to feedback, and willing to see herself as others see her, then she will find coaching useful."

Where does a person find qualified business coaches?

"The best way to find qualified business coaches is by referral. Check with your organization, in business journals, business and professional training and organizational development networks, training institutes and organizations that provide coaching skills training to individuals, and even on the Internet."

Ultimately, however, the most important person you will need to manage is you—your responsibilities and your time. As you take on increased responsibility, you'll need to free yourself up to function at that new level by letting go of some of the responsibilities of your previous position—or at least by managing them differently.

For instance, if you are promoted from laboratory assistant to laboratory supervisor, then you'll probably have to leave the day-to-day preparation of the laboratory experiments to the new assistant. As your role shifts from doer to planner, your responsibilities will involve using new skills in interviewing, selection, and employee development, as well as in communication, training, and delegating. If you spend your time performing laboratory tasks instead of directing activities, then both your job and the assistant's job will suffer. As you move from a supervisor's role to a manager's role, you will have to deal with more accountability and less direct control. You will need to develop very effective leadership and executive skills and be able to operate with a vision from a broader perspective. If you're moving into a consultant role, expect to be challenged to influence change and implement a vision without having direct power and authority.

RESOURCES

The Art of Selfishness—Can Make You a Happier Person by David Seabury (Pocket Books, 1981) is one of the best little books I've ever read for putting you in control of your life. I've carried this book around with me for fifteen years and refer to it often. It deals with the keys to problems, compromise, failure, love, laziness, achieving dynamic living, success, etc. A must-read for everyone.

Creative Life Management: Stress Reduction for an Enhanced Quality of Life by Frieda Porat, Ph.D. (Newlife Books, 1995) is a quick-read guide for managing stress. It deals with issues like procrastination, time management, productivity and planning, and life planning.

Personal Job Power: Discover Your Own Power Style for Work Satisfaction and Success by Clay Carr and Valorie Beer (Peterson's, 1996) explores seven different power styles you'll find at work and explains how to use them to enrich your own potential. It also shows you how to recognize the power style of others so that you can work with them more effectively.

Personality Types: Using the Eneagram for Self-Discovery by Don Richard Riso (Houghton Mifflin Company, 1995) expands on the material discussed in this chapter. It breaks personality types into nine categories and helps you understand your strengths and weaknesses and the impact of your personality. This material will help you make adjustments if needed to get along better with others. It offers good information in a format that's easy to follow.

CHAPTER

MOVING AHEAD AT YOUR COMPANY

I s it time to move on in your career? Moving up doesn't have to mean moving out—to another employer, that is. There may be many benefits to staying where you are, so long as you can find and take advantage of new opportunities there.

Surprisingly, many people would advise against this and tell you to start sending out résumés and networking to find work somewhere else. This is because it's a common belief that people get ahead more quickly by changing employers. I disagree. Of course, you may face some obstacles in moving from one level to another (for example, if you've been pigeonholed in a certain job or at a certain level), but the advantages of staying with the same company are many. If you've already established a reputation for excellent performance, as Jacquelyn did in "Strive to Provide Excellence," you'll be in a perfect position to go after a promotion, and it will probably be easy for you to find support for doing so. And after working at the same company for some time, you'll likely know about potential land mines and how to avoid them (see chapter 6). Once you've won your promotion, you'll also probably know how to access resources and the right people to help you meet your objectives in a job that carries added responsibility.

Before initiating a plan to move up at your company, consider any obstacles you may have to deal with so that you can incorporate a strategy for addressing them into your plan.

- **Your image.** How is your personal image? Does your attire reflect the level to which you want to move? If not, buy two or three suits, a new briefcase, shoes, and such. The expense will be worth it, because your new image will give you a psychological boost as well as make you look like someone on the way up.

- **Your performance record.** Do you have a good track record? Any glitches there? If so, check with your mentor or an understanding supervisor (if you're fortunate enough to have one that you can confide in) for the best way to address this at your company.

- **External obstacles.** Are you likely to encounter roadblocks because of your age? If so, a haircut, makeup, and some alterations to your wardrobe can help you project youthfulness and openness or seriousness and maturity. Because of your gender? Do your homework—unfortunately, sometimes women must work harder and be smarter than men just to overcome ingrained biases. Because of your race? Strive for commonalities and chemistry—they usually win out (refer back to chapter 6 for guidance in ensuring that your personality is a good match with the company culture).

  Stay focused on how your qualifications fit the needs of any job you interview for. The barriers you may face in trying to get "hired" into another department or into a higher-level job in your current department could be quite similar to those faced by people seeking employment with another company. If you suspect this might be true, then take a look at my book *101*

Great Answers to the Toughest Job Search Problems for more suggestions on how you can address a variety of difficult issues.

After you've anticipated and planned for any negatives, you're ready to evaluate the potential for moving forward at your company. Keeping all these factors in mind, take some time to weigh the advantages and disadvantages of staying or leaving.

ESTABLISHING YOUR CAREER PLAN

If you're with a large organization, arrange to meet with people who can give you an idea of your potential for advancement: managers, department heads, and human resources people. This will help you to determine not only where and how far you can go within the company, but also whether you'll be able to accomplish your long-range career goal there at all.

If you're with a small or medium-sized organization, you can talk directly with your manager (or the owner) about the potential for advancement. Because smaller companies generally have fewer actual job slots (and, therefore, fewer places to which you can advance), you may need to focus more on working to rearrange responsibilities than on getting promoted. This will enable you to take on more challenging tasks so that you can develop further skills and, in turn, enhance your marketability in the future.

Whether you work for a large or small organization, timing and tact are important here. It's best to have been in your current job for at least a year before broaching the subject of career advancement, even if you've been with the company longer in other positions. The best time to discuss advancement is during the goal-setting phase of your performance review. If you're with a small company or if performance reviews are not a part of the company's culture, ask your manager for a time when the two of you can get together to discuss your performance—without using the formal term *performance review*.

Before approaching her, you'll need to develop your strategy. How receptive is she likely to be to the discussion? Are there any factors that would prevent her from supporting the idea: A heavy workload? Reluctance to losing a key team member? Not naturally inclined to help subordinates advance? Then determine the best way to approach her based on her personal style and yours. Discuss your approach with your mentor or a colleague, and role-play the conversation if possible.

Once you sit down with your manager, the primary purpose of this conversation will be to get input on your capabilities and potential. Moreover, it's politically correct to let your manager be the first to know that you're interested in advancing—you don't want her to think that you're going behind her back to make a move or trying to separate yourself from her supervision. Also, if she plans to put up any roadblocks to your advancement, you'll want to know this right away so that you can address these issues before proceeding. It's called covering your bases. Ideally, once your manager knows of your goal, she'll help you.

Plan to discuss the skills you want to use and explore the functional areas and specific jobs within the company that would fit those skills and interests. Your side of the conversation may go something like this:

> I'm interested in advancing my career and focusing more on my artistic skill and mechanical ability. I have some ideas about how I could contribute those skills in the company, and I would like to discuss my ideas with you and get your feedback.

At this point, you're looking to set a course leading toward a goal within the company, so you want to get a sense not only of a specific job several levels above where you are, but also of the interim jobs needed to get to that level.

What if your manager seems unreceptive to your advancement? Then make the effort to find out why (if she will tell you). If she makes a good case that you still need to develop skills in your current job and can point out specifically what you need to do, then it might be best to back away from the advancement idea right now and instead talk about setting goals on your current job to build a stronger foundation for advancement down the road.

If your manager is not receptive to your advancing because she needs you for a critical project, try to get a commitment for a time when you will be able to go after other jobs. If it's not too far in the future, then it will probably be best to just wait it out. If, on the other hand, she gives you no definite time frame, then you might want to let her know that you'd like to look for new opportunities within the company anyway and that if something does open up, you will do your best to make the transition as smooth as possible for all involved.

If she doesn't have a valid job-related reason for not supporting you or a timetable as to when you can proceed, then you'll have to take a different approach. If you work in a large organization, meet with your human resources representative to talk about how you can advance. If you work in a small company, forget the advancement avenue at that company and shift your focus to your other options (i.e., start sending out your résumé!) because the other managers (or principals) will probably support your manager's assessment.

These are worst-case scenarios. The truth is, it's unlikely that your manager will refuse to support you without giving you a legitimate reason; she won't want to be stuck with a disgruntled, unmotivated employee.

If your manager is supportive, she may volunteer information about her own career progression. If not, ask her how she advanced to her current level, and ask her for advice on your own approach. I've always found people to be more than willing to share this kind of information. Also, find out whom else in the company you should talk with and then ask your manager whether it's all right to tell them that she referred you.

Your next step is to make an appointment with each of these people. When you set up the meetings, mention that your manager suggested you talk with them and that you'd appreciate about 30 minutes of their time and then give them a clear idea of the reason for the meeting and what you expect from them. Stick to your word—stay focused on your objective and specific about your goals. You don't want to ramble in these meetings and waste their time. If you prepare questions before going to the meeting, you'll be able to keep these informational interviews on track.

Finally, you'll want to meet with your human resources representative, who should be able to recommend a career path for you within the company, discuss the likelihood of relevant job openings in the future, and give you a sense of how you can prepare so that you will be considered for these openings. Additionally, the human resources representative should schedule an interview between you and the manager or a representative from the department you're interested in working in. This will give you not only a clearer understanding of the department and its needs but also the added advantage of alerting the right people about your skills and goals.

FINDING MENTORS (OR ALLOWING THEM TO FIND YOU)

The best way to get a mentor is to demonstrate good performance so that you'll be selected by someone who takes an interest in your career and decides that mentoring you would be worth the time and effort.

The dictionary defines a mentor as a "trusted counselor or guide, a tutor or coach." Mentoring is help over and beyond that which is expected in the normal course of the business world, and it is something that is given voluntarily—it cannot be requested. Of course, you can give others an opportunity to mentor you by approaching them and asking for their advice on how to advance in your field or for feedback on your performance.

"SPEAK UP"

■

"Networking is something that, from a cultural and personal point of view, we don't do. It's difficult for Hispanics to blow their own horn—and it takes a while for us to understand that it takes more than doing a good job to succeed.

"I am forever grateful to a person who unofficially mentored me early in my career. When I was first starting out, I used to bury myself in my work—I didn't look up or say anything to anyone. I felt that if I did a good job it would show for itself. But then, the person who started mentoring me began to come over each morning and say, 'Put your head up and say hello,' until I finally started doing it on my own."

This lesson, early in his career, helped teach Juan the value of speaking up, being visible, and reaching out to others. It is a lesson he has never forgotten.

Juan can't emphasize enough the necessity of networking, especially for people of color, who may not be used to this concept. "You should establish a network that will allow you to call on others if you need help. Employee-initiated, company-supported groups are great for that. At NYNEX, we have groups like our Hispanic support organization and a multicultural association where one can find good role models."

Juan advocates networking because it has been instrumental for him in achieving his own career growth. "I was on the technical side for a number of years and was sponsored by the company in a master's [degree] program. After I finished, I wanted a position as a technical trainer. I finally got the job as the result of knowing the district and regional managers. I had decision makers on the lookout for me, and it helped."

Juan knows that you cannot succeed by yourself and believes that his ability to develop relationships and get consensus has been invaluable to him. "If I could say just one thing to people who are trying to communicate with others and advance, it would be words that Jesse Jackson spoke: 'Look for the common ground to seek the higher ground.'"

People have more in common than we think. Juan knows from his own experience that success depends on reaching out and communicating our ideas, our goals, and who we are in order to make valuable connections.

■

JUAN N. RODRIGUEZ
Hispanic executive
Director of Human Resources, Manhattan Market Area
NYNEX
New York

As you advance in your career, however, it becomes somewhat more difficult to find just one person to mentor you. In her book *Women Breaking Through*, Deborah Swiss offers good advice for finding a number of mentors rather than concentrating on just one individual. Pointing out that it is not necessary to even like your mentors, Swiss includes a quote from Mary Rowe, ombudsperson at MIT, who suggests considering the broadest possible pool of mentors and forgetting about finding a saint or a perfect role model: "Seek advice from anyone who is competent and responsible. Seek out several mentors and learn different things from different people . . . even your peers."

Any conversations (networking or informational interviews) in which you seek or are given advice are opportunities to connect with someone as an adviser or guide. Most likely, if some chemistry or connection exists between you that supports a mentoring relationship, the other person will be forthcoming with help.

As you expand your network, you increase your pool of potential mentors. Here again, people in your professional groups, associations, social groups that include people who work at your socioeconomic level, associates in other companies—all have the potential to mentor you.

Hopefully, as you seek advice in how to move forward, you will gain mentors along the way. If you finely tune your listening skills during these conversations, you may be able to pick up clues for identifying potential mentors. People who have mentor potential:

- . . . empathize with you. For example, they tell you they remember going through a similar process to yours when they were establishing their own career tracks.

- . . . offer to do more than give you suggestions on developing your career track. They may arrange for you to talk with others, offer to get additional information for you, or ask for you to get back to them after carrying out some instruction or following some advice they give you.

- . . . give you positive feedback from someone else. They may even say that a particular person has recommended you for a certain job. In this case, the person who recommended you could be another potential mentor.

GOING AFTER A JOB

Planning, persistence, and patience will help you get the job you want. Beyond this, there are no set rules for advancing at this stage of your career. Now you're more on your own than you were at the beginning. At this level, you are expected to be willing to take some risks for advancement. Quite often, people secure more advanced positions by using unique strategies and approaches to go after them. Usually these approaches involve some risks and a measure of creativity; in fact, the more unique, creative, or daring the strategy, the more it will distinguish the accomplished veteran from the less confident novice. Of course, your approach should not be foolhardy. But by developing a strategy based on knowledge of the culture and your manager's personality, you won't make any big mistakes.

One experienced executive once told me of a particularly creative approach he used when he was working toward advancement in his company. He timed his visits to the water cooler to coincide with those of the general manager; once there, he would casually mention projects he wanted to promote or inquire about.

Cassie, a career consultant with a major organizational development firm, did an excellent job of going after the position she wanted—and getting it. It took eighteen months, an interim job with another organization, and a six-month volunteer stint with a social services group before she accomplished her goal. Six months prior to completing her master's degree in psychology, which she was working on while holding a full-time position as an office manager, Cassie decided she wanted to move into a consultant position at the firm. She started the process of establishing her career track by introducing herself to one of her company executives, whom she first met at a professional association meeting, and arranging to meet with him for an informational interview to discuss her career.

In the interview, Cassie learned that her degree would not be sufficient to qualify her to handle the organization's clientele. As part of its marketing approach, the company used only consultants who were highly experienced. In other words, they had no room for an entry-level consultant.

Now Cassie realized that she was either stuck in her administrative position or would have to leave the company. After obtaining her degree, she elected to leave the company and join a smaller organization where she could gain the experience she lacked. At the same time, to supplement the skills she was developing at her new interim job, she worked two evenings a week and on the weekends volunteering for a community-based social services agency. All the while she maintained regular contact with her former employer. Her dedication and commitment paid off. She got the experience and then rejoined her original company, moving into the consultant position she aspired to from the beginning.

As Cassie found out early, there are two key considerations in going after a specific job at a company: (1) whether the opportunity is worth the effort; and (2) what your chances are of getting it. John also learned this after he set his sights on the spot of vice president of finance at his company. He knew that before he could compete for the job, he would need to work at two interim jobs to gain the necessary experience. The problem was that employees with more than fifteen years of service were already well-established in those two interim positions. As the situation stood, John would have been wasting his time going after the top financial job in his company. Instead, he opted to transfer to another division in the company where he could get the experience he needed, so that he would be prepared to eventually compete for the top position when it became available.

Both of these examples point to the importance of thoroughly assessing your potential for advancing in your company before you establish a career track there. If you discover through your interviews and research that it will be all but impossible to reach your goal at your current company, then it's best to cut your losses and move on. On the other hand, you may learn that the job you want is attainable but that you will need to gain more experience at another company or within another division before you can compete for it.

EXPANDING YOUR CURRENT JOB

Expanding your current job may be one of the most viable avenues for advancement because it allows you to develop your position specifically around your strengths. To do this, you will need to take the lead role in restructuring your job and convincing your supervisors to work with you.

George, a senior marketing executive for a Fortune 100 company, managed to restructure and expand his position to become lead marketing executive. Noted for his ability to land very difficult clients as well as being able to work well with the staff, George had established himself as an excellent employee. Not only did he willingly put in the extra effort to close the loop on every deal, but he also made himself available to train other marketing executives and to pitch in when one of them needed help.

Before long, others in the department came to rely on George's help, and, as a result, he eventually became overloaded with the additional responsibilities of training and coaching his peers. At this point, he approached his division head about rewriting his job description to incorporate his expanded responsibilities. He also asked for an administrative assistant to help him with some of the follow-up activities and administrative work connected with servicing his clients. Because he presented his needs clearly and realistically (and because his firm recognized George as a real asset), he got all that he requested. The company officially rewrote his position to cover his new responsibility as lead marketing executive; he also got an assistant— and a raise.

The key to expanding your position is to meet a need your employer has by using additional skills that are outside the scope of your current responsibilities. Some possible ways to accomplish this include:

- Take on the responsibility to initiate activities that will upgrade your skills as well as those of others in the group. For example, provide training or suggest a program of cross-functional activities that will train and expand the capabilities of key individuals.

- Take responsibility for some task that needs to be done but that no one wants to do; for instance, serving as liaison to sources external to your department or company in order to carry out necessary tasks.

- Demonstrate problem-solving skills by working to find a solution to an onerous situation that has bothered a lot of people.

- Volunteer to assume some of the responsibilities that are cumbersome to your immediate manager.

CREATING A NEW JOB

Another means of advancing your career within your current company is to create an entirely new position. The key to doing this is to identify a significant need that is not being met, which could either increase revenue, cut costs, or improve efficiency—and then volunteer to step in and fill that need. Because this approach requires the greatest amount of initiative and creativity, many people are not up to the challenge.

It's more common for people to stay in their current job, hoping that someone will recognize their hidden capabilities and then offer to create a new job for them. They want to advance but they're waiting for either someone else or circumstances to create opportunities that will move their career along. Instead of taking the steps to determine where they could add value to the organization, they get stuck by giving in to prevalent career-stopping attitudes.

Don, for example, relied heavily on his good relationship with his boss as an avenue to advance, but he did not use the relationship to its fullest potential. He hinted to Mike, his boss, that he wanted a more responsible position, and he waited with the hope that something would eventually materialize. Nothing did. Don was right to use the relationship as a tool, but he would have been better off talking with Mike, not about a problem but about a solution. Rather than asking how we could have more responsibility, Don should have offered to take on more responsibility by presenting a list of needs he could address. If he had looked around the organization to determine where he could add value, he probably could have enlisted Mike's help.

Be Part of the Solution

Most any department or company has areas where productivity is low and work gets bottlenecked or where a number of complaints originate. By discussing problem areas with the people involved, you'll have a good chance of hitting on workable solutions. Often the people with the problem also have a solution for how it should be handled; it's just that no one in the group is willing to take the initiative for addressing the problem or the responsibility for implementing the solution.

As an example, suppose, as the manager of a marketing department, you were constantly requesting a variety of statistical information that your team needed for developing proposals. You could either develop a retrieval system for accessing the information quickly or research and provide information on programs that could accomplish the goal. You could put this in the form of a proposal with recommendations for your boss's signature. Your boss would then have something he could react to or forward to the next level of authority for approval.

Another career-stopping attitude is the inability to think outside of predictable patterns. When needs arise that must be addressed, such tunnel vision may translate to "It's not my job," followed by "It's so-and-so's job. Let him do it. He's getting paid for it." The interesting thing about such an attitude is that people who have it will never be paid for "it," because people who continually pass off responsibility to others are also passing up the opportunity to increase their own earning power.

I encountered this kind of thinking recently when talking with a peer about an assignment that had been offered to me and that I knew would be difficult. The client wanted to implement a huge project on a very tight deadline. My colleague advised me to stay clear of the project because it seemed destined for failure—why risk having the failure fall on me? Fortunately, I ignored that advice and worked hard to help make the project a success. When we did meet the goal, my credibility increased tenfold, ensuring future business with that client.

Of course, people can always think of reasons to avoid taking on a challenging job or, in some cases, doing any work at all. Harry is a classic example of someone who held to the last of the popular career-blocking attitudes: "That's too much work; I don't want to do it." Seeing himself as someone who possessed true leadership ability, Harry felt he should not have to get stuck in the trenches doing dirty work. After all, he had already paid his dues. He made a point of avoiding projects where he had to "get his hands dirty," or he tried to enlist the help of someone else to handle the difficult tasks. He did all right with this method of managing, but it caused him to lose out when a prestigious position that he really wanted became available. The person responsible for filling the position wanted someone with enthusiasm, high energy, and flexibility. Not surprisingly, Harry's reputation kept him out of the running.

"STRIVE TO DELIVER EXCELLENCE"

■

Jacquelyn attributes her rapid career growth at NYNEX to her ability to facilitate change; her transferable skills, reputation, and presence; and, above all, her ongoing commitment to excellence. "I joined the company with twelve years' corporate staff experience but no direct operating experience. NYNEX gave me my first hands-on operating opportunity: handling customer service and managing a staff of 120 people."

Jacquelyn focused on the tasks of the position and directed her energy toward upgrading the customer service effort and delivering excellence. As she did, she successfully elevated the level of service and quality of her role, which ultimately led to her promotion to a position created specifically around her capabilities. She attributes her advancement to vice president, quality and ethics, at one of the company's subsidiaries to her commitment to getting the job done well. "You must have standards for yourself and not be level-conscious—to do a good job no matter what level you're at. I believe that motivating my customer service team to deliver quality service signaled to management that I could lead a quality effort throughout the company, and that led to the vice president position."

Maintaining a practice of meeting high standards never goes unnoticed. Two years after her promotion, a reorganization took place within the company and Jacquelyn moved into a more corporate position as director of corporate culture initiatives and then into her current position of vice president, quality and ethics.

For Jacquelyn, visibility is a final critical element for success. "Visibility means you need to join organizations and volunteer for projects and task forces," she explains. "My participation in these organizations gave me visibility in my company that I never would have gotten otherwise. As a matter of fact, that was how I met my current boss. He was at the back of the room in a group where I was speaking, and a year later he called me about a job. Being visible is important."

■

JACQUELYN BURCH GATES
Black executive
Vice president
Office of Ethics and Business Conduct
NYNEX
New York

Take the Initiative

Smart people who take responsibility for their own careers will take a different approach—an approach that will lead to advancement.

Consider the examples of Susan, Julie, and Diane, three professionals at the same consulting company who took the initiative to create new jobs for themselves. Susan conducted management training sessions, and after working with several organizations from a variety of industries, she noticed a recurring theme in the complaints from the participants. She saw a need for programs that would bring together managers and employees for discussion and problem solving and encourage them to form closer working relationships. She developed and sold a team-building program for addressing these issues to the executive management of her company and convinced them to implement the new program nationally. Her concept resulted almost immediately in a significant increase in revenues—and a new job for her.

Julie, a branch manager, used her management and leadership talent to cut costs significantly. After two or three staff members left through promotion or attrition, Julie realigned the responsibilities without refilling the positions. The district director soon noticed the tremendous savings in overhead, combined with the more efficient operation of the office. He met with Julie to determine what it was that she was doing that made her so much more efficient than the other unit managers. Based on his findings, he promoted her to senior manager, directing the efforts of five other managers and offices.

Diane's new job came out of her ability to conceptualize and implement on a broad scale. In its start-up phase, the consulting company had operated very efficiently and consistently delivered a quality product and service. After about seven years, however, Diane noticed that staff members were experiencing frustration in trying to meet the needs of the clients. She also recognized inconsistent service and duplication of effort. Meeting with management, she suggested consolidating the administrative and system functions in the five offices in the district so that they could be managed at one office, with the aim of improving efficiency. She did so well that the responsibilities eventually grew into a new senior operations position for her within two years.

Opportunities for creating your own job may exist right under your nose if you are willing to be part of the solution instead of the problem. The following suggestions may spark ideas about needs in your organization that you could explore.

- Check out areas that a number of employees have been complaining about. Make a point of listening for the consistent theme of the complaints, and then explore ways they could be addressed.

- Discuss job issues and problems with members of your professional groups. One of the advantages of participating in professional groups is that they provide a forum for discussing issues that might bring forth a solution. Some of these "solutions" could be significant enough to create a new position or expand an existing one.

- Stay current on industry news. Often, reading about other organizations and their leadership approaches may very well give you ideas for solving problems in your own company.

MAKING RESTRUCTURING WORK FOR YOU

If you have the ability to function in the midst of chaos, you can make a restructuring work for you. This can be a real challenge because, naturally, a reorganization creates a tremendous amount of stress for everyone involved, especially if it is also associated with downsizing.

Everyone is wondering what will happen to his job and hoping he has sufficiently proved himself to ensure that his job is secure. This anxiety can cause people to react in several ways. They may close off communication with others and try to protect their turf, potentially shutting down some important processes because they are not feeding the necessary information into the pipeline. Others, assigned to complete certain projects, may delay completion by dawdling or intentionally making mistakes, assuming the company won't lay them off because it needs them to finish the work. Still others may deliberately sabotage the efforts of coworkers in order to eliminate competition.

Obviously, a person who can maintain some objectivity and perspective on work that needs to be done in the face of this kind of psychological upheaval will clearly stand out in a positive way. Janice, a trainer for a major chemical processing company, learned this when her company restructured and decentralized the corporate staff groups. Her whole department was eliminated overnight. Janice and twelve other coworkers were given four months to find a position in the company or they would be declared surplus, given a severance package, and terminated.

As angry and devastated as she was, Janice managed to maintain enough clarity to realize that she needed to focus on getting another job either at the company or somewhere else. Prepared to relocate if necessary, she started sending out résumés and networking all over the country. In the meantime, her responsibilities had been removed and she didn't have anything to do at work. Being idle increased her frustration and she felt very isolated not being part of the mainstream of activity.

She seized her opportunity to change the situation when she encountered the division vice president in the hallway. When he asked how she was doing, she engaged him in a conversation and let him know that she was bored and wanted some work to do while going through the restructuring process. She mentioned that she thought the human resources group could use some help (ironically, companies that are downsizing are often hiring simultaneously). Janice knew of this opportunity through some friends in that department who had told her how extreme their workload had become since the restructure. The executive looked into the situation and the next day had Janice working on a short-term staffing project for the personnel department.

Janice completed the project quickly and went on to provide additional support in the department. This came to the attention of the executive, and he stopped by her office to compliment her on how impressively she had handled the work. Ultimately, Janice was offered three jobs within the company, primarily as a result of how well she had carried out the temporary project. She accepted a newly created position that handled centralized professional staffing.

Look for Opportunities

If your organization is being restructured and you see or feel in others frustration similar to Janice's, keep your ears and eyes open for new opportunities. If you notice any one of the following situations and you have the necessary skills to step in, don't waste any time—seize the opportunity and go for it:

- A need for new leadership skills and knowledge. (I knew of one human resources director job that, after restructuring, needed someone with labor relations skills.)

- A project comes to a standstill because of discord and tension among the group members assigned to work on it.

- Someone suddenly leaves, is transferred, or promoted, removing key skills from the organization.

- Two or three departments are merged into one, causing some important responsibilities to fall through the cracks in certain areas and some duplication of effort in others.

- A department or a coworker has an excessively heavy workload, and you have very few responsibilities.

RESOURCES

Developing Mentor Relationships

Mentoring: The Tao of Giving and Receiving Wisdom by Chungliang A. Huang and Jerry Lynch (HarperCollins, 1995) outlines easy-to-understand principles that incorporate the Taoist teachings of self-reflection, simplicity, openness to others, and sharing in order to have mutually beneficial relationships. This is a great book that leaves the spirit feeling grounded and assured. It is perfect as a guide for developing characteristics that support the cooperation and team building necessary to move ahead in the new business world of self-directed work teams.

Career Advancement

The End of Work: The Decline of the Global Labor Force and the Dawn of the Post-Market Era by Jeremy Rifkin (Tarcher/Putnam, 1995) provides help in directing your thinking when creating your new job. This book deals with the reality of the changing business arena, new technology, and how we fit into this all. Since everything is becoming more productive, it encourages people to get on top of the new technology or be left behind.

How to Be Twice As Smart: Boosting Your Brainpower and Unleashing the Miracles of Your Mind by Scott Witt (Prentice Hall, 1983) gives very practical advice for being more effective. The book presents guidelines for handling a variety of issues that slow you down, and it offers methods for getting paperwork done in half the time, speeding up the learning process, impressing people who can help you the most, and solving problems that stump others.

The Secret Language of Success: Using Body Language to Get What You Want by David Lewis (Carroll & Graf Publishers, Inc., 1990) uses illustrations, examples, and exercises to show how to make a positive impression on others, sell yourself successfully (for example, during job interviews), communicate your ideas more powerfully, take charge without being overbearing, learn what others are really thinking, and discern and diffuse hostility in others.

Women Breaking Through: Overcoming the Final 10 Obstacles at Work by Deborah J. Swiss (Peterson's/Pacesetter Books, 1996) provides advice for any woman who has ever felt her career stalled just because she was born female. Swiss outlines strategies for overcoming the remaining obstacles to fair treatment and equal opportunity at work. Good advice for both genders.

221

CHANGING COMPANIES

After ten years or so with the same company, you can easily fall into a predictable and comfortable routine, even if you're working at a job you dislike. Most of us, either consciously or subconsciously, resist the idea of making a change from a position that feels secure. Not surprisingly then, some of us remain stuck too long in jobs going nowhere. Do any of the situations below sound familiar? If any do, it might be time to consider making a change.

Decreased Revenues

When a company starts losing money, it's just a matter of time before managers begin cutting overhead expenses. This means downsizing, which means eliminating projects and people. A company in a downsizing mode is not the most pleasant place to be and certainly not conducive to career growth for most people there.

One of the more negative aspects of downsizing is the politics. People in power tend to make decisions and act on their own behalf and on the behalf of those in whom they have an interest. This often means that if you're not affiliated with the right person or people, you could end up in an undesirable position or out the door, even if you're the most qualified person for a particular job.

The positive aspect of downsizing is that it sometimes brings with it the opportunity to pick up new skills and experience. As managers cut full-time permanent positions, stand-alone short-term projects and temporary positions often become available.

I've been involved in a downsizing myself, and, fortunately, I managed to come out on the other end with a sharper career focus as well as a better position. This required a lot of self-control on my part because, for the first time, I found myself in a position in which others had a great deal of control over my career. It took all my restraint not to let myself be derailed by my anger and frustration over my lack of power. As I struggled to maintain my objectivity, I reevaluated my career direction and looked for new opportunities that grew out of the downsizing.

Bad Press

If you've blown it pretty badly, the resulting bad press may make it impossible for you to advance for a long time. In fact, you may not be able to move up at all until an almost entirely new regime comes in—and possibly not even then because bad news is always passed along. The type of bad press you've received will dictate how much it will inhibit your career. For example, advancing in your career after an extensive history of nonperformance, bungled projects, missed deadlines, poor attitude, or not being a team player will require tremendous effort. You may even have to start over again at a new company, in a new career, or possibly, in a new location.

Less serious transgressions that have resulted in undisciplined behavior or a limited contribution—such as a short period of laziness, an instance or two of poor judgment, or letting outside problems distract you from doing your job for a certain amount of time—are less likely to leave a permanent mark, as long as you demonstrate a true willingness to change and leave the negative behavior behind you.

Incompatibility

One of the best reasons for changing companies is that the culture is no longer compatible with your personality, goals, interests, or values. Networking has long been considered the number-one way to connect with people and move ahead in a career. Naturally, networking, which is simply "word of mouth," is most effective when it occurs between two people who have something in common. It stands to reason, then, that if you are not in sync with the company's culture, you're probably not going to be compatible with a majority of the decision makers there. Most likely, this will limit your ability to effectively network in order to create opportunities for your own progress.

Dead-End Job

A popular belief holds that there are no dead-end jobs, just dead-end people. I have to agree with that to a certain extent, because a "live wire" is not going to allow herself to remain stuck in a position that offers no opportunity for growth. Upward advancement is not necessary for growth. Depending on your career goal, a job that may appear to outsiders to be dead-end may actually be a great growth opportunity for you. Before changing companies, evaluate the potential of the position to get all that you can out of it to help your career goals.

Frank's goal was to start his own consulting practice, and when he landed in a dead-end job, it turned out to be an excellent bridge to achieving his career objective. The position was not geared to any of the company's career tracks; rather it dealt with a lot of external companies. It provided Frank with the perfect opportunity to start building credibility with outside organizations, which he was able to later use as networking contacts when he started his own consulting practice.

An Executive Change

When the CEO, president, or several other top executives leave (or are removed) from their positions of power, it's time to consider a change. The head of the organization establishes the philosophy and tone of an organization. A change at this level produces a ripple effect that may create an atmosphere with which you're no longer comfortable. When a major change occurs within your organization, take the time to research the background of the incoming executive for insight on what the new corporate philosophy might be. Information on how the new executive managed a former company would be helpful.

I remember working at a company whose top executive strongly supported philanthropic causes, which was reflected in the activities to which he committed the company's efforts and resources. When he was replaced, the tone of the company changed considerably. The new head executive significantly minimized the philanthropic effort, as well as the company's presence in the community, and focused on relocating the company in another region.

To get a sense of what you might expect when a major change occurs, ask your public relations department and the executive's former public relations department for literature (e.g., a press kit) on the company where the new executive previously worked. Also, search your public library for articles on either the executive or the company. Members of professional groups may also provide a networking link through which you can gain information.

A number of services are available that provide information on databases about companies. These services can be pretty expensive, though, and may not be readily available at your local library. In addition to the databases, such services generally publish a variety of reference materials, so you can get the information that way as well. *Dun & Bradstreet's Million Dollar Directory* is one such source, as is *Standard and Poor's Register of Corporations, Directors, and Executives*— both these publications provide information on companies and officers within publicly held companies. Financial institutions (e.g., stock brokerage firms) and large corporations are likely to have these database services at their company. A good networking contact at one of these organizations could probably get you the information you need.

A Significant Restructuring

This may come after a change in top executives or as a result of market influences. A major organizational shake-up can initiate a process in which departments within the company continue to be reorganized for a while and no one actually settles into a position for any length of time. This can severely impair your ability to establish a meaningful networking system or develop a career track. It can also remove or consolidate some responsibilities you had hoped to take on as avenues to reach your goal, possibly leaving your career at a standstill.

While these examples are not the only factors pointing toward change, they are some of the most common ones. If you've arrived at a juncture where it would be best to change, you should take the time to plan your move carefully. This will give you a better chance of hooking up with the right company, one that will offer you the greatest potential for progress.

Take a few moments to look at the box Should You Stay With Your Company Or Go? An analysis of your responses should help you decide whether such a change is necessary for you to progress in your career at this time.

SETTING GOALS

If you think you're ready for a career change, you'll first need to determine the next career objective you want to fulfill. Hopefully, you've already brought your career goal into focus and have arrived at a stage where you can identify objectives and implement a plan to get there. Taking the steps to do this will not only save you time, it will also help to reenergize you and renew your commitment.

I've found it often to be true that when someone renews his commitment, he expresses it outwardly so that he sends very positive and self-directed energy to the universe. He walks with more confidence, is more purposeful in his activities, and conveys very clearly that he knows what he wants. That message is responded to by the universe, and what he receives is in direct proportion to that energy.

To ensure that the energy around your career objectives is truly focused, you need to take into account other factors that may influence your decision whether to stay or go. For example, perhaps you've been

SHOULD YOU STAY WITH YOUR COMPANY OR GO?

The following questions will help you sort out any doubts you may have about changing companies and confirm that your final reasons for deciding to stay or go are based on factors that will promote career growth. Respond yes or no to the following statements:

- I have been in the same department and job for the past five years.

- I have accomplished the goal that I came to this company for.

- The philosophy of the company has changed, and it negatively impacts my ability to progress.

- The culture of the company has changed, and I don't fit in as well as I did in the past.

- I have identified my new objectives and determined that it will be difficult to accomplish them in the current culture.

- There are a limited number of positions for the kinds of job I'd like to advance into and all are filled by people who will not likely move for a long time.

- I have had some performance or attitude problems in the past that I might not be able to overcome.

- I have heard serious rumblings that the company will be downsized and/or sold.

- My boss and I do not get along well and I need his or her support in order to advance.

- I believe that the management at my current company is poor and will inhibit the growth potential of the company.

- Since joining the company, new skills, interests, and values have surfaced that I could best develop in a different environment.

If you answered yes to any of these questions, it may be time to change companies.

looking forward to relocating to one of your company's offices in another state or region; or you may be reluctant to let go of certain benefits, such as health insurance or a retirement fund.

It's equally important that you make an honest evaluation of why you want to change companies. If you feel you must change in order to grow, that's a positive reason. If, on the other hand, you're trying to escape from something (like poor performance or bad press), changing employers will not help if you take your behavior with you to the new job. In order to succeed, you will have to improve your attitude at your current job or devise a solid personal plan for establishing a higher standard of performance at your new job.

TAKING STOCK

Take a few moments to assess your current situation so that you can be sure that you actually do need to change companies in order to advance your career. This will help you confirm that you're making the right move—before you make a change that you can't undo.

- I've evaluated where I am with my career and determined what the next growth step should be.

- My performance and capabilities reflect that I'm ready in every respect for the next step.

- I have explored all possibilities at my current company and know for certain that I cannot accomplish my next goal there.

- I'm certain that the obstacles preventing my advancement are not within my power to remove.

- I'm willing to let go of certain benefits (such as a good retirement fund or a generous vacation and holiday schedule) to go after my goal.

- I've determined that my next career step can only be achieved at another company.

CHOOSE CAREFULLY BEFORE YOU MAKE A MOVE

As you shop around for new employers, base your choices on your psychological needs as well as your career needs. If you don't carefully consider these factors before you make a move, you could end up in an organization that doesn't support your goals. For instance, if you enjoy using your leadership ability or you're a creative, independent contributor, and you discover that the new company is very rigid in its culture, policies, and organizational structure, you probably won't be happy or successful there.

Remember, too, that you should look at the big picture when changing companies. Base your decision on more than just a single promotional step. You need to ask yourself whether you'll be able to continue advancing forward within the new environment. Will there be opportunities to advance upward or laterally, and will you be rewarded for doing so? Will there be peer support for projects? Is the company advancing along lines that will provide continued challenge and growth opportunities for you? Will you have any influence in developing new directions?

Art learned too late how important it is to carefully consider the corporate culture and opportunities for personal growth before making a move. A systems engineer, he decided to switch companies several years into his career because he felt uncomfortable in his present company's highly political environment, where upward mobility depended almost completely on whom you knew. An old college friend helped him land a job at his company, and for a time, Art enjoyed his new position. However, after five years with no advancement whatsoever, he became frustrated and discontented.

In his new company, advancement depended solely on seniority. Since the department heads were entrenched in their positions, and Art had less seniority than others in the division, he had virtually no opportunity for advancement. Eventually, he decided to change companies again, but this time, he took the time to evaluate the move against a set of criteria that he developed—a series of questions about the new organization—that helped him determine whether or not he would have opportunity to advance there.

The Checklist for Your New Job Search will help you stay on track as you evaluate and select appropriate companies to pursue.

REVISING YOUR MARKETING TOOLS (RÉSUMÉS AND LETTERS)

If you haven't looked for a job in some years, not only is your résumé undoubtedly out of date, it's out of style and does not reflect your current capabilities. Ten years ago, almost all résumés were written in a chronological format; as a result, they often included superfluous company information and emphasized previous job duties. Résumés today either use a modified chronological format (leaving out the superfluous information) or a functional format (for people with lots of experience). They are viewed as marketing tools that display accomplishments rather than responsibilities. And they are more concise (1–2 pages); not the long documents of years ago. (To read about the different types of résumés, see chapter 5.)

Since most of us do not think about the skills we draw on to accomplish our jobs on a day-to-day basis, we're often at a loss when we try to describe our capabilities in a résumé or interview situation. The further we move forward in our career, the broader our skill base becomes, making it difficult for us to break down our skills into specific categories. You may have successfully brought projects to completion, proposed an idea that helped the company move in a productive direction, or identified and capitalized on an unknown talent in an up-and-coming employee—but none of these accomplishments point to a superior skill set that can be easily categorized in a résumé, even though they all clearly demonstrate your capabilities.

CHECKLIST FOR YOUR NEW JOB SEARCH

The following checklist will help direct you in researching, evaluating, and selecting the companies you target in a new job search. And the information you gather will make you more knowledgeable about the companies at which you eventually interview, which can only help to make you more comfortable during the interviews and show employers that you've done your homework.

- I've compiled a list of companies based on my interests and skills. I developed the list from information I obtained through networking and from sources like the Chamber of Commerce and business references at the public library.

- I've read literature on companies that I'm interested in working for and, through networking contacts, have spoken with their employees whenever possible. In the process, I have narrowed my search to those companies whose major policies and culture are compatible with my own values, style, and work ethics.

- Through my contacts, I've learned the names of the department heads for my profession at the companies that interest me so that I can write to these individuals directly about developing job opportunities.

- I've selected only companies where I would want to work for a long period of time.

- The companies I'm interested in all have good compensation policies and opportunity for advancement.

- The companies I'm interested in all have stable management teams.

- All the companies are in expanding or growth industries.

- I believe I could make a contribution and add value at any of the companies I've chosen.

Emphasize Accomplishments

Here are some sample accomplishments that illustrate the strong people skills, leadership ability, and technical competence that one can develop over time. They are concise examples of the action and positive results associated with handling a specific task that involves some degree of difficulty, such as working well with a limited staff, tight deadlines, and budget constraints. Any of them would be an asset to a résumé:

- Assumed responsibility for and implemented within ninety days a high-priority, past-due project that generated $5 million in revenue.

- Replaced a member on a three-person project team and helped bring the $2 million project to completion on time and under budget.

- Combined three manual financial processes into one computerized system, which was adopted throughout the company, resulting in annual cost savings of $500,000.

- Smoothed out a political bottleneck and recaptured a key account worth $3 million in annual revenues.

If you can find examples along these lines from your own experience, include three or four in the body of your résumé to emphasize your skills. If you're using a chronological format, present your accomplishments after the company name, job title, and statement of responsibility. In a functional résumé format, highlight your accomplishments all in one place—such as in a bulleted list—following the summary statement. You can also include one or two of these accomplishments in your cover letter to demonstrate a specific qualification that the prospective employer is looking for.

Let the situation you're responding to dictate how many accomplishments to use and which ones best demonstrate your skills. If you're answering an ad, choose accomplishments that demonstrate

A CHRONOLOGICAL RÉSUMÉ

John Jacobson

44 Wittenberg Road   513-555-0987 (h)
Oxford, Ohio 43590   513-555-9000 (w)

SUMMARY

As a college-level sports director for eighteen years, I have managed and promoted successful athletic programs. With my newly-earned M.B.A. degree, I want to put my marketing skills to work for a sports manufacturer.

EDUCATION

1996, M.B.A., Miami University, Oxford, Ohio

1982, B.S., Marketing, Michigan State University

WORK EXPERIENCE

Director of Intercollegiate Athletics, 1990–present
Miami University

- Direct athletic program, which produced annual revenues of $2 million and operated on a $1-million budget
- Supervise 25-member coaching staff, who have collectively improved their team's win/loss records by 25 percent
- Increased attendance at athletic events in 1994–95 school year by 20 percent to highest levels in school's history
- Played a major role in development of new $3-million sports facility on campus

Assistant Director of Athletics, 1986–1990
Baldwin-Wallace College, Berea, Ohio

- Helped coordinate an athletic program that featured three intramural teams and twenty-five intramural programs
- Evaluated and made hiring recommendations for three coaching positions
- Purchased uniforms, equipment, and supplies
- Scheduled maintenance of fields, gym setups, and cleanups
- Determined player eligibility

Head Basketball Coach, 1982-1986
University of Toledo, Toledo, Ohio

- Recruited players with academic and athletic potential
- Led team through four winning seasons

PERSONAL SPORTS INVOLVEMENT

Forward, Michigan State University Spartans, 1980-1982

Cyclist; have participated in 100 cycling events in last fourteen years

A FUNCTIONAL RÉSUMÉ

Marie Jonello
19 Webster Road
N. Miami, Florida 33138
305-555-9875

Job Objective: A position as a relocation counselor

Summary
As a counseling professional with twenty years of experience and a real estate broker with five years' experience, I can anticipate problems and offer practical housing, education, and other solutions for families being relocated by their companies. Having made five major moves in my adult life, I am sensitive to the adjustments that relocation requires and how to make transitions smoother.

Real Estate
- Averaged $1 million a year in residential real estate sales for past four years, selling part-time
- Specialized in working with relocation services of major companies; found desirable housing situations for twenty clients in last two years
- Have demonstrated a capacity to work with the most difficult and demanding clients, who were referred to me by my office manager because of my ability to work with them

Counseling
- Evaluated clients' problems and concerns by asking questions, listening carefully to answers, and comparing information gathered from close friends, relatives, and employers
- Worked one-on-one and in a group setting to make clients aware of their behavior and its effects on their work, families, and personal lives
- Received fifty letters from substance abusers in recovery who credit me with playing a major role in their return to sobriety

Administration
- Orchestrated the successful functioning of a facility employing 55 people and treating as many as 100 clients at a time; follow-up surveys indicate program success—50 percent of clients sober and working a year after their "graduation"
- Built a database of 500 clients on computer; by maintaining regular contact, successfully did business with one-third

Employment History
Real Estate Agent, Century 21, Fort Lauderdale, Florida, 1992–present
Director, Rosemont Center, Fort Lauderdale, Florida, 1989–present
Substance Abuse Counselor, The Lakeland Institute, Lorain, Ohio, 1986–1989
Resident Adviser, Evergreen Home for Girls, Lexington, Kentucky, 1981–1986
Social Worker, City of Pittsburgh, 1976–1981

Education and Licenses
Licensed real estate salesperson, State of Florida, 1992
Real Estate Certificate Program, Dade Community College, 1992
Master's in Social Work, Columbia University, 1977
B.A., English, Hunter College, 1974

Interests
Deep-sea fishing, underwater photography, bridge

qualifications appropriate for the need advertised. If sending an unsolicited letter and résumé to a company, use accomplishments that align with the information about the company that you gathered in your research.

Also, be prepared with some "success stories" (these are also accomplishments—activities carried out with a positive result) that you can (briefly) share in interviews to answer questions like: "What was one of the biggest challenges you faced in your last job?" or "What contributions did you offer to help your department run more smoothly and effectively?" (see the box Developing Your Success Stories).

Updating Your Résumé

A review of the information and Resources in chapter 5 will provide you with the basic foundation for developing your résumé. Completing the following steps should help you bring your information up-to-date:

1. Compile a list of ten or twelve of your job-related accomplishments. If you, like most people, tend to forget what you've done after the work is complete, you may find it helpful to ask colleagues, friends, and family members who are familiar with your work to help you to remember some of your accomplishments; you can also draw examples from copies of your performance reviews, memos, letters, and other documents in your career files.

2. Refine and focus the accomplishments so they emphasize the skills necessary to support your goal. For instance, a writer might say: "Wrote and edited a monthly ten-page training and development newsletter that was distributed companywide." A training manager responsible for a similar newsletter would have a different focus: "Developed a corporatewide training and development newsletter that provided state-of-the-art information to update the technical staff."

3. Choose a résumé style that fits the type of jobs and industries you will pursue. I suggest creating your résumé in both a chronological and a functional format and see which works best for you. The

chronological format is probably most appropriate when you're seeking a job exactly like the one you have or that advances your career to the next logical step. Even so, use a chronological format only if your career has proceeded in a steady upward fashion with no glitches. The functional résumé works best when you have a lot of experience and you wish to highlight just the information necessary to support your goal.

4. Review the résumé to ensure that there are no negative pieces of information and that all the information is pertinent to the goal. Be sure that your résumé does not include any negative attention-getters, as outlined in the box Oops! I Didn't Think.

JOB HUNTING WHILE EMPLOYED

You certainly want to keep the job you have while you're looking for a better one. Proceed with care and be discreet.

Should You Tell Your Boss That You're Looking for a New Job?

If you tell her, how should you word it? You need to consider the circumstances and the personality of the manager. If she is open-minded and supportive of your advancement, no problem—tell her. You can take your cues from how she's reacted in the past to other employees who've left the company for greener pastures.

If you've already explored opportunities in the company, and the two of you have discussed what's needed for your career advancement (maybe as part of a performance review process), then she may support your action. On the other hand, if she is the type of person who believes that leaving means you're being disloyal to her, then you've got a problem. In this case, be very discreet about your search, because if she hears of it, you are likely to injure your relationship with her or may even be fired. She may not be happy about your leaving, even though it is for your advancement, simply because it will create a

OOPS! I DIDN'T THINK
(AVOIDING RÉSUMÉ BLOOPERS)

If you can avoid the common mistakes listed below, you will be well on your way to creating winning résumés and cover letters that have a high probability of passing the screening process and being forwarded to a decision maker rather than to the reject pile.

- **Showing more experience than the job requires.** The ad asked for five-plus years' experience, and you show twenty. The result? The company may think you're overqualified. Better to say "experienced" in the summary and leave off dates in the body. Or, better yet, apply for jobs that fit your experience level.

- **Making it too long and too detailed.** More than two pages is too much. Get to the point—keep paragraphs to two concise sentences.

- **Highlighting demotions.** Demotions are easy to spot when titles are used. When there has been a demotion, don't list any title for any of your jobs; just list the department name and show your responsibilities or accomplishments in that job. Be prepared to explain why you were demoted in an interview.

- **Highlighting job gaps.** If you show dates, it will be glaringly obvious where gaps have occurred. Consider leaving off dates on all jobs when there have been job gaps. This will give you a chance to explain any significant job gaps in person in the interview.

- **Presenting information inconsistently.** If you leave off dates, titles, etc., for one job or in one area of the résumé, then leave off the same information in all areas of the résumé.

Continued

OOPS! I DIDN'T THINK—*Continued*

- **Not including a cover letter.** If you send a résumé in response to an ad, for an anticipated opening, or as part of a cold mailing, then it should have a cover letter and in that letter you should specify your area of interest. Refer to the ad when that's appropriate and, if possible, include someone at the company whose name you have permission to use as a reference.

- **Making it too general.** Target the language in both the résumé and the cover letter to the company (if unsolicited) and to the specific job (when responding to an ad). Every résumé sent in response to an ad should be targeted to the needs of that ad—and the language in the résumé and cover letter should be targeted to the industry.

- **Stating a weak job objective.** Be sure to be specific. For example, say: "Seeking a responsible human resources position in which I can apply my skills in benefits development, staffing, and compensation at (name of company) to enhance the department's efforts." Don't say: "Seeking a responsible human resources position."

- **Not taking the time to make it presentable.** To project a positive, professional image, print both the résumé and cover letter on a laser printer and use the same high-quality paper.

- **Stapling pages together.** Do not staple the résumé—instead put your name on both pages in case they're separated.

- **Including irrelevant information.** Do not include salary history, personal information, marital status, or references to race or gender. If membership in a culturally based association supports your objective, it is all right to list it.

- **Sending it out with typos and grammatical errors.** A misspelling or glaring grammatical error will instantly land your résumé and letter in the reject pile. Be sure to check and double-check your résumé and cover letters and then have others proofread them for you.

vacancy, which means that she has to take the time and effort to find your replacement or do without someone in your position.

If your manager finds out anyway, explain that you are investigating opportunities at this point (if you've had a discussion about your advancement, tie it in to that). Also, assure her that if you do find another position, you will discuss a departure date with her before you accept so that projects can be turned over to someone else as part of a smooth transition. Then reinforce how positive your relationship has been for you, how you expect to maintain that relationship, and that you hope she understands you're seeking a change purely for your own career growth.

Whom Do You Use as References?

Most companies (if not all of the larger ones) do not allow their managers to give references in their official capacity as a representative of the company, so prospective employers are not surprised when you do not give your former manager as a reference. Some managers will give a reference anyway and just ask that you call them at home. They will let you know when they are willing to do that.

Other good references are peers or people in your professional groups who have worked on projects with you; clients or customers; and public officials and high-ranking service professionals (i.e., doctors and lawyers).

A word of advice: Choose your references wisely. You want people who you trust will give you a strong reference and who can be discreet about your job search (you don't want word getting back to your manager). As a professional courtesy, you should speak with all potential references before you give their names—both to confirm their support and to remind them to be discreet.

What Reason Should You Give for Looking for a New Job?

Be prepared for prospective employers to ask why are you leaving your current job. They may be concerned that you're being fired or are a deadbeat. You're in great shape if your current manager knows you're looking because you can simply state that she knows, you have a great working relationship, but the opportunity you seek for growth does not exist at your current company. Then move right into the reason you're talking with this employer—because you believe that opportunity might be with him.

Never, ever say to anyone that you are making a change because you are unhappy (even if you are). It smacks of negativity and can give rise to the suspicion that you are a disgruntled employee who has a negative outlook on work. So, scream in private if you must, but put on a happy face in your search.

Should You Take Job Search Calls at Work?

Making a job change is a personal matter. I'd get an answering service with voice mail (on your home phone or through a personal service) and receive your calls there. Even if your manager knows you're looking, you don't want your job search to take time away from the work at hand. After all, you want to maintain this job—you might end up keeping it.

How Do You Schedule Interviews?

Explain to the prospective employer that since you are currently employed, you would prefer to interview in the evening or on a Saturday. But expect that most will want you to accommodate their schedules, and you will, too, if you're serious about your job search. When you explain your situation to prospective employers, they may be willing to do some initial screening by phone. If not, arrange to take personal or vacation days for interviews.

PREPARING FOR THE INTERVIEW

Having a clear sense of your prospective employers and the company's culture can save you time and eliminate some of the anxiety about interviewing. Obviously, the best way to find out some of the inside scoop on employers is through networking, but you can also gain some insight by checking resources at a public library or by contacting the

MORE JOB SEARCH ADVICE

For more basics about résumés and interviewing, take a look at chapter 5 in this book. While it addresses résumés and other job search tools particularly for job search novices, it has some advice that people who've been working for some time will find useful, especially the box Questions You Shouldn't Be Asked and the table Nine Steps to a Successful Interview.

company's media relations office (if it's large enough to have one); it will usually be happy to mail you an information packet. If your research uncovers information that makes you aware that it would be impossible to work in a particular culture, then you won't have to waste time pursuing opportunities with that company.

As you know, if you've been through several interviews yourself, there is no set format as to how the process unfolds. You may start by interviewing with a human resources person, or you may be interviewed right away by the hiring manager. Generally, you will have at least two interviews before a decision is made, and many times three. Some interviews might even take place by phone—or even by e-mail—if you are a good distance away.

Most often, interviewers will ask questions specifically based on the information provided on your résumé. For this reason, you should include information that you know you want to be questioned about so that you'll have a better chance to sell yourself. Here are some key points for effective interviewing:

Build rapport. Have a conversation—as opposed to behaving as if you're being interrogated. As a person with work experience, you are more on a colleague level with the interviewer than on the novice level of a person just starting out. Listen to questions, repeat for clarification if necessary, then respond succinctly. And ask questions yourself. Have an exchange while seeking areas of common interest and benefit (i.e., "We seem to have a similar vision about the function").

Avoid canned answers. Be prepared to share concepts about the industry, the direction the company should be going, effective management styles, and the like. Think beforehand about questions you may be asked, so you'll know what information you want to communicate. Consider what issues would be important to you if you were in the decision maker's shoes, and, during the interview, allow that information to flow naturally into the conversation.

Prepare for sensitive and tough questions. Decide beforehand how you will handle sensitive questions. Often, it's the executives who ask the very direct questions (no matter what their human resources people advise); therefore, the higher the job level you seek, the higher the probability that you will encounter questions that challenge your overall technical knowledge and vision about the work, as well as your maturity. In addition to demonstrating your functional or technical knowledge, you'll want to give answers that reveal your motivational level, political savvy, and management style, as well as your technical and administrative strengths and weaknesses.

As a person of color moving into a key position in a predominantly white environment, you may be asked questions about how you would handle situations on the job. You may have a challenging situation described to you, be asked to respond, and then have your answer probed or challenged to get your reaction.

Also, you may want to divert personal questions or look for and respond to the underlying reason that the interviewer is asking the question. For example, when an interviewer asks, "Are you married?" you might respond by saying, "Is there a family-oriented culture here?" While it's usually appropriate to deflect such personal questions, my own experience tells me to just answer them frankly. Experienced people generally rely on the value they are perceived as bringing to the company, rather than on issues that may be detractors for people just starting out.

Be prepared to explain why you want to change companies. It's not unreasonable to change because your philosophy is inconsistent with the former (or new) management or because the growth potential is limited at the company. However, avoid any explanation that would come across as petty. For all questions, honesty in your responses is the best course.

Model the behavior that fits the job. Your attire, smile, attitude, conversation, and energy should all project intellectual curiosity, confidence, self-motivation, and personality traits that indicate you will fit into the company's culture.

Close on a positive note. If you're interested in the job, say so and ask what the next step will be. Then follow up with a thank-you note. Most people don't, so you'll be ahead of the game when you do. If you found out about the opening through a networking contact, follow up with that person so that you can obtain his or her support in getting the job.

HANDLING INTERVIEWS

An interview is simply an exchange of information that, hopefully, is carried out in a conversational vein. You'll do your best in an interview when you know what to expect and have prepared yourself accordingly. I suggest you reread chapter 5 for a refresher on the basics of effective interviewing. The tips included there will make the process easier and help you as you prepare to talk with people in both formal and informal settings.

After years of working and interacting with others, you've probably received some consistent feedback about your communication style. Now is the time to take note of that feedback so that you can

DEVELOPING YOUR SUCCESS STORIES FOR THE INTERVIEW

A well-phrased (and well-timed) story of how you successfully handled responsibilities on a former job can do a lot to help you ace an interview. It allows you to display your talents, skills, and accomplishments without having to be obvious about "tootin' your horn." And it's a much more comfortable and natural way to communicate information about yourself than just responding to questions. Here are some guidelines for effective success storytelling:

- **Choose your story ahead of time.** Your story should be based on the research you've done on the company and about the job. You want to choose a story that will display skills that are in line with the position you're going for.

- **Write the story ahead of time.** Even though you will be communicating a story about something you know, you can still approach the telling from several angles. Writing it out before the interview will help you decide which would be the best slant and what you want to emphasize. Leadership? Communication skills? Team work?

- **Make sure to include your accomplishments.** Don't forget the point of the storytelling: to establish your capability for the job. Get the right accomplishments in the story.

- **Practice relating the story back to the job you're interviewing for.** Don't forget why you're telling the story. Get back to how it relates to your qualifications for the job. For example: "Do you ever have that kind of thing happen here?"

- **Rehearse.** The story may sound great when you're by yourself reading it back. No pressure there. Go through a mock interview with someone, and tell the story in this setting. You'll find it takes a little practice. Plus, the role-playing will allow you to time it. Don't go on and on with your story—keep it under 2 minutes. If you don't have a ready audience, then audiotape or videotape yourself.

develop a strategy for using the behaviors for which you've been complimented and minimizing any less desirable traits (like taking too long to answer a question, for example). Since you want to make a good, strong impression, your attitude needs to be positive in every respect. Your facial expressions and body language should be consistent with that positive attitude.

Also, keep in mind that in an interview, you can enhance the very positive impression you make initially by demonstrating that you have a goal to which you're committed. I remember being impressed with a client who, at first glance, seemed to have all the tickets—brains, education, style, and wit, as well as options. And that was the problem; she had difficulty committing to any of her options. After probing for a while and receiving only evasive answers, I concluded that she really needed to think more about her priorities so that she could decide which of her options to pursue. I could understand her dilemma, but my opinion of her capabilities diminished simply because I felt that if she really had it together, she would have had a goal before initiating her search, and as a result, she would have been more focused.

JOB AND SALARY NEGOTIATION

Salary is always based on the job and not necessarily on what you want or feel you are worth. It's based on the current market value of the position. Never discuss salary, except in general terms or in context of a range, until the job responsibilities and reporting relationship have been agreed to.

I've noticed that handling salary negotiations is where most experienced professionals blow it. Many people tend to fixate on a certain salary, whether it is appropriate or not; they base their expectations on what they were paid previously and on their experience. The irony is that the salary you expect might be too low.

Understand that when an employer wants to interview you and make you an offer, you have some power—and you can exercise your power to elevate the amount you're offered. If you have a realistic ballpark figure in mind going into the interview, then you can start the negotiations at a higher point and work down if necessary. Network with associates and check trade journals, associations, and other sources to find out an appropriate salary range for the position. Also, remember that you are an experienced individual, not a recent college graduate, so the salary will be dependent on the job, its market value, and your experience rather than on a standard rate that may be used for entry-level new hires.

On the other hand, if you quickly give up your power in the salary negotiations, you can easily reduce the amount the company is prepared to pay you. For example, poor image and lack of research may lead you to say to the employer something like, "I know I'll have to take less than I did on my last job." You certainly will now that you've mentioned it!

In some cases, however, it may be wise to accept a lower salary than your former position paid. For example, if your technical skills are not up to par or you're relocating to a geographic area that typically pays less, you'll need to take such factors into consideration when developing an appropriate salary range for yourself. Your primary consideration in these instances is that the job is one that will advance your career. Whatever the case, don't immediately advertise your willingness to accept a lower salary; let the employer be the first to take the negotiations in this direction.

The keys to successfully negotiating salary include:

- Deciding what you want in terms of job responsibilities, salary, benefits, and other perks. Before salary negotiations begin, make a mental note of what you hope to get, the least you'd take, and where you might be willing to compromise.

- Determining what reasons you should give for getting what you want—what your discussion and/or argument will be—then, switching sides and looking at the picture from the employer's point of view—anticipating objections and planning a response to them.

- Being prepared to compromise, as long as the compromise does not affect your future career growth.

- Not playing games. Counteroffers after the top offer has been put on the table generally do not work out well. If the employer feels pushed into a corner because he has an immediate need for your services, he may accept the counteroffer, but your future may not be too bright at the company—if you're even retained beyond his immediate need. Even worse, if he feels like you're playing games or being too pushy, he may very well reconsider the job offer.

SETTING UP FOR THE NEXT JOB

Unlike the novice whose value has to be proved, you will start at a new company as a confident, experienced professional in possession of your career and your work skills. It's all right to let it be known that you have your sights on developing in a specific area or that you aspire to a certain job or want to take on more responsibilities. Look for such opportunities to open up and then volunteer for them—such initiative and commitment are two of the traits that lead to further success. As a matter of fact, this type of behavior is expected from professionals— and the higher the job level, the more it is expected.

RESOURCES

The New Rules of the Job Search Game: Why Today's Managers Hire—and Why They Don't by Jackie Larson and Cheri Comstock (Adams). Written by people on the hiring side of the table, this book explains why job hunters who are not the best fit for a job usually get it and how to become the sort of person that companies want to hire. It also demonstrates how to use conversation to bring you closer to the job. Very helpful and informative for the committed professional.

Power Networking by Donna Fisher and Sandy Vilas (Mountain/Harbour) provides fifty-five strategies for effective networking, as well as an assessment to determine your networking quotient. A good book for experienced people who are looking to change companies.

Rites of Passage at $100,000+: The Insider's Lifetime Guide to Executive Job-Changing and Faster Career Progress by John Lucht (Holt & Co., 1993) is a very upscale approach to the job search. Covers everything from clothes to the style of pen you should carry—and why. A great guide for that executive who has grown beyond the job and needs to make a change but doesn't know how—and may not even realize that he or she needs to make a change. (Lucht also has a comprehensive workbook of the same title supporting this book, which includes information on taxes, outplacement, and negotiating an ideal employment contract.)

Reference material available at public libraries

Dun & Bradstreet's Million Dollar Directory, Dun & Bradstreet, Inc., 3 Century Drive, Parsippany, NJ 07054. An annual guide to 160,000 public companies in the U.S.; lists the products offered by each company.

Standard and Poor's Register of Corporations, Directors, and Executives, 25 Broadway, New York, NY 10004. Published annually, this directory lists products and key people in more than 45,000 public companies in the U.S., including biographies of over 70,000 individuals.

CHAPTER

GIVING BACK: COMPLETING THE CYCLE OF SUCCESS

In establishing my own success pattern, I set some goals (and was pushed into others) and worked to achieve them. Gradually, in my small way, I began to be viewed as a success, and, by some, as a role model. I overheard people I knew comparing me to others. "She's an 'Ollie" or "She's not an 'Ollie," they sometimes said. How does one get to this place called success?

For me, it has simply been a matter of being motivated to set a goal, accomplishing it by whatever honorable means possible, then using that as a step up to my next goal—and accomplishing that new goal by whatever honorable means possible. Out of curiosity, I began to look at the careers of highly visible, very successful people and those of others I know personally who have achieved success. I found there to be certain qualities that all successful people share:

- They are moved by the spirit of love of something or someone. They are motivated by something beyond money and, usually, beyond themselves. Great athletic performances, unbelievable acts of courage, and other extraordinary achievements usually stem from a desire to do something for someone the person cares for deeply or for something (often an ideal) that inspires her passion.

Carol Maninger, a social worker at Redwood Coast Regional Center in Clearlake Park, California, is such a person. For over twenty years, she has dedicated her life to working to ensure that developmentally disabled people would have the chance to live a quality life and be able to live in their own homes instead of being institutionalized. "My challenge is to try to figure out a way to substitute negative behavior so that the people can be successful in the community. Success for me is seeing a person develop new, positive behavior."

• They have charted a path and stay on it to reach their goal. These highly motivated and self-directed people haven't copped out, taken a job just to get by, or been persuaded to follow someone else's path. Rather, fueled by a passion or a mission, they have allowed themselves to be divinely guided to use the gifts that they have been given for the highest good of all.

Johnnie Savoy, executive director of College Bound, in Cerritos, California, is such a person. She founded the organization with her husband to help African Americans, Hispanic Americans, and Native Americans get into college. "You don't take on something like this unless you have the heart for it," she says. "You have to have a real commitment to the cause and the kids. When I look into their faces, I can't give up. One of the greatest rewards I get is when I see them make it and become successful. When I see something in a kid and that kid passes my expectation, or when someone beats the odds by being accepted into the school of their choice—when they didn't think they would make it—my fulfillment is in seeing their joy." In helping others beat the odds, Johnnie, like all successful people, knows that her success comes from a strong desire—in her case to help young people get the education they need. If your desire is strong enough, you can achieve the same kind of success, too.

- People who achieve success ultimately speak a similar language, which evolves from the spiritual strength and character they've developed by achieving a tough goal. And they project their faith by behaving in a way that shows they believe in their ability to accomplish their goals. This is why when successful people say "Yes, you can!" with such certainty, it's because they have accomplished their goals in spite of insurmountable obstacles.

- People who achieve success go through a similar process in achieving that success. They are challenged to overcome roadblocks that seem to appear out of nowhere. Remember Kerry Strugs, the Olympic gymnast who hurt her leg in the 1996 Summer Olympics just before her final jump but jumped anyway? And took the gold medal? Clearly, a roadblock is just another challenge to a success-oriented person—something that causes her to stretch in one or more skill areas and go beyond what she thought she was capable of.

- Successful people do not limit themselves, nor do they limit others. They know the process is ageless, timeless, nongender-specific, and colorblind—and that, fueled by a belief in their vision, enables them to set a goal at any time or any age and accomplish it.

Anyone who has accomplished a difficult goal needed the motivation to do so. And while this motivation may be different for each person, it is always something more than money. You know that you are on a plateau of success when you are motivated by your commitment and belief rather than money or glory, and you allow this motivation to take you where you want to go.

You should go as high as your motivation will carry you. And you will know how high that is by how you respond to the challenges or opportunities that will be presented to you at each step along the way. At the point that challenges become burdens and new opportunities no longer interest you, you will know that you have reached your pinnacle.

Maybe the challenges will never become burdensome, and new opportunities will always be exciting—if so, there is no limit to how high you can go.

"WHAT DO YOU MEAN BY WHAT YOU SAY?"

■

To succeed, we've got to be involved with other people—we cannot do it alone. Those of us who desire to accomplish a goal need to acquire as part of our mix of skills the ability to deal successfully with others; it is our responsibility to learn how to do that.

As a diversity consultant, Roberta has wise advice about interacting with others: "I believe in the platinum rule, which is to do unto others as they would have done unto themselves. Everyone does not want to be treated the way that you want to be treated. For instance, not everyone in the corporate world would consider it a reward to be the focus of a big lunch—some cultures consider that kind of glory embarrassing. Or a Hispanic man who's offered a promotion that takes him away from his family may not see that promotion as a benefit at all; while a white male probably won't understand why the Hispanic male doesn't appreciate it. Neither one of them is wrong, it's just a case of different values and a need for communication on both sides to gain understanding."

Roberta, quoting Workforce 2000, a study conducted by the Hudson Institute,* points out that 75 percent of new entrants into the workforce in the future will be people of color, immigrants, and women. "Obviously, we cannot concentrate on just dealing effectively with the white race. We have to

---

* The Hudson Institute, an Indianapolis, Indiana, think tank, worked with the U.S. Bureau of Labor Statistics to develop Workforce 2000, a 1987 study that predicted what the workforce would look like in year 2000.

learn to deal with each other. We have to learn to be cognizant of what is going on and not be exclusionary. We need to understand that people in all cultures simply express themselves in ways that are comfortable for them and which may be different from the culture we know. We all need to learn to value each other and respect our differences."

"The 1992 riots in Los Angeles showed what happens when we don't reach out and try to understand one another. Blacks and Koreans were in a conflict that may have been avoided if there had been better communication between them—then perhaps the Koreans would have learned how blacks feel about their not making eye contact, while blacks would have learned that the Koreans mean no disrespect by that."

Clearly, to advance, we all need to increase our self-awareness by taking time to find out where the other person is coming from. The ability to live and work in harmony with others comes from an understanding heart.

■

ROBERTA YOUTAN KAY
Caucasian-American
Corporate trainer, Camarillo, California
Specialty: Cultural diversity, team building, and communications

THE RESPONSIBILITY AT THE TOP

So far, I've stressed the importance of acquiring skills, developing effective networks, creating opportunities, drawing on your motivation—in short, doing all the things necessary to grasp the golden ring of success. Having reached the pinnacle of success, should you then just set yet another goal and climb higher? Should anything be different after you're there? Surely, new dimensions of your life will have opened up—a new home, cars, clothes, investments, maybe a boat or a vacation home. But still—is that all? Will all these luxuries that come with success give you true satisfaction?

I think not.

True success, with all its satisfaction and fulfillment, comes when we complete the cycle of our success by giving back to others who are struggling to reach their own goals. Actually, the higher you go, the more opportunity you will have to give back to the universe and to help others. And when it is time to give that help, you will know because people will come to you for advice. You may be asked to give on an individual basis (personally mentoring or coaching someone) or to join others in movements for social change. To continue evolving, you will have to willingly give more of yourself.

Does this mean that you are responsible for giving indiscriminately to anyone who asks for a handout? No. You are not in the business of giving handouts. It is your responsibility to give a hand—a word of encouragement, an introduction, a tip on how to do something, but not to do it for them—not to get in the way of their growth. You should be there to support their effort.

As you move to increasingly higher levels, you will find yourself serving as a mentor for others. Effective mentoring is a positive way to help others—but it's serious business, says George Fraser in *Success Runs in Our Race*. "As young people receive the benefits of mentoring, they grow and achieve. Their roots go deep into the community and, once established, they give back," Fraser writes.

LET YOUR HELP BE COLORBLIND

When I attend conferences and professional meetings, I am often approached by both white people and people of color for guidance in their careers. These are the people who have had a chord struck in them by something I have said or done that provides the encouragement they need. I don't let myself be inhibited by their color or gender or by sticking to some preconceived plan that I have for helping others—I just simply respond.

Recently, I attended a community support group, looking for a way to use my services to help support its program (whose target population was mostly people of color). I made a presentation outlining

MENTORING: A NETWORKING NUDGE

Being a good mentor means that you endeavor to bring out the best in those you focus on. Here are seven important keys to successful mentoring.

- Be attentive and listen. Once you have committed to mentoring someone, you must accept that your attentions have to be focused during mentoring sessions.

- Keep your word. Chances are disappointment has been a big part of the lives of those you are mentoring. You must not add to those disappointments.

- Bring something to the party. Have a story to tell, an experience to relate, something intriguing to impart.

- Nurture the spirit as well as the mind. Mentor the spirit, too. Uplift the person you're mentoring.

- Put yourself in their shoes; try to understand the particular mind-set of the age group and background of those whom you mentor.

- Cheerlead, encourage, praise, salute. Generally, those who seek mentors have been deprived of positive feedback. One of your biggest jobs is to give that to them.

- Don't always assume that those whom you are mentoring will get the point. Make sure they understand or see the value in what you are telling and showing them.

Reprinted with permission of William Morrow & Co., Inc. from *Success Runs in Our Race* by George C. Fraser, 1994.

the kind of service that I could provide. A young white woman in the group came up to me after the presentation and asked me if I would give her private counseling to help her with her career. She told me all the things she had already done and how she was stuck. She had done her homework and was not expecting something for nothing or for someone to do it for her. She simply wanted guidance, and my message had struck a chord in her; she felt that I could—and would—help her.

It is not unusual for me to be approached by a white person after a lecture or seminar, but in a presentation that was directed specifically to people of color and given to an audience that was 99 percent black, I was surprised that the message most strongly reached a white person.

It shouldn't have surprised me really, because the simple truth is that the universe is colorblind. No doubt, you've been helped along the way by white people as well as by people of color. You, in turn, must do the same. And, when you are led to give that help, give the person what she needs, not what you think she needs (see "What Do You Mean By What You Say?").

Also, keep in mind that helping others does not mean that you no longer need help in accomplishing your goals—because you do. Not only will you need help, but you will also have to reach out to people who are different from you, both to ask for help and to offer your help. Part of the process of expanding, progressing, and succeeding involves learning about and interacting effectively with others.

RESOURCES

Control Your Destiny or Someone Else Will: Lessons in Mastering Change by Noel M. Tichy and Stratford Sherman (HarperCollins, 1994). This book is based on the principles Jack Welch used to revolutionize General Electric: face reality as it is, not as it was or as you wish it were; be candid with everyone; don't manage, lead;

change before you have to; and if you don't have a competitive advantage, don't compete. It includes a test for determining if you have what it takes to lead. This is a great book for giving you the kick in the pants to move forward. It won't ensure you won't make mistakes—it just encourages you to move forward.

The Eleven Commandments of Wildly Successful Women by Pamela Boucher Giberd (MacMillan, 1996). Provides good resource material that is applicable to anyone. She reinforces the idea that women are in charge of their careers and their lives, and in so doing, encourages you to clarify goals, values, and personal definitions of success that can lead to new insights and action. Addresses mainstream business, career, and personal challenges. Gives some lively, practical advice and information.

PART 3

REENGINEERING YOUR CAREER

W hat comes now? Now that you've been successful working within "the system"? Now that you know you can set tough goals and achieve them? Now that you know that the only limitations that truly exist are the ones you place on yourself?

Perhaps one of the greatest rewards of arriving at this stage is knowing that you have a number of options for redefining your path if you so wish. And years of experience have given you confidence. You know that once you define that path, you can make it work because you bring more to everything that you're involved in now—more skills, more wisdom, a greater sense of yourself, your capabilities and priorities.

At this stage, you might find yourself asking some new questions about your career. Should you work on changing your job so you can focus on the parts you like? Would a less stressful job be the answer—doing some part of the work you enjoy but leaving a lot more free time and energy for other pursuits? Or should you expand your career in some way, even take on new challenges? Is this the time to make that significant career change you've dreamed of making for years? Or to work more independently? Should you consider contracting or consulting or working part-time—or even starting your own business?

This last part of the book looks at the issues and concerns you may face as you reassess your work and career and the role you want them to play in your life now. It's at this stage that you will most likely develop and live your own version of the American dream.

■

SETTING SHORT- AND LONG-TERM GOALS

The time may come when your career assumes a significantly different value in the overall scheme of things. For some people, it becomes less of a priority; for others, parts of it take on an expanded, richer role in their lives. This shift may occur quickly and dramatically; for example, as the result of a major event such as a serious illness or the loss of a loved one. Or it may be less dramatic; perhaps turning 50 or 60 or reaching a certain milestone in your life or career causes a subtle and gradual realization that a change is in order, as you experience decreasing interest in activities associated with your profession, your job, or the way you work.

A friend described his change to me this way: "The alarm clock went off one morning, and I rolled over, looked at it for a moment, and wondered why it was ringing. At that point, I knew it was time to restructure my life. I had just returned from a month at my cabin in the country, working at my other business, and had absolutely no desire to return to my corporate job."

Whatever the catalyst for change is for you, when the time comes you will have a sense of it within yourself. It may even happen at a high point in your career, when you find yourself feeling that something is missing or that there's a new interest developing in your life.

This process of restructuring and refocusing is much like what you did in the first and second stages of your career; the difference now is that, hopefully, you have more options because you bring more to the table. Having already proven yourself, you're in the enviable position of being able to shape your career on your own terms.

GOLDEN HARVEST OR DUST BOWL?

First, you need to consider where you are at this point in time and how much leverage and choice you actually have. If you've developed a career based on what you truly enjoy doing and you've successfully passed through stages one and two, then you'll probably be well-positioned to take on and achieve whatever you choose to do at this point in your life. If, on the other hand, the first two stages didn't go as well as you would have liked—or they did, but you didn't plan or organize the other aspects of your life well—you may have to struggle through and scramble to set your career on track now. At a time in your life when other priorities and psychological needs may demand that you redistribute your energy and devote less time to your career, you may find yourself still having to operate at the high energy level and with the same financial concerns of stages one and two.

Because of poor planning or bad circumstances, I've known people to arrive at stage three, after years of working at a successful and lucrative career, with no real financial stability or savings to speak of. Katherine is one of them. A contractor who commanded high fees handling very difficult issues for a branch of the city's housing authority, Katherine was well-respected and her services were in demand. She enjoyed an affluent, even extravagant lifestyle, wearing fashionable clothes and buying a new luxury car every two years.

Katherine's comfortable lifestyle came to an abrupt halt, however, when a change in the department's policy forced management not to renew her contract. Katherine had not planned at all for this possibility. She had no financial reserves and had not developed or explored any other avenues for marketing her skills to maintain her lifestyle. Not surprisingly, at 47, she had neither the drive nor the time to begin again, to develop a new career that could support the lifestyle she'd been accustomed to. Eventually, she was able to find another job through networking contacts, but the pay was considerably less than what she'd gotten in the past. Poor planning had left Katherine ill-prepared for the future.

Like Katherine, Hank had a successful career, but unlike her, he prepared and planned well for his future. As a result, he found his later years to be the best time of his life. At 62, when failing health necessitated a change in lifestyle, Hank restructured his tax preparation and financial-planning business so that he could work only four months a year. He had prepared ahead of time for this eventuality by bringing on and developing other talented people so that they could manage the major responsibilities of his business. Hank had also invested in property rentals that gave him a regular income without many demands on his time. He'd managed career stages one and two and his own finances so well that stage three turned out to be for him what it should be for everyone—a time of golden harvest.

NEW PRIORITIES, CHANGING INTERESTS

You don't have to spend your entire career preparing to accommodate a future change you may want to make. Often, just a little advance planning is enough to refocus and ready yourself. For Louise, the catalyst for reassessing her priorities came when some family members were diagnosed with life-threatening illnesses. As she struggled to cope, supervisors at the high-tech firm where she worked asked her to take on the more responsible position of senior consultant. Faced with the decision to accept or decline the challenge in order to move forward in management, Louise realized that her next move would determine the quality of the rest of her life. She got subtle pressure from her peer group to take the new job, but Louise had reached the point where the opinions and judgment of others carried little weight. She decided that the need to have less stress in her life and spend more time saying "I love you" to the people she cared for had become her top priority.

Once she had made the decision, Louise set about organizing things to accommodate this shift in priorities. She began by cutting her spending, eliminating anything she could do without. Then she set a goal to continue working full-time for eighteen months to pay off bills and to prepare herself to live with less income. After those eighteen months she left her job and got a part-time position that allowed her to use some of her skills. She knew that to satisfy her long-term financial needs, she would have to continue working, if only part-time, for at least another ten years and, possibly, until after age 65. Because of this, she included in her new plan a strategy for staying competitive in her field; it involved setting aside time and money to regularly update her skills through school and professional courses.

Unlike Louise, money was not really an issue for Trent, which meant that when his priorities changed, he had the freedom to make choices from a different perspective. A systems engineer who worked full-time while running his own consulting practice, Trent felt happy and productive. However, when he was laid off from his full-time job during a company restructuring, he found that at 67, he needed to reevaluate his goals. He soon realized that he actually did not need to work for the money; in fact, at this point in his life, money had no motivational value for him at all. For him, true enjoyment and professional satisfaction came from intellectual stimulation and the sense of being valued for his knowledge and contribution.

When a technical professional group asked him to serve on its board, he knew that it was something he wanted to do. The position came with no salary, but in every other way the many responsibilities of the position satisfied Trent's work needs for stage three in his career. Not only that, but members of the professional group often passed on information about short-term project assignments that enabled Trent to continue to participate in his field and stay challenged and involved.

Clearly, Louise and Trent were ready to advance to the third stage of their careers and were, in their individual ways, prepared for it. Are you ready? The following statements should help to clarify things for you.

- You're ready if you've established a career that you've thoroughly enjoyed and that has provided for you financially so that you're at a comfortable level.

- You're not ready if you've only recently begun a career or if the work you do does not support your financial needs.

- You're ready if you're experiencing less desire and motivation to continue doing the work you've been doing.

- You're not ready if you're still thriving in your career, waking up each morning excited and raring to go to work, and positioning yourself for more responsibilities. In this case, you're still working in stage two.

- You're ready if other interests constantly conflict with career demands for your time.

- You're not ready if your current career is still the number-one priority in your life, if you still get much of your identity from your work.

FOCUS ON YOUR SATISFIERS

If you know you're ready to redirect your career, the next step is to choose those aspects of your work that you enjoy and on which you can draw to establish new work. You can do this by identifying your most significant accomplishments and the motivators that were behind them. Look at the table here that describes the key information that Trent used to decide what he would do in stage three.

IDENTIFYING AREAS ON WHICH TO DEVELOP A CAREER GOAL	
Accomplishment	The Positive Motivator(s)
Technical director of a start-up company. Developed processes and a line of successful industrial products.	• Feeling needed as a result of role as a key contributor. • Creative challenge.
Electrooptical engineering and technical management of various projects for military systems, automotive displays, data communications, and sensor systems.	• Variety of assignments. • Expansion of experience. • Expansion of personal network.
Developed complex laser instrumentation systems for industrial processes, the military, and consumer instruments.	• Creative challenge. • Variety of assignments.
Member of the editorial board of applied optics, patents' section.	• Recognition as expert in the profession.
Eight patents and publications.	• Creative challenge. • Developing something of value. • Recognition.

You may want to use a similar process to clearly identify the aspects of your work you enjoy most. This is a personal decision, so go through this process before you seek input from your colleagues or friends and risk being influenced by their feedback. If you've developed a good reputation that's based on certain pronounced traits or skills, people are likely to encourage you to go in a direction that uses them, but this might not be what you really want. For instance, if you have been very effective in a leadership role at your company or as part of community efforts, colleagues may advise you to continue doing that, even though you may be getting a sense that you're ready to shift your focus.

Take the following steps to arrive at the set of positive motivators you want to use now:

- Make a list of the most significant accomplishments you've made in the past decade (ten accomplishments would be good; that's one per year).

- Ask yourself what led you to your accepting the task. Were you pushed into it? Did you volunteer? If so, why? Next to each accomplishment indicate whether your motivation came from external sources (e.g., everyone thought you ought to) or internal ones.

- Ask yourself what felt good about accomplishing the activity. These are the positive factors that came after completion of the tasks.

- If you had a chance to do these things all over again, would you? And, if so, how would you do them differently?

- If you had to choose the top three most significant accomplishments, which would they be? Why? Which would be number one? Writing out your response to this question will be very helpful in determining career direction.

Your analysis will help you more clearly identify your motivators, whether you are influenced by external factors or an internal drive (either is all right as long as you know what it is), and the factors that you should give priority to in setting a new goal for yourself.

FUTURE OUTLOOK—PRESENT ACTION

Naturally, the lifestyle you expect to enjoy in the coming years will greatly influence your career goals at this stage in your life. Now, perhaps more than ever before, you will have to weigh your choices carefully to ensure that you will be able to support for the long-term the lifestyle you desire. Begin by determining how much income you'll need to meet your responsibilities and maintain your lifestyle, as well as how little you can live on and still be content.

Analyzing your finances can be a little tricky at this stage. Often, career phase three coincides with significant personal changes that greatly impact in both positive and negative ways your financial picture. For example, you may be financing the education of college-age children or have just finished paying those bills, you may still be struggling to build up your retirement fund, you may have your heart set on buying that vacation home you've always dreamed of, or you may have finally achieved financial security, with enough money saved so that you don't have to worry about working to earn a living.

In Colleen's case, a significant decrease in her financial responsibilities allowed her to let go of a high-paying stressful job and spend some time just living. With her daughter finishing her last year of college, Colleen realized that she no longer needed to provide extra money in her budget for education. Set free of this huge responsibility, she had the opportunity to make a career decision based solely on her own needs.

This, however, proved to be something of a dilemma because Colleen had never based a career decision simply on her own needs. All she knew was that she no longer needed to drive herself to maintain the six-figure income she earned as an account executive. Ultimately, she decided to switch to an administrative position within the same company and take some time to reassess her career and her goals. The transition was easy because Colleen already knew the company culture, products, and services, and the new position provided her with enough of an income to support herself while she pursued outside interests and decided on her next step.

Like Colleen, Ted also wanted to cut back on his work. While his executive-level position with a car manufacturer provided a lucrative income, it left him little time to spend with his family. As he made the psychological transition to middle age, he realized he wanted to spend more time with his adult children, his grandchildren, and his parents. He decided he needed a new job with fewer responsibilities and fewer demands on his time. His solution was to relocate his immediate family from the East Coast to his small hometown in the Midwest and work with his brother in the family store.

Take A Good Look at Your Situation

As Ted's and Colleen's examples show, it's important to be flexible, open to new ideas and as aware as possible of factors, especially the financial ones, that will affect your life during stage three. Your responses to the following questions may help get you thinking:

- Do I still have school-age children or children who are or will soon be in college or living on their own? If so, what impact will this have on my time, money, or resources?

- Do I have a working spouse who wants to retire or wants to expand his or her career? How would his or her decision impact my career plans?

- Have I had a complete physical recently? Am I in good health? Are there any limitations that I need to consider?

- What are the majority of my friends or peers doing? How do I feel about the changes, if any, in my social circle? How do they impact my decision?

- Do I have a stable financial plan that allows me to entertain a variety of career options, or do I need to put finances first in my decision?

- Are my parents well-provided for? If they need help, would they have to rely on me?

- Do I have a stable marriage? If not, how would a divorce or breakup impact my career?

- Do I have enough leisure time in my life now?

- Am I willing to relocate?

- Do I need to get additional education/training to follow a new career path, and if so, will I be able to do this financially?

- Have I planned for my retirement? Do I have enough money saved to comfortably stop working at the time I hope to retire?

- Do I need to generate an income, and if so, how much? Do I have enough money in the bank today to stop working tomorrow?

IT'S YOUR TURN NOW

In stage two, it's not unusual for career choices to be motivated by a wish to provide security for family; and often, your need for security will take priority over your need to be challenged and creative. But in the third stage, as your financial responsibilities decrease, you finally have the opportunity to put your needs and desires above everything.

Surprisingly, this can cause some initial discomfort or negative feelings if you're not accustomed to putting yourself first. I had occasion to experience this sense of uneasiness myself recently when my daughter left home to attend school in another state. I decided I wanted to move to a smaller living space, one that would better fit my new lifestyle, but I encountered a certain dilemma as I considered the move. Where I lived had always been dictated by a need to be close to good schools for my children. Now, with that factor removed, I had the freedom to concentrate just on my own needs; in other words, I had to make a choice in the face of unlimited possibilities.

Making a good choice with so much freedom can be difficult at any age. But if you approach the decision making with the sure knowledge that it is your time to enjoy and fulfill any unmet dreams, you'll likely soar with this freedom rather than be weighed down by it.

New Goals for the Peak Period of Your Career

Give yourself some quiet time and space away from others to assess your situation and arrive at new goals. If you've been on a fast-paced treadmill, you may find yourself still in "go" for awhile, even though you are trying to gear down so that you have time to reflect.

Start by asking yourself what kind of work activities you enjoy and can visualize doing in the future. Don't feel pressured to come up with an immediate answer (that's a need that reflects the "go" mode you will still be operating in for a while). Write the question down on a pad, and jot down ideas that come to you over a period of several days.

After that, consider how the activities you enjoy are different from or similar to what you have been doing. Does anything stand out as being a significant addition? For instance, you may enjoy providing individual help to people in your department rather than attending a strategy meeting focusing on the company's new direction; or you may prefer being a contributing member on committees rather than the head of them. If either is true, you may be a person who wants to get back to the rewards of being directly involved in the action (the implementation) rather than in the planning (the conceptualization).

You might want to estimate how much time you would like to devote to certain activities or interests: how much time you'd allot, say, to research, writing, leading workshops, or marketing. Start keeping a daily journal listing your activities and the time devoted to each so you get a sense of how you are actually prioritizing your time—and if you are doing it in a way that satisfies you.

You can make this process even more worthwhile if you set priorities the night before, and then the following night compare this list to what you actually did. A significant departure from what you planned to do (especially on a consistent basis) should help show you your real priorities. In evaluating any departure, consider if what you actually did was more enjoyable than what you planned and why you changed your plans. Maybe you think you should be doing one thing, but deep down you're really more satisfied doing something else. If so, you'll want to factor that into your planning.

Make the process of this self-evaluation and goal-setting fun. Don't think of it as a task that you're pressured to complete. It will not only help you get the most out of the next phase, it will also enable you to give to each area of your life the priority that it deserves.

Once you have pinpointed your career priority, you can begin to look at your options for making it happen. The following chapters will review options and present strategies for realigning your career. Chapter 13 gives ideas for renegotiating your current job, chapter 14 shows how you can change to a less stressful job, chapter 15 provides guidelines for making a major career change, and chapter 16 explores new ways of working.

RESOURCES

Transitions: Making Sense of Life's Changes by William Bridges (Addison-Wesley, 1980) provides strategies for coping with difficult times. It shows us how to recognize endings as opportunities as well as losses and how to get reoriented and set new priorities. Reengineering a career, especially one that has been high profile and demanding, can be traumatic. The information in this book can help you understand the transition and make it easier for you.

Workforce 2000: The Revolution Reshaping American Business by Joseph H. Boyett and Henry P. Conn (Dutton, 1992). An excellent book to help you understand the changes in business and better determine how you can fit in. It offers valuable personal guidance and charts the education, skills, and attitudes that positions in the new workplace will demand. The title implies this is a book for the future, but the information is very relevant for the present.

CHAPTER

RENEGOTIATING YOUR CURRENT JOB

I f you are ready to change how you work, you may not have to look too hard for ways to make it happen. In fact, the opportunity to accomplish your new goal may be right under your nose—in your current job. In *Breaking Out of 9 to 5*, Maria Laquer and Donna Dickinson explain that today, more than ever before, increasing numbers of people are renegotiating their jobs: "These redesigners cross all occupations. They include accountants, attorneys, career counselors, computer specialists, engineers, health-care providers, lobbyists, public relations specialists, secretaries, and word processors, just to name a few."

Interesting? You bet.

The simple truth is that progressive companies recognize that they need to be more flexible in defining work schedules and work roles, and this is creating opportunities for new ways of working for many of us. If you're already working in a company you like and in a job that brings you some satisfaction, renegotiating your position may be a better way to make a career goal change than changing to another job or company. What does renegotiating involve? It depends on what you want. It can mean downsizing your current job (i.e., working fewer hours or days) so that you have more time to pursue other interests; realigning your responsibilities so that you take care of only those duties you enjoy; or taking on increased responsibility (either in your current job or a new position) so that your work becomes more stimulating and meaningful.

PRIORITIZE YOUR NEEDS

If pressure from other parts of your life, unpleasant or distracting work responsibilities, or plain old boredom are driving your desire to restructure your job, you may feel like just getting out. Resist this urge, however, and take a few days off to relax and regain your perspective instead. Rather than chucking it all and quitting, think about how you might be able to rework your job to solve your biggest problems. Sometimes we want it all. And we usually can have it all—just not all at once or not without some compromise.

Start by evaluating your current life and career needs and determining the importance of each in the hierarchy of your priorities. Ask yourself the following questions:

- Is time spent on the job beginning to feel like a burden, taking me away from other pursuits that I'd rather be doing? Am I yearning for more time now to spend with my family, to travel, to pursue outside interests? (Maybe the children are away at school or married and gone, and now you have more free time—and energy—and want to do things a bit differently.)

- Am I feeling unstimulated by my current job, yearning for more challenge and fulfillment? Do I see ways that I could take on new responsibilities and challenges by addressing certain needs in the company?

- Am I happy with my job and generally fulfilled by it, but find that certain parts of it have grown tedious? Which aspects of the job would I like to do more of? Which would I like to do less of or have eliminated altogether?

Whether you want to enhance your position or realign or reduce your responsibilities, understand that you have to make it happen. You'll need to choose the option, develop the proposal, and convince your management that it fits the needs of the department. Don't expect anyone else to figure it out for you. You have a powerful advantage if you've developed a good track record at your company—the powers that be will at least listen to you when you have a proposal. Take the time to think it through and present a well-thought-out idea (both orally and in writing) as enthusiastically as you can to your higher-ups.

DOES YOUR JOB LEND ITSELF TO RESTRUCTURING?

Before you approach management, you need to figure out if it's even possible to restructure your job in the way that you envision. If your position could not feasibly be handled a different way, then you'd be wasting your time trying to restructure it. For instance, if you supervise very delicate processes in a research laboratory or on a production line, your job may have little flexibility built into it. Or if you work in a capacity that requires a lot of personal appearances and community involvement, you probably could not get away with working only 9 to 5. In such cases you'll need to look at other options.

But usually this is not the case, and it will just take some creative thinking on your part to come up with a plan to make it work. You'll have to present some good reasons to convince your boss to go along with your idea. And to do that, you need to look closely at your responsibilities and determine how they can be effectively handled in the change. Remember that managers are always going to be primarily concerned with what is best for the company, and this means that you and your change proposal will have to add to—not take away from—the effectiveness of the department.

Let's say you've decided you want to cut back to a three-day work week. Start by categorizing your job into major areas of responsibility; then look at how the various responsibilities are being handled now. Could any of them be dealt with differently? For instance, if you have a staff of fifteen direct reports who handle a variety of functions, you might consider reorganizing the group into three sections, with a lead person responsible for supervising some of the day-to-day activities of each section.

You could maintain quality control by meeting with these group leaders on a weekly basis to discuss issues and resolve problems. On your days off, they could contact you by phone if a serious problem arose. Making these changes would give you more free time and eliminate some of the necessity of being on-site.

In addition to your responsibilities, you also need to consider the people, places, and things that might be affected by your change. Are there meetings you are required to attend? People you need to maintain regular contact with? Are serious decisions made in informal situations—lunch, coffee breaks, in the hallway outside someone's door—where you may no longer be available? If so, add a column to your list of responsibilities and write out the impact your change will have on people and processes. Start a third column next to that showing how you will address these issues or, if you cannot, how it will hinder your effectiveness.

Finally, you'll need to ask yourself whether a job restructuring will affect your benefits or other perks. Start a fourth column listing things you might have to give up if you redesign your job. Are you driving a company car? Do you have retirement or other benefit plans that are tied to full-time hours or a specific salary level? Companies often offer fewer benefits (as well as a lower salary) to people who work fewer hours. Would a three-day week affect any benefits that are important to you?

After you've looked at each of your major responsibilities and how a change might affect them, look at the information you've gathered and decide where you have some flexibility for restructuring and where you don't. If you think that you could effectively redesign your job, then read on for ideas on how to do so.

ARE YOU READY TO DOWNSIZE?

For many people at this stage, renegotiating their jobs often means cutting back on their working hours. If this is true for you, look at the best way to accomplish this so that you can still be effective on the job. For instance, let's say you're considering flexible working hours because you need more time to run errands and take care of family matters or because you want more time for a hobby or new project. What are your options? Would taking off early every Friday or Monday give you the time you're looking for? Or would you do just as well committing to four days, without designating which four. If you're in a job that has work you can control somewhat and often has downtime, this might work for you and cut costs for the company (although that might mean a lower salary for you).

Jason, a counselor at a social services agency and a single parent, found he was much more productive in a four-day week than in a five-day one. Not working on Wednesdays gave him the boost he needed to be more productive on the job and the extra energy to handle the responsibilities connected with the children. By managing his caseload differently, he got all the work done and saved the company a day's pay.

Joy also wanted to downsize her job, for reasons different from Jason's. When her youngest son married, Joy decided that she wanted to work less so that she would have time to travel. Because the demands of her human resources position barely allowed her to take regular vacations, she could not foresee much flexibility in being able to take the time off that she wanted.

Her first thought was to leave the company and get a part-time job that would be less demanding on her time and give her the flexibility she wanted. But one of her peers suggested she try working as a contractor for the company instead. The company had been using quite a few contractors for recruiting and training, and Joy had experience in both these areas.

She proposed to her manager that she leave the company as a permanent employee and join the contractors' pool, which would allow her to work on an as-needed basis providing support both in recruiting and training. Fortunately, Joy had developed an excellent performance track record with the company and, because of this, got management's support when she proposed a new working relationship.

Options for reducing your hours include job sharing, part-time, flex time, contracting, and temping. (Chapter 16 offers detailed information on some of these.) Talk with people about the options they see being used at their companies. A professional group like the Association of Part-Time Professionals (APTP), a national organization that promotes flexible work options to both employers and individuals, may be able to help you examine your options and suggest strategies for implementing them.

REALIGNING YOUR RESPONSIBILITIES

You may have no interest in cutting back your work time but only in letting go of responsibilities that have grown unpleasant and unrewarding. You may want to restructure your job simply to get rid of certain administrative or managerial responsibilities so that you have more time and focus to do the work you truly enjoy.

When Sharon got married, she closed down her consulting business and relocated to another state with her husband. With twenty-five years' experience in business systems consulting, she had no problem getting a position with a management consulting firm. She worked for six years as one of the company's most valued consultants and, for a time, enjoyed her position. At a certain point, however, she became increasingly overwhelmed by the "administrivia" of the job. She made up her mind to quit and return to consulting so that she could use her working time more constructively. She wanted to use her creative skills while freeing herself from administration duties so that her job would be more satisfying. She also wanted to reduce her hours somewhat to pursue leisure activities with her husband.

Just as Sharon started to develop her plan for moving on, however, the company's leadership announced a new strategic direction that coincided perfectly with her career goals and the skills she enjoyed using. They proposed a new service that would use consulting partners who would have the flexibility to work from home part of the time. A junior partner training with each partner would handle the administrative tasks.

Sharon saw an opportunity here to use her creative skills to help develop a new product for the company, and by participating in its development, she could minimize her involvement in the administrative work she disliked. She submitted a proposal to her manager outlining a new area of responsibility for herself and, after getting his buy-in, worked with him to structure a new job for herself. Because she had, like Joy, established such a high level of credibility within the company, the next two levels of approval were relatively easy to obtain. After negotiating a revised compensation package, Sharon had a new job and had let go of the day-to-day duties that had grown so tedious after thirty years.

If you've decided you want to restructure your job so that you can focus on using the skills you find most rewarding, you'll have to figure out how your other responsibilities can be effectively handled. Is there someone else in your department who could take them on? Or could they be divided among several people? What would be the impact of dividing the work, and how would you then interact with these people? Maybe it would be best to leave your position but continue working with the company on a consulting basis. Try to determine whether there are portions of the work that could be done by a consultant or contractor. How is your type of work handled in other companies? Do they provide examples you could use?

"UPSIZING" YOUR POSITION

Is your desire for change motivated by a need for more fulfilling work and, perhaps, increased responsibility? Quality assignments? More autonomy? Increased creativity? Project assignments that permit bringing closure to an activity rather than an ongoing management responsibility? Look at areas in your department or company that appeal to you and see if there might be room for you to contribute—either by changing your job altogether or by enhancing your current position to include more challenge.

The best way to find these growth opportunities is to be on the lookout for changes in the company or for departments that are not effectively accomplishing their goals. The following scenarios will give you some places to look for opportunities to enhance your responsibilities so you can upsize your job:

The company moves in a new strategic direction. A new business strategy usually opens up opportunities for meeting new corporate needs. Talk with people connected with the new plan to determine if there might be a niche for the skills you enjoy using.

Company merger. When a merger occurs, new opportunities always exist. The keys to maneuvering for a good job fit during this time is to be very good at what you do; to be flexible about whom you are willing to do it for; to align yourself with the acquiring company; and to let it be known to all that you see the change as a great opportunity. As the dust settles, stay in touch with the internal network so that you'll hear about new opportunities for developing work around those skills you enjoy using.

Change in leadership. Be alert to the subtle (and sometimes not so subtle) messages from a new department, division, or company leader. For instance: "I'm not so sure that we're going in the right direction"; "That new plan doesn't seem to be working out as we expected"; or "The competition is doing something that seems to be working more effectively than what we're doing." These messages could signal impending changes. Sometimes a little brainstorming (maybe around the water cooler) with peers will uncover a niche for your skills in these anticipated changes.

Global changes within the industry. Typically, when one company in an industry comes out with a new bell or whistle, other companies in the industry follow suit. Stay current on industry trends by reading trade magazines, attending professional meetings, and subscribing to relevant on-line news groups. If you're quick enough, you may find an opportunity for a new job as part of the group or department that will be helping your company align with the industry trend.

Functional problems. Wherever chaos exists, so does opportunity. When a functional area (e.g., accounting, engineering, public affairs, or human resources) is not effectively providing the service it should, it's usually a strong indication that certain needs are not being met. These voids may provide a niche that you can fill by using the skills you enjoy, either as an employee, consultant, or contractor.

People problems. This is possibly the greatest of all areas for the use of expanded skills. When the people in a department are not working together effectively as a team to meet departmental objectives, it's usually because of one of several things: an ineffective organizational structure, politics, or deficits in the skills of the people or the existing leadership. These situations provide an opportunity to solve problems and come up with creative solutions. Evaluate them to determine if the skills you enjoy using can be developed into a job here.

Money problems. A company is in business to make a profit, which it cannot do if revenues do not significantly exceed costs. You're sure to have a winning proposal if you can identify profit issues and then come up with a solution to decrease costs or increase revenue.

BRING ANSWERS, NOT PROBLEMS

To some degree, it's human nature to complain and place blame when a problem exists in the company or within some area of management. But let's face it—what good does it do to just complain? It is far better to direct that energy toward developing solutions to the problem. The restructuring and downsizing mania that companies have been struggling with for the past decade often creates problems that you may want to address. Before approaching management with your solution, be sure you have covered all your bases. The following checklist will provide some guidance in doing this.

- Make sure that the problem is affecting others as well as you; if the situation bothers you only, then it may be more of a personal issue and not something that needs to be addressed companywide.

- Gather input from others about the problem as well as possible solutions so that when you propose an "answer," you're confident that it has been well thought out.

- Be sure that the skills needed to solve the problem are ones you have and want to use. Some of the same people you talk with about the solution would also be good sources for information about the skills needed to improve the situation.

- Have alternative solutions that will also fit the skills you want to use.

- If taking on new responsibilities means your plate will be too full, you'll have to eliminate some others. Be prepared with suggestions for how these responsibilities can be handled after you move into your new role.

A PROPOSAL FOR RENEGOTIATING YOUR JOB

Has your job become a problem for you? Do you want to change it—work different hours or a shorter work week or perhaps increase your responsibilities? Look at the following hypothetical scenario to get a sense of how to go about putting together a proposal to enhance your job or to change the way you work.

Problem Analysis

This first step is for your eyes only (and perhaps a mentor's or confidant's). Begin by writing down the problem clearly and completely (e.g., a need for more flexible hours, greater challenge, more autonomy). Include all the important factors surrounding the situation, then spell out options for solving it before you approach your boss. Here's a sample analysis:

State the situation:
As the manager of a customer service function, I am responsible for supporting three product lines and overseeing a staff of sixty-five spread out over three offices within a large region. When I accepted the job ten years ago, it had a staff of fifteen. My boss is a demanding, action-oriented taskmaster who looks for immediate results. Whenever there is a problem, he expects me to stop whatever I'm doing to handle it. I've reached a point where I would like time to use my creative skills to develop systems to make the operation more efficient, but cannot do this while handling all the day-to-day staff problems and acting as a troubleshooter.

State how you will handle the problem:
I want to address this problem by restructuring my job so that I will be relieved of the day-to-day supervision of the staff as well as the troubleshooting responsibility. This way, I can focus on designing new systems to make the overall function more efficient. In essence, I want to make the transition from a managerial role to consultant role.

Continued

Determine what factors will impact the outcome:

- *My boss has come to rely on me as the source for answers and would not know to whom to go if I were not in the role.*

- *No one on my staff has the overall knowledge to troubleshoot all the problems the way I do.*

- *No one could step into the manager's role and handle supervision and staff problems while keeping the operation running smoothly.*

- *Whenever I've tried to subtly suggest to my boss that the operation could be more efficient, he has brushed me off by saying he'll discuss it at some indeterminate time in the future.*

Assess the pros and cons of maintaining your job versus changing it.

Option 1:   Keep my job as it is (essentially supervising and fighting fires)

Benefits	Problems
Boss has high level of confidence in my ability to handle all situations.	I'm getting burned out trying to handle all facets of the operation independently.
I have complete control of the operation.	No backup systems in place to manage any portion of the operation if I'm not available.
	No time to be proactive in developing systems for increased efficiency.
	I'm concerned that I really don't have a handle on everything the way I'd like.

Option 2:   Restructure my job into a consultant position (to provide supervision, troubleshooting, and cross-training)

Benefits	Possible Problems
Give me more time to develop new ideas and make the opera-tion more efficient.	Boss would be insecure about working with new, inexperienced people.

Benefits	Possible Problems
Opportunity to implement backup systems.	*Some inefficiency during the learning curve of the transition.*

Communicating the Idea

You should communicate your proposal both orally and in writing. Saying it right depends on your nature, your boss's nature, and the strength of your relationship. If possible, before making your proposal, talk with someone who has had a proposal accepted by your boss (or other company manager) to get an idea of what is likely to work best.

If your boss is open to new ideas, you may be able to be very direct in communicating your proposal. If, however, he or she is more closed and needs to be involved in every aspect of a decision, you may be better off outlining the problems, offering several options for addressing them, and suggesting to your boss that you work together to develop the best solution.

With an action-oriented boss, take the direct approach. Be sure to stress the benefits of the change, while recognizing and minimizing any resistance. Make sure that the benefits that are currently being received will continue, but make a strong point that if the change is not made, there will be definite problems that will get worse. Also, be sure to suggest a timetable for making the transition that would allow time for everyone to be trained before final implementation.

After you've gathered your thoughts and organized all the relevant information, you should have a clear sense of the problem and the solution. Now you're ready to make the proposal. The letter and the conversation might be communicated in a format along these lines:

I started my present job as manager with a staff of fifteen; it has grown to sixty-five with no change in how the function is handled. The job requires that all my time be devoted to day-to-day supervision of the staff and troubleshooting problems. This leaves me no time to work on developing a more efficient cost-effective operation, provide advancement opportunities for the staff, or set up any processes for cross-training. The current arrangement is no longer efficient and is beginning to affect the quality of service delivered.

Continued

I propose that my position be restructured from a manager's role into that of consultant. Along with that, I propose that the departmental staff be realigned to include a group leader at each of our locations.

These changes would:

- Allow me to concentrate on assessing the needs of the department, evaluating the feasibility of new processes and equipment, and developing new systems to make our service more efficient.

- Place the primary supervisory responsibility within each unit, thereby increasing operational efficiency and creating a backup system of management support.

- Provide an opportunity to develop potential candidates for vacancies as they occur within the department and establish a logical and natural avenue for upward mobility for the staff.

I am the only person in the department who handles the immediate staff problems and troubleshoots service areas. I realize that people count on me to perform these duties and that it will take time to transfer these responsibilities to others.

I appreciate the need for this transition to occur smoothly, so I suggest making the change over a ninety-day period, during which time the group leaders would be selected, trained, and given an opportunity to function within their new roles while still under my direct guidance. This would provide you and the department with three qualified people who could be relied on for troubleshooting problems and supervising the staff after I assume the consultant responsibility.

I look forward to a favorable review of the proposed change.

Making the Pitch

Identifying a situation in the company that you can address and that
will allow you to use the skills you enjoy most can be the easiest part of
renegotiating your job. The most difficult part may be just ahead, when
you start making your pitch to the decision makers. Using the
following approach will increase your chances of success:

- **Clearly identify the problem.** As explained earlier, it is
  important to focus on a situation that a number of people agree
  is a problem. It should be something that is not being handled
  well through the established processes and that is apparent to
  people whose work has been impaired because of it.

- **Gather support.** It is very important to get the support of those
  who would be impacted by your new job and who could
  influence the acceptance of your idea. They may be people who
  are concerned about turf issues and who need to see that what
  you propose will help them perform their jobs better. Getting
  input from these people and addressing any issues or objections
  they have will help you lay a proper foundation for succeeding
  with those at the management level, who will have to give final
  approval to your proposal.

- **Put your proposal in writing.** You'll probably make your
  proposal in person, but the process of writing it out will force
  you to bring clarity to your thoughts; also, it will usually be
  necessary to have the idea in writing for those who will have to
  take it to the next levels for approval. Your proposal should
  include: the problem, quantified by statistics, costs, or
  situations; how it can be addressed by the new job you propose;
  your qualifications for the new job; and how the excess
  responsibilities of your current job could be handled.

- **Consider the personality of the decision maker.** Proposals are
  not sold in writing, they are sold in person—to another person.
  You can increase your chance for success tremendously by

gearing your presentation to the personality and values of the decision maker. For example, if you know the person likes to talk ideas through thoroughly before making a decision, allow plenty of time for that. For a more analytic type, make sure you have all your facts straight and that your presentation is organized, logical, and systematic. If you are pitching it to a very warm and personable manager, then you can probably present your proposal somewhat informally. Finally, for the really action-oriented manager, your presentation should be concise, with the bottom line expressed first, and a clear outline of your plan for action.

- **Go for the win/win solution.** Your proposal may be accepted verbatim, but don't be surprised or disappointed if it is not. At every level, expect input that could alter your ideas. If you wish to be successful, you'll need to listen nondefensively to any and all suggestions and either incorporate those ideas into your proposal or demonstrate how you will address any objections.

RESOURCES

Breaking Out of 9 to 5: How to Redesign Your Job to Fit You by Maria Laqueur and Donna Dickinson (Peterson's, 1994) explains how to sell your boss on a new arrangement and then negotiate the best salary, benefits, and vacation package possible. The book also shows you how to stay on your career track with a job that doesn't conform to a rigid 9-to-5 schedule every day—week in and week out.

How to Manage Your Boss by Roger Fritz and Kristie Kennard (Career Press, 1994) provides tips on working with your boss to get the support for the things you want to do. An excellent aid for the person who wants to make a pitch to renegotiate a current job.

CHAPTER

TAKING A LESS STRESSFUL JOB

Y ou may arrive at the third stage of your career with no interest in renegotiating your job or realigning your career but rather with an eye toward reducing your focus on your work and the stress that goes with it. As a person of color, you may have unique reasons for wanting to jump off the corporate ladder. Often, the upward climb for us is more difficult and considerably more stressful than it is for other people. Every day, we have to operate by one set of values in the workplace and then switch to a different set when we get home. This balancing act takes such a toll on all parts of our life that the signal that it's time to make a change often comes as welcome relief.

AN ADDED CHALLENGE

Taking a lesser job is initially stressful for anyone because it requires making lifestyle and career adjustments. As a person of color, however, you may have the added stress of dealing with the subtle but pervasive message that says, "You should be grateful you have such a good job—how dare you think about giving it up?" We've had to work hard to achieve our success and status, so be prepared for people to ask you if you've lost your mind when you tell them you want to give it up or take a lesser job. Expect some to believe that you just couldn't cut the muster. Understand that when people express these attitudes, they are operating from their own value system and are not considering your needs.

When I left my corporate job, a white peer flatly told me that I was going to starve to death, and an older black friend asked me if I were nuts. In a sense, I felt they were both communicating the same thing: How dare you (a black person) leave when a good job is so hard for black people to get. Their message to me, I believe, was that a person of color doesn't have a right to make this change and that we should always value a job above any other consideration.

This kind of attitude can stop you from making a change if you let it. You have to remember that you have achieved what you have because you did not let negative attitudes like these stop you before, and you shouldn't let them interfere now with your new decision. In America we have the freedom to come full circle in our careers and give ourselves the option of taking a lesser job if it's better for our overall life-career plan.

A Lesser Job Will Affect Your Whole Life

Before you make a drastic change, however, realize that while changing to a lesser job will probably reduce your work stress, improve your health, and allow you more time to spend with your family and to do other things you enjoy, making the transition will bring new stress to other areas of your life. You will be adjusting to a new routine, different responsibilities, and a different level of authority—or no authority at all. If you're starting out on a new path, expect the stress to be even greater and to last for a longer period of time. Transferring your skills into a new profession or starting over in a new career will bring on the additional stress of a culture change and probably a different work location. Plus, you may have to get more training to bring your skill level up for the new job, even though it's at a level lower than your former job. Be prepared for the change to be a little bumpy at first, as every area under your life-career umbrella adjusts.

For starters, you'll be earning less money, which means you'll probably have to make changes in your lifestyle. Perhaps you'll be dining out less, taking fewer vacations, keeping your car longer, or moving to a smaller, more affordable house or apartment. You may also find that your circle of friends will change to realign with your new values and priorities. Don't be surprised if, for a while, you feel pulled between the new friends and the old, as well as between the activities of the old lifestyle and the new. Family members may be happy that you have more available time but may also take a while to accept that the change will affect the things they can do or have, too.

MAKE THE CHANGE AS EASY AS POSSIBLE

You can make the change easier if you do some work beforehand. First, get your family's support by discussing with them how they will be affected in both positive and negative ways. Second, take time to fully understand all the ramifications of the job you're considering so that you will know what to expect. If you prepare yourself in both areas of your life, the change can be positive right away. These pointers may help:

- Before changing a job you enjoy, consider the other factors in your life and your career that may be causing you stress and determine if changing any of them will remedy the situation. For instance, could you rearrange how you work, get help for ailing parents, join a gym to develop better health, or better prioritize your activities to include more "rose-smelling time"? You may find that it's not your job that needs changing after all.

- Analyze the situation surrounding your work. Could your stress be reduced by changing from the culture that you're in or the activities that you have felt compelled to be involved with to support your job? For instance, could you eliminate golf, association meetings, or conferences that take you away from your family?

- Consider taking a leave from your current job to try out a new goal before making a commitment to it.

- Think about the factors that may surround a lesser position or different profession and how easily you'll be able to adapt to them. For instance, the change may require you to work with a more youthful group, possibly doing routine tasks with little challenge. Is this going to add to your stress or reduce it?

- Write down the advantages and disadvantages of taking a less stressful position—and consider a change only if your evaluation shows the advantages outweighing the disadvantages.

TAKING A LESSER JOB WITHIN YOUR PROFESSION

Some of the most successful transitions I've seen involved individuals taking jobs in the same or a related profession but at a less responsible level. Usually, you can accomplish this more easily by changing companies, since you, as well as your colleagues, may find it difficult to adjust to your change within the company. Typically, when you change jobs at your company, you will find that others are not making the adjustment as quickly as you are; they're still coming to you for the information and support you gave them in your previous position.

Either way, whether you change to a lesser position within your company or move to another company, you'll be an asset in the job. You'll be able to carry over some aspects of the former work that you enjoyed, while bringing added value to the function. For instance, if you step down as a human resources director with several functional areas reporting to you and move to a position of recruiter, you will better appreciate your manager's need for receiving timely staffing reports. You could also be an asset to your colleagues, willing to share information and support their efforts since you're not competing with them to move up a ladder you've just descended.

For John, the career transition in stage three presented less stress because he stayed within a field that he knew and loved. As director for a community program in a major city for twenty years, his high-profile role demanded he be in the public eye a great deal and attend a lot of social events. He relished his many responsibilities but decided to change jobs when they began to consume the better part of his waking hours, including weekends.

Two factors contributed to John's decision to make a change. His father, whom he considered his best friend, contracted cancer and needed a lot of his son's attention. Around the same time, John developed diabetes. It became clear to him that his job was one of the things he could alter to relieve stress and leave more time to spend with his family. In deciding what he could do next, John asked himself a few questions, some of which are listed below.

If you can answer yes to the following questions, then taking a lesser job in your field, either at your present company or at another company, could be a good move for you.

- Would your stress be reduced by eliminating some of the secondary functions in your job, or is the stress caused by the major responsibilities?

- Is it feasible to move to a lesser position in your profession, continue to use the skills you enjoy, and still reduce your stress?

- Will you be accepted by your peers and management in a lesser role in your profession and be expected only to make a contribution at that level?

- Is it really feasible to move to a more flexible job without feeling awkward about it—or without feeling pressure to carry out some of your previous responsibilities?

- Can you let go of the power and influence of the higher level position and adjust psychologically to having less influence, especially if you remain in your present company?

- Can you deal with the possibility that others may perceive you as being not as competent as before if you accept a lesser position in your profession?

VENTURING INTO A NEW FIELD

Some people look at stage three as a perfect opportunity to make a major career switch—to move to a completely unrelated position of reduced responsibility or to an area that one has always wanted to be involved in. One way of making a major change like this easier is to align yourself with people who are also undergoing a career change. You may meet them in a class that you take to support your new venture or in one of the new professional groups you're likely to join; maybe even at a new health club or in a new sport or hobby. Look for them, because I believe the universe will supply them.

Think about other times when you've made a major change in your life. You may have thought it a coincidence when you began to meet people doing the same thing. It was no coincidence—you've been drawn together because of what you now have in common. The people you meet as you make this change will also be experiencing a major career change, and by talking with them about your concerns and fears or just discussing your plans and ideas, you'll start building a new support group. At the same time, you'll make some contacts who may prove to be a link to finding out more about your new venture.

I've noticed that we people of color tend to not be open to communicating our plans to people outside our families or safe social circles, and that can work against us. Understand that you have to be open to support from whomever or wherever it comes. The universe supplies people with no regard to race or gender—the connection is based on commonality of need. Do not restrict yourself to talking about your plans solely with people of your own race or gender because if you do this, you might miss an important link to information you need.

Draw on Foresight, Not Hindsight

Find out as much as you can about the job you want before you go after it. This will keep the stress down by helping to prepare you mentally for the change. You'll want to make sure that you have the skills for the job you'll be going after, that it will be less stressful than your previous position, and that you'll be compatible with the new culture. Contact people in your network and ask for referrals to someone who is doing the work and can give you the real scoop on the job you're interested in. Also consider joining forces with search consultants (head hunters) who specialize in placing people in the type of job you seek. These consultants could help critique the résumé you prepare for your new job and give you an idea of your chances of getting the kind of job you want.

Donna learned too late the value of research after she moved into an entirely new field. She took an early retirement to leave the stress and politics of her job as a personnel manager in a major national corporation. After nine months in retirement, however, she became bored and decided to pursue a position she had always wanted—a department store sales clerk. In her corporate position, Donna had been respected by her peers and the company executives; the position made her feel important, but it was very demanding. She loved to shop, and decided that a sales job would be a perfect change for her. By regularly saving while working at her former job, Donna had prepared herself financially to live on less income; she did not, however, take the time to get herself ready mentally and emotionally by researching what she could expect in a sales job.

Through her contacts, Donna had no problem landing a job as a sales clerk—and at first, the job was a dream come true. But soon, she realized that the job wasn't at all what she expected it to be. She thought she'd have time to shop and browse at her leisure—in between helping customers. As it turned out, she had little time for anything but work. Having been removed so long from that level of work, Donna had no frame of reference for assessing what the job would require. Had she picked a lesser job closer to the level of responsibility she was accustomed to, it may have been easier for her to anticipate its realities.

When workers treated her as the junior person on the sales team, Donna realized how accustomed she had become to being deferred to, and she wasn't comfortable with the role reversal. As she adjusted to customer attitudes—which ranged from condescending to downright rude—customer service took on a whole new meaning for her. And her feet, they ached all the time.

In spite of the unexpected stresses, Donna made the adjustment. She eventually worked her way to a better sales department and managed to negotiate a shortened work week (her corporate human relations experience came in handy here). Eventually Donna grew happy with her decision; however, she realized, with 20/20 hindsight, that the change would have been easier if she had mentally prepared herself by finding out more about a sales job before going after one.

Ease Into a New Commitment

Unlike Donna, Norma took the time to investigate and try out a different job before making a full commitment to it. After working as an elementary school teacher for twenty years, she had reached burn-out. She evaluated her strengths and areas of interest and decided she would enjoy a job using her personal computer skills. She took a couple of evening courses to expand her computer knowledge and, during her summer break from school, registered with a temporary agency to do office work. Three weeks into her first assignment, Norma realized she had found her next niche—working as an administrative manager on a part-time temporary basis. She enjoyed the work and liked the flexibility that temping offered. Her strong English and grammar skills, coupled with her organizational ability and patient personality, kept her in demand, which gave her the freedom to choose her assignments and negotiate her working hours.

If you have skills that you think can be transferred to a new profession, do as Norma did—do your research:

- Talk with people who are doing the kind of job you are interested in. Find out what additional skills you'll need. Ask them to describe the work culture so you can determine whether it's compatible. Also, try to get a sense of the stress factors that come with the job—no point in jumping from one intolerable position to another.

- Ask your sources about the training or education you'll need to acquire any additional skills necessary to handle the new position.

- If possible, try the job out before committing to it. If you can, do the work on a temporary or volunteer basis so you can observe the processes connected with the job. (For example, if you've decided you want to work on an administrative or admitting level in a hospital, find an appropriate clerical temporary or volunteer hospital job so that you can observe the position in action and get a sense of whether or not you'd like it.)

Developing a Résumé That Fits the Goal

Whether you go after a different job in your current field or one in a different field, you'll need a new résumé to go along with your new career goal. In revising your résumé, keep in mind that you will be seeking a position that is less than what you are capable of handling. A chronological (the standard type) résumé that lists your full work history and accomplishments may make you feel good but probably won't help you land a lesser job. Prospective employers might be intimidated or consider you overqualified for the positions you'll be applying for.

As a staffing professional for a Fortune 100 company, I had an opportunity to assess résumés and compile a list of promising candidates for managers to review for their openings. I remember feeling quite satisfied with the first list of candidates I submitted and then feeling extremely disappointed when most of them were rejected—without being interviewed. I had mistakenly thought the manager would be pleased to see the most qualified applicants available. As the manager discarded most of the people on my list, he jokingly commented, "Some of these people are more qualified than I am. What do you want me to do, lose my job?"

While logic would seem to dictate that the manager would benefit most by having a highly capable person, emotion most often rules in such situations. Managers might worry that every time they interacted with an overqualified employee or contended with his questioning of an idea or policy, they would be reminded that the employee might be more experienced and possibly have once commanded a higher salary than the manager does.

Employers seek the best fit for their openings, which is not necessarily the most experienced or most impressive person who applies. Most believe that if they hire an overqualified person, they'll end up with a disgruntled, hard-to-manage employee who is only using the position as a stop-gap measure until he gets something he really wants. Most managers consider hiring an overqualified person a bad investment for the long term.

In spite of these obstacles, changing to a lesser position can be done successfully with some forethought and planning. The information outlined below will guide you in developing a résumé that will help you get consideration as a viable candidate. This résumé will also set the stage for a good interview.

Downsizing Your Résumé

When downsizing, develop a new résumé rather than using an edited version of your old one. (Refer to chapters 5 and 10 for tips on résumé writing.) Follow these steps:

- Use a functional résumé format. The traditional chronological résumé, which typically reveals your age, years of service, titles, and levels of responsibility, may wind up being your kiss of death. Employers looking at it may think you're overqualified or feel that your last job doesn't qualify you for the position you're seeking. Eliminate dates and group accomplishments by function to fit your new job target.

- Develop a résumé targeted to the goal. At the top of the paper, write down the job you want to get—for example, "product representative." Then test all the information you put in the rest of the résumé against this objective. If you prefer not to include an objective on your résumé, you can delete it after you have developed the résumé and done your test.

- Develop a summary statement at the top of the résumé. After the objective, in five to seven lines summarize the skills, traits (the way you work), experience, and knowledge that you would bring to this position. Refer back to the information that people gave you when you talked with them about this type of work. Emphasize the skills, traits, knowledge, and experience they told you were needed. Include skills that you used in your old job only when they fit the new job, and at the same time, use only the portion of those skills and traits that will transfer to the new job. (See the box Developing a Résumé for a Lesser Position.)

- Provide examples of accomplishments in your résumé that support the information in the summary. Word them so they fit the needs of the job.

- Describe your previous jobs in the most generic terms possible to avoid any issue of you being overqualified.

- Have someone review your résumé. Try to find someone who does the kind of work you want to do or is at least knowledgeable about that field.

FINDING NEW POSITIONS

Ads and agencies should certainly be used to help you find new positions outside your company, but networking will probably be the

DEVELOPING A RÉSUMÉ FOR A LESSER POSITION

Imagine that a newscaster is looking for a new job as a product representative in sales or customer service, and consider how his skills and experience might be used in his new résumé. The information below on the left is appropriate; that on the right is not. While the right-hand information is indicative of what most newscasters would be inclined to include in their résumés and is impressive, it does not align as well with the new job requirements as the information on the left. Rather, it underscores what a high-achieving go-getter the job applicant is and would create doubt in the prospective employer's mind about the newscaster's ability to be happy as a customer service representative.

Do's	Don'ts
Objective: A position as a product representative where I can apply my experience in influencing others to make positive decisions.	**Objective:** A responsible position in a progressive organization where I can make a contribution.
Summary: A seasoned professional with more than ten years' experience developing and communicating information. Excellent analytical and problem-solving skills. Easy to talk with. Projects corporate image. Politically savvy. A resourceful self-starter who can work independently or as part of a team.	**Summary:** More than twenty years' experience as a newscaster for three major stations. Knowledgeable director and producer. Traveled extensively in China, Caribbean, Germany, Switzerland, and Thailand. Considerable experience handling investigative and on-the-spot news stories. Fluent in Chinese and Spanish.
Selected Accomplishments: Developed, sold to upper management, and implemented a proposal that expanded company's service by 10 percent. Independently handled all functions of a satellite location for eleven months. Worked with division within a client company to identify and resolve resistance to a major proposal, which resulted in $350,000 in revenues.	**Selected Accomplishments:** Received a national award for top investigative story in 1991. Special commendation for work with Chinese businessmen to establish a positive link with U.S. television stations. Part of team that developed KPPC access station.
Professional History: KNWC News, News Department; ACCX NEWS, Community Relations Department; VMES News, Media Division (Note: No titles given, just departments)	**Professional History:** News Anchor, KNWC; News Producer, Community Relations, ACCX News; Media Director, VMES News

best method for finding the new job. This is not the time to restrict your search to a small circle of close friends. You should talk with everyone of both genders and all races. As people of color, we tend to be very closed about wanting to make a change to a lesser position (that old pride gets in the way) because we don't want anyone to think that we couldn't handle the last job. But, interestingly, if we discuss it with other people, especially people in the age group, they will probably relate, no matter what their race, because they may have some similar feelings themselves about changing their priorities.

For John, whom I spoke about earlier in this chapter, networking proved to be an excellent avenue for his job change. Because he was known for strong performance, all his contacts considered him an asset. Before talking with anyone about a change, John evaluated what he could do next so he would be able to discuss with his contacts the skills and activities he enjoyed. He decided to look for work placing people in jobs and to minimize his involvement in the social and administrative part of the work.

John used his networking contacts to help him land a new position as a job development counselor with a citywide job training program. He worked flexible hours, had one major responsibility instead of several, and was still involved in the kind of work he enjoyed. In his new role, he reported to a director, someone at the level John was at in his former job. This didn't bother John because he had willingly given up the old position and was not at all envious of the demands that went with the director's role. Rather, John's experience enabled him to serve as a valuable resource to the director; he could help ensure the program's success without having the responsibility and stress of being held accountable for it.

INTERVIEWING FOR A LESSER POSITION

It is pointless to spend time researching the position you want and tailoring a résumé for it—just to get to the interview and blow the opportunity to show them how right you are for the job. Unfortunately, this is exactly what can happen if you don't come to the interview well-prepared. Your past successes and experience have probably left you feeling quite confident in your abilities, but this heightened confidence can be a drawback in an interview situation. If you've been working at a very responsible job, you probably have the authoritative attitude that goes along with it. The new position may not call for all that strength and poise, so it's wise to adjust your interviewing style in advance.

For Ken, an ulcer, concern over ailing parents, and intense company politics forced him to give up his position as program manager for a high-tech supplier of defense parts. Years of leading a team of professionals and winning contracts worth millions of dollars had made him into a confident individual with a commanding presence.

To help him with his job search, Ken signed on with a permanent placement agency. The staffing consultant assigned to his case pegged Ken as a professional who would be an asset to a number of companies. After interviewing him for about 45 minutes, however, the search consultant had some other feedback for Ken that caught him by surprise. He told Ken that his attitude was almost too authoritative for the positions for which he would be applying. He pointed out that Ken had taken control of their interview and seemed impatient with answering the types of questions that would probably be asked on a job interview. The consultant warned him that some of the interviewers might be younger than Ken and that they could well feel intimidated by his manner—he advised him to work on being more relaxed and less intimidating. Fortunately Ken took this advice to heart and adjusted his interview style—he ended up being offered and accepting a systems engineering position with a small company, where he clicked well with the executives.

Acing the Interview

You can make your change easier by using the tips below to prepare yourself for the interview. During the process, remember to consider the point of view of the employer, who may be concerned that you are a deadbeat or couldn't cut it in your former position. Because of this, your entire approach should be upbeat, open, and positive to convince him or her of your interest in the position and your value to the company. (Also see chapters 5 and 10 for more information on interviewing.)

Be prepared for a new interview process.

If you haven't interviewed in years, you can expect a different process than you remember from ten or twenty years ago. Much work now is project-oriented and handled by teams. You may be interviewed by several people, either in a group interview or individually, to determine if you will fit with the "team." And don't be surprised if the selection process takes six to eight weeks.

Because most companies tend to follow the current market patterns, the interview process at your current company should reflect what you can expect at another company. You can get a sense of this process by talking informally with someone in your human resources department. If you're not currently working or are working at a small company with no human resources department, join forces with a reputable search consultant. He or she will be able to give you an idea of what to expect in the interview, as well as offer feedback and tips on your interview style.

Know about the company and the interviewer.

You can get general information on most publicly held companies at the public library or by calling the firm's public relations or public affairs department and requesting it. But the unpublished information you can get through networking sources will be the most valuable. Use your contacts to find out as much as you can about the interviewer, the department, company culture, and major projects underway in the functional area for which you'll be interviewing.

The better your understanding of the backgrounds and motivations of the decision makers, the better your chances of selling yourself in the interview. For instance, if you discover that the decision maker believes that everyone has to prove himself before taking on prize projects, then it will be to your advantage to approach the interview ready to express your willingness to do just that—even if you already have experience handling similar projects.

Look and act the part.

I've learned through experience that a job candidate should always dress and behave according to the level of the position for which he or she is interviewing. If you usually dress well—in expensive, designer clothes—you may have to tone down your look a bit. You don't have to look drab or bargain basement, but a Pierre Cardin suit for an engineering position may be overdoing it. The standard middle-of-the-road blue or gray suit always works—and leave off the expensive watch or ring.

On the other hand, if you have never made your appearance a priority, your image may need to be updated. Dressing out of style can be just as bad as overdressing because it could signal to a potential employer that if your wardrobe is out of step, your thinking might be as well. If this applies to you, update your whole appearance before starting the interview process. Get your hair styled and buy a good new suit and a pair of new shoes. No need to be trendy; go for a conservative look consistent with the current styles.

Be sure not to be condescending or patronizing in the interview. Have an air of respect for the process and the interviewer (even if the person is your son or daughter's age). Be open, flexible, and friendly. Let the interviewer lead the session and don't make any references to him or her sharing some similarity in style or experience to your children. Before going to the interview, you may want to practice interviewing with someone about the same age as your prospective employer.

Prepare for key questions.

Here are some sample questions often asked at interviews. Be prepared by having good answers worked out ahead of time.

- **Tell me about yourself.** Keep your answer short and relevant to the job. This is not the time to expound on all your accomplishments (just those that are relevant to the position). Use the same approach in the interview that you used for the résumé: Give an overview of your career, using generic terms as much as possible; only highlight those skills and characteristics that support this lesser position. I recommend something like: "I've been in the industry for a number of years. I've had an opportunity to work with ABC Company, Universal Defense, and High-Tech Incorporated. I've enjoyed it most when I've been able to use my creative and technical skills, which is why I'm very interested in your opening. I believe it's one where I would be fulfilled and where I could add value."

- **Why do you want this job?** It's important that you have an enthusiastic, convincing answer here, or the interviewer is liable to think that the only reason you're making a change is because you became deadwood in your former position. Something along the lines of the following answer might effectively sum up your thoughts and give a positive impression: "I have reached a point in my life and my career where I want to concentrate on doing just those things I enjoy. I found my former position to be very challenging and am proud of what I accomplished in that job. Now I'd like to return to using my creative skills and believe I can bring that expertise to this job."

- **Why did you leave your last company?** The prior answer will work well for this question, too.

- **What kind of salary do you expect?** Do not expect to receive a salary consistent with your last job; remember, this is a lesser position. Be sure to know what a fair range would be if you have to suggest a salary and begin with something like this: "I would expect to receive a fair salary consistent with the market and the skills I will be using in the job. I'm sure that if we agree on me for the position, we'll be able to work out a fair salary."

Follow up.

Sending a thank-you letter is still in style. It makes a very positive point, shows that you follow through, and may be the deciding factor that gets you the job. In the letter, mention something that seemed important to the interviewer to let him or her know that you were listening to what was said. Also, be clear that you would like to have the job, if that's the case.

RESOURCES

Take This Job and Leave It: How to Get Out of a Job You Hate and Into a Job You Love by Bill Radin (Career Press, 1993). This book provides help for dissatisfied workers, unfulfilled employees, and stress-filled wage earners to seek and land a job they enjoy. It contains excellent job-hunting basics for creating an effective job-changing strategy, working through job description makeovers, recreating a winning résumé, evaluating compensation, and adjusting successfully to your new job.

To Build the Life You Want, Create the Work You Love: The Spiritual Dimension of Entrepreneuring by Marsha Sinetar (St. Martin's Press, 1995). Making a career change to a less stressful job should not mean taking a position that you don't like. This book will inspire you to search your soul and mind for the factors that are important in your own decision-making process.

CHAPTER

MAKING A CAREER CHANGE

Most people do not make dramatic career changes; rather, they develop and build on their skills until certain ones become strengths, and then they gradually take on challenges in new areas of interest. Those who do seem to make extreme changes—for example, from bartender to doctor, personnel clerk to veterinarian, personal trainer to record producer—generally have been working toward that second career for a long time before they eventually make the final transition.

It is not unusual to know for years in advance that you want to make a career change. You may have commented to others about what you plan to do "when the kids finish college," "when the major bills are paid off," or "when I finish school." Knowing what you want to do at some point in the future can give you plenty of time to plan and build the necessary foundation while you continue in your current career. In fact, if you plan your career change while working in another job, you may discover that you can draw on company resources and contacts to help make the transition to your new career easier.

A personal trainer I know learned the value of working at one career while laying the foundation for his move into record production. He networked among his clients and met professionals in the entertainment business who helped him. As a trainer he was an entrepreneur; he was self-disciplined, accustomed to working independently, and skilled at developing and implementing a plan to accomplish his goal. He could transfer these skills to his new career, making the change less difficult than it might otherwise have been.

It takes drive, energy, and focus to successfully make the leap from one career to a totally different one, and few people are up to the challenge. For most, such a change involves taking the skills you already have and combining them with new interests, setting a new or modified goal that is a better reflection of your self-knowledge, then deciding where to market the skills.

"BURNED OUT AND RENEWED"

■

The opportunity to create a new career for yourself will come when you're ready for a change, whether you immediately realize you're ready or not. Often you can anticipate coming changes and new areas for growth and opportunity when you see existing situations begin to deteriorate or come to an end.

Ed managed a consulting group at Digital Equipment Corporation for seven years before making his first career change. He realized after a heated discussion with his boss that he had outgrown his job and was ready to move on. An offer to stay with the company and start a new division selling software solutions allowed him to use his technical knowledge while he developed new skills in marketing and sales. Working at this position for another seven years, he helped to build up a $12-million business. Then an industry downturn forced the company to downsize, and Ed, finding himself dealing daily with office politics in order to survive, decided to accept the company's buyout package.

"I was going to find another job but discovered it wasn't that easy at my age [50] to get a job as a middle manager. And after a long time in middle management, I had lost many of my technical skills, making it hard to find another job. Also, corporations were flattening and moving to high-performance teams, so there were fewer positions available like the one I'd had."

A visit to his uncle in the Caribbean, where Ed went to do some consulting work, inspired him to start his own business. "My 75-year-old uncle was a tremendous motivating force for me," Ed explains. "I was trying to figure out what I wanted to do and was fearful of starting my own business. I had an opportunity to interact with him and observe what can be done when one has no fear of failure. Here was a man who had constructed a twelve-unit villa at 70 years of age. He had been motivated to do so by a promise he'd made to himself years ago; at the young age of 7 he looked up to the mountain and said, 'I will have a villa up there someday.'"

Ed spent some time evaluating his career path and looking back on his experience writing business plans in a corporate environment. In doing so, he realized that nearly all his significant positions involved starting up new ventures within the company. So it was natural for him to begin a new business venture of his own—his current consulting practice.

"If you want to make a career change, make sure you have a clear motivation and objective—you'll need this focus to give you the steam to reach your goal. While in the Caribbean, I realized I was adept at working with people; now I know that my enjoyment comes from working with people, not with technology. That's what drives me."

■

ED CHAPMAN
Black entrepreneur
President
Business Development Concepts
Laguna Niguel, California
Business: New business development, business plans for startup and expansion

A MODEL FOR IDENTIFYING TRANSFERABLE SKILLS

Regardless of how a career change comes about, once it does, you'll need to identify a new goal. If you've been in the workforce for several years, you can usually do this by analyzing the pattern of your past accomplishments to determine the direction in which your skills are now pointing. After that, it's a matter of honing in on the assets you want to market.

Start by putting together a list of your accomplishments, as described in chapter 10. These are accomplishments you've achieved in the last ten years or so, but use a longer time span if necessary. Highlight relevant accomplishments from both work and outside activities. Concentrate on identifying accomplishments you made while involved in activities you truly enjoyed. Then analyze them for the skills and traits you developed as a result of each. As you do this, you will likely note: (1) significant accomplishments that led to bigger accomplishments involving the use of other skills; and (2) overall patterns of skills and traits that run throughout all or most of your accomplishments. Those that appear often are probably your dominant ones and the ones that you will want to transfer to another career.

To get an idea of how to identify transferable skills, look at the table on the next page, which lists a history of Ed Chapman's accomplishments (see "Burned Out and Renewed").

COMBINING SKILLS AND INTERESTS INTO NEW CAREER OPTIONS

After identifying your strongest skills, your next step is to identify those you most enjoy using and consider what types of work would allow you to use them. Just as important, you need to determine the functions that, over the course of your career, you've come to find uninteresting, unpleasant, or uncomfortable to perform. All of this requires an honest

ED'S ANALYSIS OF HIS ACCOMPLISHMENTS

Accomplishment	Result	Skills and Traits
Played in a band to finance college education	Declined music scholarship because of dislike of lifestyle and, instead, chose to finish business school	Creativity, resourcefulness, self-knowledge
Excelled in college: graduated in upper 2 percent of class in computer information systems	Led to job developing new systems and applying innovative computer skills to the company	Analytical ability, perseverance, concentration
Developed an automated evaluation and compensation system allowing people to be placed in their job at an equitable pay scale	Leadership skills surfaced; successfully engendered support and cooperation from others	Negotiation, influencing upper management
Promoted to upper management position with staff of sixty	Discovered people skills	Selling, influencing, proposing, tracking, managing, working well with people
Set up a new business for software development within a major company	Established and implemented a business plan	Business startup, ability to secure financing, initiative, vision, resourcefulness; product development, marketing, consulting

self-analysis of the activities you do and do not enjoy. Essentially, your aim is to to ensure that your new career options reflect the inner you that has surfaced since you set your original career goal years ago.

Carolyn, an accounting supervisor, made a careful self-analysis when she grew dissatisfied in her position. By determining what she didn't want to do, she was able to make a smooth and personally rewarding career switch. Looking back on her work history, she realized that although she had significant experience as a supervisor, she disliked managing people. She had originally accepted a supervisory role simply because it offered a significant increase in pay.

Now ready for a change, she evaluated her skills, along with her likes and dislikes, and incorporated them into a new focus. Knowing that she wanted to stay in accounting, Carolyn decided to move into a role where she would tackle work assignments as part of a team but where she would not directly supervise, give performance reviews, or handle the grievances of others. Her new job, as a member of the finance team with a management consulting firm, allowed her to do just that.

If you can identify the skills you enjoy using most, while taking into account the ones you're sure you no longer want to use, you have a good basis for developing options for a career change. The following steps will help with the process.

- On a sheet of paper, write out a list of the skills you enjoy using. Try to express each in one word or two-word phrases; avoid listing skills in broad categories. For instance, instead of using the broad term *leadership*, break it down into specifics: *communicating information; convincing others; writing letters; conducting meetings; supervising others.*

- On another sheet of paper, make a column for each job that interests you. Three jobs is a manageable number. (Reread chapter 2 if you need help with this step.)

- For each job, do research to find out the required skills. The reference or career librarian at your local library will be able to direct you to books that describe most occupations. But the best way to determine what real-life skills that are necessary for a job is to ask a person already employed in that occupation. If you don't have a direct contact, ask your friends and peers to help you locate such a person. In questioning these contacts, ask them to give you examples of how the skills are used so that you get a clear idea of what is required. Try to come up with a list of five to seven primary skills, then write them in the columns below each job heading.

- Now compare the skills you most enjoy with the skills required for each of the jobs you listed. The job that best matches your skills is probably your best bet for a new career.

Take steps to explore that option. But plan to research the other two options as well. You may find as you explore your first option that it is not feasible for any number of reasons (e.g., money, timing, educational requirements). If so, you can focus on your next strongest option.

In the following model—Ed's Analysis of His Career Options—a further evaluation of Ed's background demonstrates how he combined skills and interests into new career options and then through a process of elimination chose the best one. He chose option 1 because he assumed the next logical step for him was to get a job at another company doing the same thing he had done. During the process of trying to find that type of job, however, he discovered he wasn't really motivated to continue doing the same job elsewhere. Option 2 came from his uncle in the Caribbean, who had asked Ed to help with the family business for a while. After exploring this second possibility, Ed decided he was not interested in pursuing it either. He then decided to start his own consulting business using the skills he was comfortable with. This turned out to be his best option, even though it was not his first choice.

The previous box—Ed's Analysis of His Accomplishments—identifies certain patterns in Ed's career, including a progression from using analytical skills to using people skills, a transition from managing to visionary leadership and then to consulting, and a successful history of handling start-up operations or projects. For Ed, recognizing this pattern helped him get a clear picture of the skills he enjoyed using most. This information, listed in the left column of that box, represents a group of skills that he used most often and against which he evaluated his options.

When you have settled on a new career option, be sure to compare it to your list of skills to be certain that it will not eventually lead to using many of the skills you wish to avoid. Finally, evaluate the

---

ED'S ANALYSIS OF HIS
CAREER OPTIONS

Skills I enjoy using the most

Management skills, leadership, consulting start-up activities, technical knowledge

Option 1
Job with another company.

Result: Couldn't find job at desired salary and location. Wasn't motivated.

Option 2
Work outside of corporate America in hotel management in Caribbean.

Result: Discovered skills were transferable but location was not desirable for long-term.

Option 3
Consulting business writing and developing business plans for start-up and expansion. Result: Best choice. Able to transfer skills and maintain options

---

feasibility of your interest options against the information you've discovered about yourself. You may discover, as Ed did, that the process is essentially one of elimination.

EVALUATING YOUR OPTIONS AND SETTING A GOAL

In an ideal world, your strengths would align perfectly with one of your options and you could just go for it. But the world, as we all know, isn't perfect. And it may actually be "less perfect" for you than it was ten years ago because family, new responsibilities, and other social and economic factors have made it more complicated. More than likely, you probably now have issues and considerations that you didn't face when first starting out. The following list should help you identify the realities that apply to your current situation. These are the concerns you may need to consider as you pinpoint your career options and develop the objectives to reach your goal.

How High Should the Goal Be?

You'll need to think about developing a goal for which you'll have the time, energy, and drive to support. Be realistic; don't set yourself up for failure by developing a goal you know you can't reach. Of course, if you are an exceptional person—like Ed's uncle, who fulfilled a dream at the age of 70—then age is truly just a number. But many people find their drive diminishes, at least temporarily, around middle age.

Lifestyle Change

One action, like embarking on a new career, can cause a ripple effect that can change your whole life. You may find that some friends drift away; you may find yourself interacting with new and different professional groups and business associates. You may have less personal time to spend with friends and family if you have to go to school a couple of nights a week. You may have to accept a lower salary. How do you think you'll handle the adjustment? What about your family?

Family Support

It's a good idea to talk over your plans with your spouse (and children). Involvement produces commitment. If they're involved in your decision, you'll have their support and understanding. This will be especially important if you plan to start a business or make a career move that means reeducation, a new work schedule, or a reduction in income.

Time—Is It Worth It?

Even if the learning curve is relatively short and the transition smooth, a career change requires time for you to adjust to a new role and then come up to speed. You may have to return to school for additional training or spend extra hours in the evening boning up on required information. Obviously, if you start at a lower position than you've normally held, it will take time to move up to the level you're accustomed to. How much time are you willing to commit to a career switch?

Culture Shock

Consider the impact of possibly working with younger, more experienced people. You may have to adjust to being the oldest person in the group. Of course that can have its advantages in certain professions—real estate or financial planning, for example—where your age can work to your advantage by making you seem more experienced and wiser and, thus, enhancing your credibility.

Starting at the Bottom

If you're accustomed to having a secretary and staff, starting over without these may seem like a real handicap, especially if you're lacking in organizational and administrative skills. It could be particularly problematic if you're starting your own business because there will be no more company supplies or services at your disposal.

What If It Doesn't Work?

It's always wise to have an alternate route to your goal, as well as a backup plan. You can gain valuable insight into what to expect in the new career if you take the time to research it beforehand; for example, by talking with people who do what you want to do. In exploring your alternatives, make sure you choose ones that allow you to use the same skills; for example, coaching at a university or coaching at a junior college, with a backup plan for earning a living if coaching does not work out at all. Go through the same process for developing backup options that you used for developing your original career goal. The more thoroughly informed you are about what to expect, the more assured you can be about your decision.

CHANGING AT YOUR COMPANY

You may decide after this process of evaluation that you can actually accomplish your new goal in your current company. If you do, refer back to chapter 8 for the essential factors you need to consider in making a career change there. Of greatest importance here will be your current job level. Is there a position at this level or above in the work that you want to do? If not, will you be able to function effectively at a lower level, or will you be uncomfortable with what may seem like a demotion?

Two of the biggest advantages of staying with your company are credibility and money. If you have established a good reputation and your philosophy is in line with that of the company, you will likely be given serious consideration when you propose a career change. Since you've already proven yourself, management will have faith in you and assume you'll perform well in a new job. Also, many companies, especially large ones, will keep job changers at their current salary though they move into positions that would normally pay less.

But not everyone finds it easy to make a career change at their present company. I know a number of people who found it difficult to make a lateral or a downward move; the stigma of not moving up when they had the opportunity took a long time to wear off. If you do move up, you may find that your new salary is not as much of an increase as you expected because you came into the job with a low pay basis. Decision makers often give salary increases based on a past job or title rather than on the new position itself. In other words, someone promoted from associate director to director of sales will generally receive a higher salary than someone who makes a bigger jump from, say, sales assistant to director of sales.

If you decide there is opportunity for a career change within your company and the advantages outweigh the disadvantages, you may want to use some of the following approaches to find a new position.

- Define clearly what you want to do. Have a specific job or clearly defined responsibilities in mind.

- Let your current manager know that you want to make a career change, and enlist that person's support in accomplishing this goal. (Of course, this isn't a good idea if you suspect that your manager won't be supportive, possibly because the chemistry between you two has never been right. In this case, think of someone else whom you could turn to for help: a mentor, a higher-up who's always supported you, or an influential colleague, for instance.)

- Talk with the person who manages the area you want to change about the possibilities in that area. Your current manager may be helpful here in setting up that conversation if she is supportive of your change.

- Talk with the human resources manager about job openings and new opportunities within the company. Sometimes job openings are posted in the HR department or, for instance, in the company eating area or lounge.

MOVING TO ANOTHER COMPANY

Making a career change and moving to another company simultaneously may be more challenging than making a change within your current company. You will probably start out at a lower salary and in a lesser role and then have to work your way back up both the economic and corporate ladder. When making a simultaneous career and company change, you can increase your chances of success by incorporating the following factors into the process:

- Research your industries of interest and know about the companies to which you're interested in applying.

- Think about the advantages of hiring you from the prospective employer's viewpoint, and be prepared to use those points to sell yourself on your résumé and in interviews.

- Rethink your résumé in light of the new type of work you want to do (see the before and after samples on the next pages).

- Practice interviewing with someone who is knowledgeable in your targeted profession so you'll have a strong handle on the skills that the employer will be interested in and be able to show how your past experience demonstrates the necessary transferable skills.

- If you're truly serious about the change, be flexible in starting your employment with a new company. Be willing to begin on a trial basis if necessary or at a trial salary level (three to six months) while you demonstrate your value to the company.

A New Résumé for a New Career and a New Company

When changing careers, just as when downsizing, develop a new résumé rather than using an edited version of your old one. (Refer to

THE "BEFORE" RÉSUMÉ
(CHRONOLOGICAL FORMAT WITH A CUSTOMER SERVICE FOCUS)

FRANK WALES
2300 Park Avenue
New York, New York 20023
(212) 555-1223

SUMMARY

As a customer services professional for eight years, I have managed groups supporting retail, product, and services industries. Strengths include strong organizational ability and team-building development of systems for efficient processing of information, complimented by effective management and interpersonal skills.

WORK EXPERIENCE

MANAGER, CUSTOMER SERVICE
Hi Tech Computer Company
1995–present

Hired and supervised a staff of fifty people to service the needs of the highest revenue commercial accounts. Assumed responsibility for managing a remote location of fifteen people for nine months while that supervisor was on medical leave.

Held quarterly "Your Best" training programs for entire staff, which kept quality at the forefront and helped maintain an account retention percentage of 99 percent.

Kept revenue loss through credits to less than 1%.

CUSTOMER SERVICE—TELEMARKETING MANAGER
Excel Communications—Northwest Service Center
1990–1995

Hired and developed a staff of sixty customer service–telemarketing representatives and supervisors.

Managed heavy workload of inbound and outbound call activities.

Resolved a major conflict with another department, which prevented a serious work stoppage.

CUSTOMER SERVICE SUPERVISOR
Cirro Retail Outlet
1987–1990

Supervised division customer service site and provided support to the sales force and sales management.

Promoted from Customer Service Representative after three months.

EDUCATION

1995, M.B.A., University of New York
1984, B.S. Marketing, Syracuse University

THE "AFTER" RÉSUMÉ

(FUNCTIONAL FORMAT, CHANGED FROM CUSTOMER SERVICE TO HUMAN RESOURCES FOCUS)

FRANK WALES
2300 Park Avenue
New York, New York 20023
(212) 555-1223

SUMMARY

An experienced manager who has successfully influenced direct and indirect reports to provide quality service within retail, manufacturing, and service environments. Effective interpersonal skills have been an asset in training, counseling, and arbitrating conflicts. Strong analytical skills help with planning and project management. M.B.A. degree and professional strengths would enhance the quality of a human resources function. Computer literate.

SELECTED ACCOMPLISHMENTS

Communication/Interpersonal
—Trained seventy new hires in five classes within thirty days. Productivity increased by 13 percent within ninety days.
—Advised upper management on major hiring decisions after a division reorganization.
—Counseled a difficult employee who was abusing alcohol to independently sign up for an employee assistance program.
—Convinced upper management to establish a special awards program to recognize top performers.

Project Management
—Part of a team that reviewed and developed new benefit programs, which were offered to all employees.
—Hired and supervised a staff of fifty people to service the needs of company's highest revenue commercial accounts.
—Assumed responsibility for managing a remote location of fifteen people for nine months while that supervisor was on medical leave.

Problem Resolution
—Established a system to handle an unexpected heavy workload involving large volumes of paper.
—Resolved a major conflict with another division and prevented a serious work stoppage.
—Scheduled maintenance of fields, gym set-ups, and cleanups.
—Determined player eligibility.

PROFESSIONAL HISTORY

High Tech Computer Company, Manager of Customer Service 1995–present
Excel Communications, Customer Service—Telemarketing Manager 1990–1995
Cirro Retail Outlet, Customer Service Supervisor 1987–1990

EDUCATION

1995, M.B.A., University of New York
1984, B.S. in Marketing, Syracuse University

chapters 5 and 10 for tips on résumé writing.) Follow these steps, which are very similar to those you'd use if you were looking for a downsized job (see chapter 14):

- Use a functional résumé format, which enables you to place similar and relevant accomplishments in categories for stronger emphasis.

- Develop a summary statement at the top of the résumé. Write one that focuses on the skills, knowledge, and traits that are in line with the position you seek.

- Provide examples of accomplishments in your résumé that support the information in the summary. Reword the accomplishments slightly as needed to downplay references to your old occupation. Make them as targeted as you can to the new position and arrange them in order of importance to the position you seek.

- Use regular type, not bold, in references to former jobs. Don't give them unnecessary emphasis.

- Have someone review your résumé. Try to find someone who does the kind of work you want to do or is at least knowledgeable about that field.

RESOURCES

Careers for the '90s and Beyond by Rea Staff, compiled and published by Research & Education Association (1995). This resource includes very comprehensive information on areas such as earnings, job descriptions, education and training, working conditions, advancement opportunities, résumés, cover letters, interviews, tomorrow's jobs, and the outlook for the future.

Dictionary of Occupational Titles, Volume 1, Fourth Edition developed by U.S. Department of Labor Employment and Training Administration (VGM Career Horizons, 1991). This is the recognized source for standardized occupational information. It provides descriptions of thousands of jobs, including such vital information as tasks performed, skills required, job locations, related careers, and working conditions.

Finding Your Perfect Work: The New Career Guide to Making a Living, Creating a Life by Paul and Sarah Edwards (J.P. Tarcher, 1996). If making a career change means working on your own, this book can show you how to blend your personal goals and dreams with the practical realities of having your own business. Intertwined in the book are the essential points you need to decide upon and factor in to any good business plan. Includes real-life examples of people who successfully implemented a plan for their own businesses.

101 Careers: A Guide to the Fastest Growing Opportunities by Michael Harkavy (John Wiley & Sons, Inc., 1990) provides information on top jobs for the 1990s, training requirements, working conditions, salary, regional trends, and advancement opportunities.

The Princeton Review Guide to Your Career by Alan B. Bernstein, CSW, PC, and Nicholas R. Schaffzin (Random House, 1996). A very helpful book that gives a good overview of what is required and what to expect for over 150 professions. It highlights job requirements and salary ranges and provides self-assessment profile information for helping you identify your potential. It deals with "a day in the life" of each career, "paying your dues," and related careers. Lists major associations and employers, what to read, and the types of clients and other professionals you'll encounter.

Survive & Profit From A Mid-Career Change by Daniel Moreau (Random House, 1996). Geared specifically toward people working in companies that are downsized, this book provides a good model for examining yourself, your job, and your career before making a change.

To locate what industries use specific types of professionals:

The Career Guide: Dun's Employment Opportunities Directory, Dun's Marketing Services, Dun & Bradstreet Corporation, 49 Old Bloomfield Road, Mountain Lakes, NJ 07046 (published annually in November). Lists more than 5,000 companies—with 1,000 or more employees—that may offer job opportunities in sales, marketing, management, engineering, life and physical sciences, computer science, mathematics, statistics planning, accounting and finance, liberal arts fields, and other technical and professional areas. Also lists personnel consultants and some government employers.

CHAPTER

NEW WAYS OF
WORKING

U ntil fairly recently, most people, if they were lucky, got a job with benefits at a "good" company and stayed until they reached 65, when they retired and stopped working altogether. This "thirty-years-and-out rule" gave them job security, but it limited their options. Today it's different. The restructuring of business as we knew it hasn't been all good news for workers, with downsizing and layoffs occurring at record rates. But it has opened up alternatives to the traditional job, and such alternatives are more popular than ever—now part-time, temporary, contracting, and consulting opportunities exist and even abound for professionals. Not only do these ways of working offer freedom, flexibility, and variety, but some may also pay better than a regular 9-to-5 job.

When George, a black attorney, entered stage three of his career, he had no choice but to look at other work options after a company merger eliminated his position. But it took him some time to get accustomed to the change. He was 55 and had worked for twenty-five years in the same job, as an in-house attorney for a manufacturing company. For awhile, at his wife's insistence, he made halfhearted attempts to get another position in manufacturing. But finally he had to admit that he really had no interest in returning to his old working pattern. He realized that he wanted to explore new career ideas, and he needed time to be able to do that.

Fortunately, George and his wife had planned carefully, and they had a solid financial foundation. His wife worked, so there was one regular income they could count on. And their children were married and settled in their careers, so they had no dependents.

After his layoff, friends and networking contacts started coming to him for legal advice, and George realized that he enjoyed the variety and flexibility that this kind of consulting work offered. He also felt good about providing service at a small fee to people in his community who otherwise could not afford legal counsel. George found his answer; here was work he enjoyed, using the skills and experience he had spent years acquiring. It was a simple transition for him.

Like George, you may very well find that you can use the professional skills you've acquired over the years and apply them to part-time or more flexible work. Making the choice to work in a new way allows you to adopt a slightly different "business mind-set," one that you'll probably find a lot more comfortable. In fact, redefining your work may be the most rewarding time of your career—personally and, perhaps, financially, too—because you get to work on your own terms, not someone else's.

TEMPING

When we think of a temp, we usually envision someone in a clerical or blue-collar job. While most temporary openings do, indeed, occur in such jobs, today a temp can be almost anyone, in almost any type of job. For many professionals, temping has become a very good, very legitimate way of working; it often offers a good deal of flexibility and variety without the stress and responsibility of managing a career and marketing one's skills. Temp workers only have to prove their skills, show up for assignments, and do a good job. The agency, if it's a good one, does the rest: handling the legwork of getting the assignments, interceding to negotiate salary, dealing with any problems that arise, and securing a new assignment when one ends or doesn't work out.

For Naomi, temping proved to be the perfect work option for stage three of her career. She had been retired for five years, when she decided to go back to work to help put her daughter through college. She did not want to return to her career as a costume designer; the work was too competitive, too demanding. Instead, Naomi wanted a low-stress job that would allow her to work three or four days a week and leave the cares of the job at the company when she went home each night.

When she registered with a temporary placement agency to do general clerical work, Naomi found out that she would need to beef up her computer skills. She took an adult ed computer course at a local high school and landed her first assignment, as a receptionist at a high-tech firm. From the start, Naomi made an outstanding contribution. The organizational and administrative abilities she had developed in handling her freelance costume design work served her well in this new role. The assignment was initially slated to last a week, but two months later Naomi was still with the company. By then she had become such an asset that the managers wanted her to stay on. The company negotiated with the temp agency to let Naomi work flexible hours (6-hour shifts four days a week), and it raised no objections when the agency asked for a higher hourly rate for Naomi's time.

Of course, not every assignment will be an immediate entree into a good part-time job as it was for Naomi. Temping does have its downsides. In fact, many temporary assignments consist primarily of grunt work and can be very unfulfilling. Also, temp workers are usually paid less than regular employees, and a portion of their pay goes directly to the agency for their fees. But an important advantage of temping is that when you get on an assignment that you just can't stand, you have the option of making a quick change. And most temp agencies offer benefits and vacation time after you've worked a certain number of hours.

If temping seems like a viable option at this point in your career, check out the temporary placement agencies that exist in every city. Look for listings under "Employment" in your local phone book. You can register with as many agencies as you like, but eventually you will probably work exclusively with one.

When choosing a temp agency, make sure it will be able to offer you assignments in areas that interest you and that are at your skill level. Less specialized temp agencies tend to offer more clerical or labor jobs and assign their workers to shorter-term assignments (e.g., a day to a month). However, executive temp agencies exist to handle management-and professional-level employees (check *The Directory of Executive Temporary Placement Firms* in your library for listings). Executive agencies often offer a variety of assignments, ranging anywhere from as long as three months to three years, and allow people to work with them on a contracting basis.

If you choose temping as a new way of working, make it work for you by keeping the following tips in mind:

- Determine a goal based on skills that fit with temporary positions, and register with as many temporary placement firms that handle your skill level as possible.

- Develop a résumé that emphasizes skills and experience appropriate for the type and level of job you seek. (The information and resources in this book, particularly in chapter 14, will assist you in doing this.)

- Determine your work criteria: number of days, hours, variety of assignments, restrictions, and other preferences. Be prepared to clarify these with the agency representative before you start accepting assignments.

- Determine what industries (or companies) you are interested in temping for, and register with agencies that support these industries and agree to your work criteria.

- After you're on an assignment, if it doesn't fit, feel free to let your agency know and to request reassignment to something else.

- If you believe you rate a higher hourly rate after a period of time, approach your agency—not the company—about this.

CONTRACTING

Unlike temping, contracting as a way of work involves providing services independently and for a specified period of time to a company, either on- or off-site. Generally, contractors perform their services for a preestablished fee and are not on the company's full-time payroll. Many corporations consider contracting an efficient and cost-effective means of quickly getting work done without having to make a commitment to the worker. It is becoming an increasingly viable and lucrative way of working that offers flexibility, independence, and variety.

After working as a contractor for fifteen years, my friend Jerry still prefers the flexibility that contracting offers him, as well as the fact that he can remain on the sidelines of company politics. Even so, he readily admits that contracting, like temping, has its downsides. For example, he says, some companies tend to misuse contractors. They often expect them to work ceaselessly and they dump a lot of work on them that they can't get their regular staff to do. Companies often expect contractors to work odd hours, handle rush assignments, or perform their services at an undesirable location.

Jerry has found that sometimes it's the contractors who give contracting a bad name. He's worked with some whose bad habits, like alcoholism or difficulty getting along with people made it impossible for them to maintain regular employment. Bad experiences with a few contractors make some companies reluctant to continue to contract work out, and this, in the long run, reduces the number of contracting opportunities available. It can also lower the pay scale for contractors because they're perceived as being less-valued workers.

Another downside to contracting is that, unlike temps, who work through agencies, contractors are self-employed businesspeople who must handle their own taxes, market their services to companies, stay current on new market trends, and budget for financial ebbs and flows.

You may not need to market yourself for each new assignment if you work under contract with a consulting firm that uses contractors; you join the firm's regular pool of contractors and are sent on assignments as they become available. You negotiate a per diem or per hour fee, sometimes with benefits, and you are paid at the completion of an assignment or at regular intervals throughout the course of the work (usually at the same time as the regular employees) for the amount accrued during that period. An excellent source for identifying consulting organizations in your field is the *Consultants and Consulting Organizations Directory*, which is available in the reference section of the library.

The best source for contract work may be your former employer. Not uncommonly, an employer will downsize a group within the company and then offer some of the individuals in that group the opportunity to come back as contractors. You may find that your hourly rate as a contractor is higher than it was when you were on staff, but you no longer enjoy benefits like life and medical insurance and may need to pay your own income and social security taxes.

You will also want to network to find new contracting opportunities. If you adopted the business mind-set in the beginning of your career (as described in chapter 1), it will surely pay off now. Make a point of approaching friends and former colleagues to tell them that you're now contracting and looking for new projects.

JOB SHARING

Job sharing involves two part-time employees sharing the responsibilities and working hours of one job. Job sharing is a unique type of teamwork, sometimes difficult to set up and maintain. The key is to find a compatible partner who has similar goals and skills. If working

TAX IMPLICATIONS OF CONTRACTING

Because there are tax advantages to being self-employed, and because contractors can be in a position that seems very much like being an employee, the IRS issued a ruling in 1987 that established a 20-point guideline for determining whether someone is an employee or a contractor. The distinction between independent contractor and employee has to do with whether or not the organization you work for has control over when, where, and how you do your work. A good tax consultant can advise you about your particular situation.

this way interests you, you will most likely need to locate your own partner and decide how you will work together before proposing the arrangement to your employer.

Some, but not all, companies are amenable to job sharing. The obvious advantage to employers is that the company, in effect, gains the mind power of two people for the price of one. The advantage to the job sharers is flexibility and part-time work. The disadvantages include the possibility of working with someone who does not pull his or her share of the load or the burden of having to find yourself a new partner if yours quits or you find you're not compatible. Each person in a job share usually negotiates her salary and benefits independently with the company. Each typically receives a limited benefit package similar to the one offered to part-time employees, which in most instances is substantially less than that offered to full-time workers.

If you think job sharing might be a good work option for you, here are some tips that can help make it happen:

- For sources for a partner: check with the human resources departments of companies you're interested in working for to see if someone has expressed a similar desire, run an ad, check with placement agencies, and network with colleagues. Women just coming off of maternity leave and people looking to downsize their jobs are good candidates.

- Set up an interview with your potential job-share partner to determine if you can work together and if you have similar goals for the job and the job-sharing arrangement. There is no need to commit to working with someone who sees it only as a short-term transitional job if you plan to make it a permanent way of working. During the interview, check for skills, motivation, chemistry, and strengths and weaknesses. Even though you will be at the job at different times, you'll be communicating and working together behind the scenes to be most effective, so you'll need to know how you fit as a team.

- Work up an agreement about how you want to divide the hours, days, work responsibilities, time off, emergencies, and vacation coverage. Try to think of all possible situations that might arise and how you would handle them now, before you have to deal with them on the job.

- Agree on a salary range and benefits for the job. Although you will be paid separately, you should be in agreement about the pay range before you begin negotiating with your employer. Since you will be doing similar work, you'll probably be receiving similar pay and benefits.

CONSULTING

To me, consulting is the creme de la creme of the new ways of working. Webster's describes a consultant as "one who gives professional advice or services." This can mean many types of professionals: artists, writers, editors, trainers, marketing consultants, managers, engineers, computer experts . . . you name it. As a consultant, you will have truly moved beyond working for someone; you've assumed all the responsibilities, risks—and rewards—of having your own business. You are marketing yourself—your skills, your expertise, and the results you can produce for clients. To do this well, you need to have highly marketable skills and expertise and the motivation to succeed.

"DON'T JUST DO IT"

■

"There is risk in being an entrepreneur," says industrial designer William Barlett. "It's not for everybody. Even with careful planning, you still have to be comfortable with not knowing just what to expect next."

After twenty years as a consultant, Bill doesn't mind taking risks, and he still loves his work. The hard part, he says, is managing the business and dealing with the responsibility involved. "The actual work is the fun part of being an entrepreneur, but managing the business is another thing all together," he says. "Anyone thinking of being a consultant or pursuing his own business needs to do some serious planning and have reasonable financial resources.

"Most people think only about the excitement and freedom of being their own boss without considering the downsides. For instance, there are the tax implications, like double FICA and a higher tax rate than salaried employees. Medical and life insurance are not completely tax deductible. Then there's the matter of vacations; when you're your own business, you don't get paid when you don't work. I didn't take a vacation for more than ten years. Also, working alone, with no support or camaraderie, can be difficult. You can't rely on anyone to back you up when you need help. One thing that has been helpful is having a supportive spouse. She is an entrepreneur also, so that makes it easier for me."

Still, Bill willingly takes on the risks and management of his business activities. He admits that his entrepreneurial drive comes sometimes from his confidence in his ability and sometimes from the simple need to make money. Over the long run, both have paid off. His business successes include attaining a copyright for new computer software, several patents, and numerous international design awards.

Like most entrepreneurs, Bill is driven to accomplish his goals and needs, which he describes as creativity/design satisfaction, variety, personal responsibility, and financial reward. When the business demands it, he takes night classes to upgrade his skills or learn new ones. "It's always necessary to maintain state-of-the-art knowledge in your field. Anyone who wants to be a consultant has to make a commitment to do this in order to stay in business," Bill advises. "But the most important thing is to have a well-thought-out business plan and keep working toward your goals.

■

WILLIAM L. BARLETT
Hispanic-American consultant
Barlett Design Associates, Inc.
Santa Barbara, California
Business: Industrial designer

MAINTAINING YOUR OWN BUSINESS

Working for yourself involves not just doing the work you've been hired to do as a consultant or a contractor; it also involves taking on the management and administrative duties associated with maintaining a business. You'll be responsible for everything from answering the telephone to negotiating fees and paying taxes. Some people find it very stressful making the transition from working in an office with structure and support to being an independent entrepreneur with no fixed workday or office environment. Handling all the administrative and clerical details can add to the stress, especially if you dislike such tasks. If you're an extrovert who needs to be around people much of the time, you may find it difficult to deal with the personal isolation that often goes with consulting and contracting.

CONSULTANT VS. CONTRACTOR

A consultant is different from a contractor. Companies look to contractors to produce repeatable ongoing tasks, not give advice. They expect consultants to be experts in their fields and to have enough influence that others are willing to listen to them and follow their advice.

For instance, if a company asks a consultant to perform a certain function, the consultant should have the knowledge and expertise to view the function in context, so that she can advise company managers about what they may need in addition to—or in place of—the requested service. Managing this process requires proven expertise and experience, as well as strong interpersonal and communication skills that can be used to overcome resistance and influence clients to change their current policies, practices, or systems.

If you've decided to be a consultant because you want more time and freedom, you may have chosen the wrong work option. In switching from the role of employee to entrepreneur, you'll likely find that consulting can be an intensive, all-encompassing profession, requiring a greater commitment of time, resources, and energy than you anticipated.

Is Consulting For You?

To help you decide if consulting would suit you, take a look at this list of personal traits and priorities found in many successful consultants and see how many describe you:

- **Control and freedom.** You feel more comfortable trusting your future to yourself than being dependent on a company.

- **Self-confidence.** You believe in yourself and your ability.

- **Resilience.** You are emotionally stable and are not overcome by disappointments.

- **Money.** A good income is one of your career motivators.

- **Sales skills.** You're a good networker and have the ability to market yourself.

- **Good interpersonal skills.** You have the ability to get along well with all kinds of people.

- **Good communication skills.** You have strong oral and written communication skills.

- **Skills.** Your research has shown that you have the right combination of skills and experience to meet current market needs.

     If you've worked in the field before, you probably have a good sense of what these needs are. To be sure, you might want to do some research. You can start by talking with colleagues and then expand to members of professional associations. If you don't belong to such an association, this is the time to join! Look up the association that represents your area of expertise (check the *Encyclopedia of Associations* at the library); then contact a local chapter, attend one of its meetings, and talk with the participants about the skills and experience needed in your field. Also, check with department heads at your company (before you leave) and ask what kind of skills they look for in the people they use as consultants. Since contracting and consulting can be closely connected, talking with a representative at an executive placement firm who specializes in your field, might also provide good information.

- **Marketing ability.** You can identify how your skills and experience should be packaged and presented in the market as well as to whom they should be presented. In other words, you can determine who benefits most from your expertise and is willing to pay for it. Then evaluate how you stack up against the competition (i.e., what you have that they may be lacking).

You may want to take this additional skill and make it one of your specialties.

For instance, if you're a competent leadership trainer but know that there are already plenty of trainers selling their services, identify something that makes you unique. Let's say you're bilingual. You can either work directly with a company that has a multicultural employee base or work in conjunction with other trainers servicing a contract that involves bilingual work.

RESOURCES

Jumping the Job Track: Security, Satisfaction and Success as an Independent Consultant by Peter C. Brown (Crown Trade Paperbacks, 1994). Explains why you don't need to be an expert to succeed on your own and covers everything you should know, from the basics of getting your employer's help to finding clients. Addresses issues like estimating your income, setting up an office, dealing with the IRS, and adjusting to your new independence.

Temp by Choice by Diane Thrailkill (Career Press, 1994). An excellent guide addressing all the major issues of making the transition from full-time employment to temping. Focuses on how to earn money quickly, reenter the workforce after a long absence, ease into retirement without leaving the workforce completely, diversify your work life without committing to one employer, and more.

The Temp Track by Peggy O'Connell Justice (Peterson's, 1994). Another fine book that explains how to take advantage of the increased opportunities in temping for people in almost all professions. The personal experiences of temps and the advice about how to work with executive and specialized temp agencies is particularly insightful.

Selling Your Services: Proven Strategies for Getting Clients to Hire You (or Your Firm) by Robert W. Bly (Henry Holt and Co., 1991). An excellent, comprehensive guide for people interested in contracting their services. Includes information on marketing techniques, identifying prospects, landing new clients, setting fees, drawing up contracts, proposals and letters of agreement, and more.

Zen and the Art of Making A Living: A Practical Guide to Creative Career Design by Laurence G. Boldt (Viking, 1993). In addition to self-assessment and practical steps for finding or creating work, this guide includes tips on starting a business, working freelance, establishing a nonprofit corporation, and managing multiple careers. It also helps you learn to love what you're doing until you're doing what you love. Includes 120 easy-to-use worksheets.

SOME FINAL WORDS

■■■

No matter what stage you're at—what age, gender, or cultural group—by making a commitment to a new career or a different way of working, you have set yourself on a challenging and eye-opening course. You will continue on your path of lifelong learning, improving and expanding your skills in your profession so that you can make the contribution to society that you were called to make.

This book represents the collective voices of many who share your quest for professional excellence. We hope that our stories and advice will help you reach your goals. And we also hope that you use the information you've found here as a springboard for further research and exploration.

If this book has served to whet your appetite for more, stimulated your intellectual curiosity, and challenged you to seek perfection in your skills and reach for higher levels of achievement, then we will have achieved our goal in writing it. We can now look forward to the quality contributions that you will be making to complete the cycle of giving.

Index

■■■

Graham, Lawrence Otis, 70, 86, 87
The Great Jobs Ahead, 71

Hadley, Joyce, 101
Harkavy, Michael, 323
Harvey, Al, 22–23
Henderson, Charsetta, 57–58, 195
Hispanic Americans, cultural values of, 20
Holton, Ed, 21, 25
Hook Up, Get Hired!, 89, 100
Hopson, Barrie, 181
How to Be Twice as Smart, 221
How to Choose the Right Career, 44
How to Make Use of a Useless Degree, 70
How to Manage Your Boss, 288
Huang, Chungliang A., 220

Incompatibility with company, 224
Industries
  global changes within, 281
  selecting, 53–56, 84–86, 97
Initiative, taking, 216–18
Internet, job research on, 87–87, 89–90
Internships, 64
Internships 1997, 69
Interpersonal skills, 60–61, 156
Interview Power, 133
Interviews, 114–29
  clothing for, 117, 126, 304
  discrimination and, 115, 117
  informational, 91
  for lesser position, 301–6
  for new job, 240–45
  phone, 125–26
  questions at, 118, 120–24, 242–43,
    304–5
  salary discussed at, 124, 305
  steps in, 116
  types, 125–29
It's Who You Know, 100–101
I Went to College for This?, 24, 142

Jackson, Ellen and Tom, 132
Job offers, negotiation and, 129–32, 245–47
Job placement agencies, 94–95
Job research, 72–82, 105
  for lesser position, 295–97
  location of jobs, 82–84
  methods, 88–100
  resources, 100–102
  selecting industries and companies,
    84–88, 97–98
Jobs. *See also* Careers
  creating, 213–18
  dead-end, 224
  expanding current, 212–13

first, 75
leading to other jobs, 160–61
less stressful, change to, 289–306
new ways of working, 325–38
renegotiating current, 273–88
sought within company, 210–12
starting new, 134–61
Job search, 103–33. *See also* Job research
  for changing to lesser position, 299,
    301
  checklist, 231
  interviews in, 114–29
  for new company, 230–45
  offers and negotiations, 129–32
  organizing and managing, 104–6
  résumés and cover letters in, 107–14
Job sharing, 330–32
Job Shock, 71
Johnson, Johnnie, 44
Jumping the Job Track, 337
Justice, Peggy O'Connell, 337

Kastre, Michael F., and Nydia Rodriguez,
  25
Kay, Roberta Youtan, 252–53
Kemp, C. Robert, 66–67, 195
Kennard, Kristie, 288
Kennedy, Joyce Lain, 89, 100
Knowledge, career vision and, 38, 40

Laquer, Maria, 273, 288
Larson, Jackie, 247
Latino Success, 41–42, 44
Lewis, David, 221
Lifestyle changes, 261–72, 315–16
Live Your Dreams, 26, 44
Location for work, 83–85
Lucht, John, 248

Maninger, Carol, 250
Marketing, for self–employed, 336–37
Medley, Jerry, 68–69
Meetings, 142–43
Mentoring, 220–21
Mentors. *See also* Coaching
  becoming successful mentor, 255
  finding, 10–11, 136, 157, 207, 209–10
  value of, 138–40
Mergers, 280
Mind–sets. *See* Business mind–set;
  Cultural mind–sets
The Minority Career Guide, 25
Miramontes, Omar, 27–28
Mission of company, 140
Miyoshi, Phyllis, 35–36
Moreau, Daniel, 323

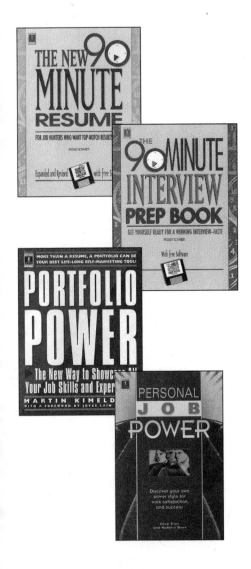